Leadership Counts

Jay —

To Someone
Who is Taking
Leadership Count.

— Rob

LEADERSHIP COUNTS

Lessons for Public Managers

*from the Massachusetts Welfare,
Training, and Employment Program*

Robert D. Behn

Harvard University Press
Cambridge, Massachusetts
London, England
1991

First Harvard University Press paperback edition, 1994

Library of Congress Cataloging-in-Publication Data

Behn, Robert D.
  Leadership counts: lessons for public managers from the
  Massachusetts welfare, training, and employment program / Robert D.
  Behn.
    p. cm.
  Includes bibliographical references and index.
  ISBN 0–674–51852–7 (cloth)
  ISBN 0–674–51853–5 (pbk.)
  1. Welfare recipients—Employment—Massachusetts. 2. Aid to
  families with dependent children programs—Massachusetts.
  3. Political leadership—Massachusetts. I. Title.
HV98.M39B44 1991
362.5′84′09744—dc20
91–3557
    CIP

To Judy
For friendship, love, and fun

Contents

Preface   *ix*

Prologue: Important Events along the Way   *1*

1   The Idea behind ET CHOICES   *9*

2   The Birth of ET CHOICES   *21*

3   The Structure of ET CHOICES   *36*

4   Managing for Performance   *49*

5   An Emphasis on Marketing   *83*

6   Making Government More Businesslike   *104*

7   Management by Groping Along   *127*

8   Managing and Evaluating Social Programs   *151*

9   Evaluating ET CHOICES   *171*

10   The Necessity of Leadership   *198*

Notes   *221*

Index   *245*

Preface

In 1979, The Urban Institute released an analysis of how state and local governments had implemented the federal Work Incentive (WIN) program, which was designed to help welfare recipients find employment and increase their income. The authors of the report sought to determine what "organizational, managerial, and service delivery characteristics . . . differentiated higher performing programs from low performers."[1] They found that the better programs had a number of distinguishing characteristics:

- Staff had a much better understanding of the program's goals and of the balance sought between the quantity and quality of the job placements.
- Training for staff was more frequent, more extensive, and more varied.
- Reporting systems were more accurate and more trouble free.
- Performance monitoring was more intensive and more sophisticated.
- Communication was not limited to the traditional downward communication of regulations and technical support. Upward communication from the field provided feedback on problems and for planning; lateral communication helped local units solve common problems and learn effective practices.
- Flexibility combined with accountability permitted the delegation of more responsibility to subordinates and local units as well as less rigid interpretations of work rules and office procedures.

Massachusetts's WIN program, ET CHOICES, possessed many of The Urban Institute's characteristics of high-performing programs. This book is not designed, however, to determine where ET ranks on The Urban Institute's performance scale. Rather, my objective is to examine *how* public managers can create the characteristics that The Urban Institute found in high-performing programs and that ET possessed.[2]

How can public managers ensure a clear understanding of complex goals? How can they create and then best utilize a performance monitoring system? How can they ensure that they receive communications—particularly the bad news—from the field? How can they provide for flexibility yet still be sure that the program's mission is being achieved? Any public agency is a complex organization. It is difficult to manage. It is one thing to determine the characteristics that make an agency effective. It is another thing to determine *how* a public manager can create them.

I began this research in 1987 at the request of the Ford Foundation. Gordon L. Berlin, then a program officer at Ford and now vice president at the Manpower Demonstration Research Corporation, thought the management of ET CHOICES might be worthy of investigation. I am grateful to him for his encouragement and to the Ford Foundation for its support. Neither, however, is responsible for my words or interpretations, which are mine alone.

The management of the Massachusetts Department of Public Welfare was also interested in this project. Michael S. Dukakis, Charles M. Atkins, Thomas P. Glynn, Jolie Bain Pillsbury, and Barbara Burke-Tatum spent many hours with me, describing their managerial philosophy. They had clear ideas about the relationship of their managerial efforts, agency behavior, and policy outcomes.

Indeed, the leaders of the department took management seriously. They worried about it constantly. They talked about the development of their people—about everything from formal training, to temporary tours of duty to broaden perspectives and reward individuals, to the necessity for on-the-job training. They focused on developing and articulating their agency's mission and on different ways to dramatize it. They worried about incentives—about how to eliminate perverse ones and how to create productive ones. Each had a personal management philosophy that reflected his or her different obligations and opportunities.

Moreover, they were enthusiastic about their jobs. They were willing to talk and animated in conveying their ideas. Occasionally, at a conference or after a meeting, I would eat lunch with people from different levels and regions within the department, and I was struck by the energy with which they talked shop with each other.

They did not, of course, always remember the events in the same way. Each remembered them from his or her own perspective. Sometimes people spoke about how "I" did something when really "we" had accomplished it. Other times, people (even the same people) were *too* willing to give out credit—even bashful about describing their own roles.

Sometimes I was there as events unfolded. I watched when ET awards were distributed and praise lavished, when outside contractors criticized the department, and when the leadership team debated how to fix problems. But, again, what I saw may not be what others saw. What I heard might not be what others heard. What I thought was happening might not have been what others were trying to make happen or what others concluded was happening to them.

This book examines the first five years of ET CHOICES—from April 1983, when Charles M. Atkins became commissioner, through June 1988, when the department achieved its goal of placing 50,000 ET participants in jobs. Throughout this period, the program was constantly evolving. Consequently, the information presented here is part snapshot, part moving picture. And the various snapshots were taken at different times throughout the five-year period.

Further, ET CHOICES continues to evolve. Any sentence written in the present tense may soon describe things that no longer are. I have therefore chosen to write about ET in the past tense. Nevertheless, some of my sentences will still describe the situation today.

The following saga is not reality. Instead, it reflects reality as seen by different people through different lenses. It reflects reality as remembered by different people, often months or years later. Sometimes, I am sure, my memory, my notes, and my tape recorder left gaps. And in attempting to organize everything I saw, everything I read, and everything I was told, I had to choose. Sometimes, a worthy observation did not make it onto the printed page simply because I could not find a good place to put it.

This book is not a historical chronicle of ET CHOICES. Rather, I have attempted to extract from the program lessons about public management that can be employed—though always with adaptation—by other public managers in other public agencies. I hope that these lessons will serve to improve public management.

My usage of third person singular pronouns is as follows. The first time I refer to a generic individual, for instance an ET worker, a supervisor, or a member of top management, I use the expression "he or she." I want to make it clear that any such unnamed individual may be either male or female. After this first mention, so that the text will flow easily, I use "he." Whenever I use "he" generically, I am referring to any member of a group that is composed of both males and females. There is, however, one group composed almost entirely of women: welfare recipients who receive aid under the program Aid to Families with Dependent

Children (AFDC). In Massachusetts, as in the United States generally, approximately 95 percent of the families receiving aid under AFDC are headed by one parent, a woman; therefore I use "she" to refer to these welfare recipients.

Some portions of Chapter 7 appeared in an earlier form in "Management by Groping Along," *Journal of Policy Analysis and Management,* vol. 7, no. 3 (Spring 1988), copyright John Wiley & Sons, Inc. Publishers.

Dozens of people in Massachusetts—from the governor to ET workers—were willing to spend time with me, to analyze and reminisce about ET, and to talk into my tape recorder. These people include Desdemonia Alexander, Charles M. Atkins, Jean M. Bellow, Kevin Brennan, Lisa Brinkman, Paul L. Broughton, Jr., Nancy Brown, Barbara Burke-Tatum, Lee A. Chelminiak, Cindy Courtney, Philip Cummings, John Currivan, Kristin S. Demong, John DeVillars, Janet Diamond, Michael S. Dukakis, Richard Finnegan, Matthew E. Fishman, Elizabeth M. Tracy Green, Thomas P. Glynn, Ken Hamilton, Walter E. Holmes, Jr., Vivian Juusola, Paul Kussman, John Lanigan, Ann Linehan, Carol VanDeusen Lukas, Joseph W. Madison, Ruth S. Malenka, Bill McKennon, Joan Miller, John Mudd, Margaret Mulligan, Thomas O'Connor, Jay Ostrower, John O'Sullivan, Mark Pelofsky, Jolie Bain Pillsbury, Dorothy F. Renaghan, Ronnie C. Sanders, Thomas P. Sellars, Anthony Silva, Rod Southwick, John Speropoulos, Leah W. Sprague, Sylvia Tate, Michelina M. Tawa, Fred Trusten, Elizabeth W. Vorenberg, Howard L. Waddell, Dan Walsh, and Alan Werner. To all of them, my thanks.

A number of people who devote quality time to thinking about public management or about employment and training programs offered ideas or commented on drafts. They include Alan Altshuler, Eugene Bardach, Gordon L. Berlin, Maria Cohen, Patricia A. Cole, Olivia Golden, Judith M. Gueron, Stephen B. Heintz, Frank Levy, Michael Lipsky, A. Sidney Johnson III, Lawrence M. Mead, Mark H. Moore, Richard P. Nathan, Demetra S. Nightingale, Robert Reischauer, Stephen R. Rosenthal, Jeffrey L. Sedgwick, Richard Silkman, Deborah A. Stone, Carl Van Horn, Aaron Wildavsky, Michael Wiseman, and Linda A. Wolf. I appreciate their advice.

In addition, I had help from my colleagues at Duke University's Institute of Policy Sciences and Public Affairs, particularly Regina K. Brough, Philip J. Cook, Dan Durning, Helen F. Ladd, Fritz Mayer, Micheline Malson, Steven Smith, and Duncan Yaggy. They read drafts, suggested ideas, and offered critiques during faculty seminars. Finally, graduate students enrolled in Duke's course in public management read draft chapters—admittedly not as volunteers—and provided helpful comments.

These people are not responsible for any of the ideas, interpretations, inaccuracies, or idiocies in this book. A wild pitch is always the pitcher's fault. Fortunately for the pitcher, a diving catcher sometimes blocks that wild pitch in the dirt, converting what might have been a fatal error into something few remember after the game. For those who were willing to get their uniform dirty on my behalf—or who simply read a few chapters and marked the typos instead of going off for a pleasant afternoon at Fenway Park—many thanks.

What would have happened to Don Newcombe without Roy Campanella? To Luis Tiant without Carlton Fisk? To Nuke Laloosh without Crash Davis? Every pitcher needs a catcher to handle him with a combination of subtle psychology and direct truth-telling. Through this project—and many others—my catcher has been Judith H. Behn. To her, my most grateful thanks.

March 1991

Leadership Counts

Prologue

Important Events
along the Way

On November 5, 1974, Michael S. Dukakis was elected governor of Massachusetts. As a state legislator, Dukakis had built a liberal reputation, and he won the governorship with much liberal support. Yet he quickly alienated these constituents. His transition team reported that the state faced a deficit of over $300 million, with over $200 million coming from the welfare department. A reporter asked the governor-elect if he might have to take a scalpel to the state's social-service budget. "He's generous when he talks about a scalpel," responded Dukakis. "It might be a meat cleaver." Indeed, Dukakis made major cuts in social services.[1]

During Dukakis's term as governor, the number of Massachusetts families receiving assistance under the federal welfare program, Aid to Families with Dependent Children (AFDC), grew rapidly. In response, the Dukakis administration proposed a mandatory "workfare" program to provide AFDC parents—specifically fathers—with the employment history necessary to obtain a regular job. This proposal, which would have required AFDC fathers to work for fifty-two weeks or lose their welfare benefits, quickly generated vigorous opposition. The original proposal was never adopted, but the state did implement an experimental Work Experience Program that required AFDC fathers to work for thirteen weeks. But this fifteen-month experiment produced no lasting results.[2]

On September 19, 1978, Dukakis lost the Democratic primary to Edward J. King, a conservative. But Dukakis also lost liberal support to a third candidate, Barbara Ackermann, who took 7 percent of the vote; other former Dukakis supporters simply stayed home. So while King took 51 percent of the vote and Ackermann 7 percent, Dukakis won only 42 percent.

On January 6, 1983, Dukakis, after defeating King in a rematch, 54 to 46 percent, took the oath of office for a second term as governor. "Thousands of homeless wander our streets without permanent shelter," said Dukakis in his inaugural address. "And we must provide it."[3]

On Monday, May 9, 1983, Governor Dukakis appointed Charles M. Atkins to be commissioner of the Department of Public Welfare, an agency that, the governor said, had "an extraordinary mandate to act on those forces which threaten the stability of families and individuals in the commonwealth."[4]

That Friday (May 13, 1983), *The Boston Globe* reported on its front page that Mary Badger and her daughter had lost their welfare benefits and were "homeless today as a direct result of the actions of the state Department of Public Welfare, a lead agency in Gov. Michael S. Dukakis' campaign to end homelessness in Massachusetts." That Badger's daughter was a special-needs student "is not our problem," said the department's legal counsel. "I don't want to sound callous but housing is not our responsibility." Concluded the *Globe:* "Badger's case demonstrates the difficulty of translating priorities established in the governor's office into practice in the bureaucracy."[5]

Atkins, however, called the *Globe* to say that Badger's file would be reexamined, that her emergency benefits would be continued, and that she would "not be thrown out on the street."[6] Then he fired the legal counsel (who was a holdover from the King administration) because of "policy views that are not in concert with this administration's commitment to the poor." Said Atkins: "If housing isn't our direct responsibility, helping her find housing is. If we can't do it, we should find the proper people who can. That's the kind of coordination across agencies that the governor has been talking about. I want a legal staff that understands that."[7]

On August 16, 1983, Atkins sent the federal Department of Health and Human Services (HHS) a proposal to create an Employment and Training Program (to be known by its first two initials, ET) to find jobs for 40,000 welfare recipients over the next five years. Calling the program "a bold message to all that we are committed to attacking the problems of poverty," Atkins wrote that he was "committed to insuring that viable opportunities for economic self-sufficiency and long-term employment exist for welfare recipients."[8]

On September 30, 1983, HHS approved the new program. It began the next day.

On June 27, 1984, the Department of Public Welfare announced that, in the first eight months of ET, it had placed 6,000 welfare recipients in jobs paying, on average, $5.00 per hour. "Jobs plan pays off," was the editorial headline the next day in *The Boston Herald*, a newspaper that was not often a fan of the Dukakis administration.[9]

On July 6, 1984, William Raspberry reported in his column in *The Washington Post:* "I had called Massachusetts to talk to the director of the state's new jobs program for welfare recipients. The return call, when it came at 10 o'clock that night, was from Gov. Michael Dukakis himself. That should give you an idea of what Massachusetts officials think of their Employment and Training Choices program."[10]

On January 16, 1985, in his State of the State speech titled "Opportunity for All," Governor Dukakis spoke of Marie Bouchard: "Ten years ago, untrained and without day care for her children, she had to go on welfare. Today, a successful graduate of our ET Choices program, she is off welfare, back in the mainstream, and employed full-time at the Cliftex Plant in New Bedford as a Computer Scanner Operator. 'My kids look to me as an example now,' she says. 'My seventeen-year-old daughter loves computers. She won't miss a day of school because now she knows how important it is.'" The governor focused on the same benefit of ET CHOICES: "It is not simply the increased income that is important, crucial though that obviously is. I have met with dozens of our ET participants, and the change in their sense of self-worth and self-esteem, in the feelings about themselves and their futures is a wonderful thing to see and experience." He continued, "Our goal is fifty thousand placements in the next five years." This was news to Atkins. The original five-year goal had been 40,000 placements. But Dukakis was excited about ET's accomplishments—13,000 placements in fifteen months—and he exercised his gubernatorial prerogative. In his speech, he simply upped the placement goal from 40,000 to 50,000.[11]

On February 9, 1985, Governor Dukakis presented a diploma to Cherly Liberatore, the thirteen thousandth ET graduate, who began work the following day at a wage that was three times her AFDC check. Said Liberatore, "The program has given us not only the ability but also the confidence to go out with our resumes in hand and look for a job."[12]

On May 12, 1985, the Public Employees Roundtable, in Washington, D.C., gave the Massachusetts Department of Public Welfare its Public Service Excellence Award for ET CHOICES.[13]

On October 29, 1985, Governor Dukakis announced that the AFDC caseload was down 9.4 percent over the first two and a half years of his new term—the largest decrease of the twelve states with the largest number of cases. "The difference is unquestionably ET," said Dukakis. "There is no other way to explain the numbers you see on these charts."[14]

On April 19, 1986, Dukakis spoke at an ET graduation ceremony at Greater Boston YMCA Training, Inc. "I'm glad this program was here when I needed it," said Diana Whiteway, the twenty-five thousandth ET graduate who had obtained a job as a clinical secretary at the New England Medical Center. "My two daughters are proud of me. I can be a more positive image."[15]

On December 17, 1986, the Massachusetts Taxpayers Foundation (MTF), which described itself as "fiscally conservative," gave Commissioner Atkins its 1986 Lyman H. Ziegler Award for outstanding public service, saying that he had "saved the taxpayers of the Commonwealth [of Massachusetts] untold millions." MTF cited Atkins for reducing the AFDC error rate (from 11.6 to 2.5 percent), for improving child-support collections by 32 percent, for "the Employment and Training Choices Program, or ET, which has placed more than 30,000 welfare recipients in full- or part-time jobs, and has served as a model for other programs across the nation," and for having "set up management practices that have made the Department of Public Welfare among the most efficient and effective state agencies."[16]

Because the award was named for an individual known for working quietly but effectively behind the scenes, MTF's director of communications described Atkins as an appropriate recipient: "I'll bet most people don't know what he looks like."[17] In an editorial, *The Boston Herald* said that "Atkins richly deserves" the award, noting that "the state could use a few more like him."[18] Observed MTF's communications director: "This fellow is one class act. In his acceptance speech, Atkins called up a half-dozen senior staffers, one at a time, and made them stand before the crowd as he explained how each contributed to the department. No wonder he's a successful leader."[19] The people Atkins recognized included three who had significant responsibility for ET CHOICES: Thomas P. Glynn, deputy commissioner; Jolie Bain Pillsbury, associate commissioner for eligibility operations; and Barbara Burke-Tatum, associate commissioner for employment and training.

In January 1987, in an interview with the *Boston Business Journal,* Governor Dukakis was asked to name his "favorite accomplishment of the last four years." Dukakis was hesitant about "singling out one thing" but, when pressed, finally responded: "I'd say ET. The fact that we've demonstrated that you can literally help thousands and thousands of people lift themselves out of dependency and become wage-earning self-sufficient people . . . That there are people who have been on welfare for eight, 10, 12, 15 years, and today are proud and working, and supporting themselves and their children, and contributing to their community and their state, and that we're doing it in a way that is just so very positive—I think it's terrific."[20]

On April 29, 1987, Michael S. Dukakis announced his candidacy for the presidency of the United States. On the Boston Common that day, the speakers included the traditional political figures and Ruby Sampson, an ET graduate. Sampson told the campaign rally:

> I know what it is to be down, to be on welfare for fourteen years, to be isolated in poverty, to have no hope. Because of Michael Dukakis, his vision and his idea which became the ET program, I also know what it is like to be offered an opportunity. ET became my route out of poverty because it allowed me—a seventh-grade drop out who had worked in a laundry—to take a 44-week training program to become a health care professional.
>
> I never worked so hard in my life. It was the best decision I ever made. I graduated. I got a job at Brigham and Women's Hospital where I am an operating room technician in the day surgery unit. I am a health care professional.
>
> My life has changed. My children's lives have changed. Michael Dukakis and ET made me a promise that, if I took the first step, things could change for the better. Michael Dukakis kept that promise. Today, I am standing here for Michael Dukakis because he stood with me when I was all alone. I remember that, and I want to say thank you from the Sampson family.[21]

Dukakis himself said: "Ask what we have already done. Ask more than whether we have new ideas. Ask whether we have already made new ideas work."[22]

One of the new ideas to which Dukakis was referring, reported David S. Broder in *The Washington Post,* was "an innovative employment and training program that he [Dukakis] asserts has moved more than 30,000 people off welfare."[23] Dukakis's "reputation as a presidential contender has been buoyed by ET's success," said *Newsweek*.[24] "Dukakis's showcase," wrote Ronald Brownstein in *National Journal*, is "his widely discussed training and job placement program for welfare recipients."[25] Nicholas Lemann, national correspondent for *The Atlantic*, wrote that "state-initiated welfare reform has made Massachusetts Gov. Michael Dukakis a presidential contender."[26]

On June 22, 1988, at what *The Evening Gazette* of Worcester called "a festive rally," Governor Dukakis announced that his administration had achieved its goal of finding jobs for 50,000 welfare recipients.[27] A fact sheet distributed to the press presented the following data:

- Seventy-five percent of the 50,000 individuals placed through ET were off welfare.
- Eighty-six percent of the ET graduates who left welfare were still off welfare one year later.
- From October 1, 1983, through June 1, 1988, the Massachusetts AFDC caseload had declined by 6 percent (from 88,600 to 83,400), the average length of stay on AFDC had dropped by 27 percent (from 37 months to 27 months), and the number of families who had been on the caseload for more than five years was off 34 percent (from nearly 20,800 to less than 13,700).
- Over this same period, Massachusetts's AFDC benefits had increased by 47 percent while its eligibility standard grew by 70 percent.
- The average ET wage was $6.75 per hour, or $13,500 annually.
- ET had saved the state $280 million.[28]

But as was traditional at these ceremonies (Dukakis observed that this was his twenty-fifth ET announcement), the emphasis was on the people rather than on the statistics. Standing before several dozen ET graduates and their children and a banner proclaiming "ET: 50,000 Success Stories," Dukakis declared: "We have helped 50,000 families trade their welfare checks for paychecks and we have watched them share in the American dream—a good job at good wages."[29] The governor was introduced by Dawn Lawson, an ET graduate, who called him "an inspiration to all of us."[30]

The next month, Dukakis had an opportunity to return the compliment. In his acceptance speech at the Democratic National Convention, the governor said: "When a young mother named Dawn Lawson leaves seven years of welfare to become a personnel specialist in a Fortune 500 company in Worcester, Massachusetts, we are all enriched and ennobled."[31]

On November 8, 1988, George W. Bush defeated Michael S. Dukakis for the presidency of the United States. Dukakis won ten states and 46 percent of the vote. While he campaigned for the presidency, the Massachusetts state budget accumulated a significant deficit.

On January 13, 1989, Dukakis announced that he would not seek reelection in 1990. Later that month, he submitted a $13.4 billion budget, which included $1 billion in new spending and $600 million in new taxes. In July, the legislature enacted a $12.7 billion budget, which many legislators knew was out of balance. From that budget, Dukakis vetoed 700 different line items, calling the cuts "the worst thing I've ever had to do in my political career."[32]

On December 13, 1989, Standard & Poor's lowered Massachusetts's bond rating to BBB—lower than the state of Louisiana but higher than junk bonds—criticizing Massachusetts for its "poor financial operations and a paralyzed budgetary process." Meanwhile, Dukakis's unfavorability rating in the state rose to 79 percent.[33]

On January 3, 1990, the Massachusetts legislature adjourned for its 1989 session with a deficit of half a billion dollars.

On January 17, 1990, Dukakis submitted a $13.4 billion budget, which he described as "painful." To balance this budget would require over a billion dollars in new taxes.[34]

On April 10, 1990, the governor's Revenue Advisory Board reduced its revenue projections; as a result, the projected budget deficit for fiscal years 1990 and 1991 grew to $2.3 billion.

On April 12, 1990, George Keverian, speaker of the Massachusetts House of Representatives, declared that, if Dukakis resigned, the House would pass the necessary taxes. "If Dukakis quit?" asked the speaker rhetorically. "We'd win tomorrow." The state's voters were angry with the governor, said the speaker; legislators were reporting that the voters were saying, "We're not giving any more taxes to him." "Who is the most hated man in the state?" asked Keverian. His answer: "Dukakis."[35]

On July 19, 1990, Dukakis signed a $1.2 billion tax increase—the largest in the state's history.

What is this ET CHOICES program that brought Michael Dukakis to the attention of Russell Baker's "Great Mentioner" (that mysterious person who "mentions" people for president)? What was it about the program that convinced a former welfare recipient to speak out for the governor's candidacy? What features of the program deserve to be considered a "national model"? Who is this commissioner of public welfare who, said the guardians of the taxpayers, "has managed to turn a mess of a department into a very efficient operation"? Who are these deputy and associate commissioners who brought down the error rate and convinced welfare recipients that they wanted to work? What exactly was ET CHOICES? How did it work? Was it as good as the Dukakis administration claimed? How can we evaluate such an ongoing program? How was ET managed? What can public managers learn about leadership from ET?

The summer of 1988, when he was nominated for president, was Michael Dukakis's political high-water mark. He never recovered politically from his defeat that November, and Massachusetts state government will not recover financially for years. Nevertheless, one of the major accomplishments of the five years prior to Dukakis's presidential nomination—indeed, one of the accomplishments that helped him win the nomination—was ET CHOICES.

What can be learned from ET? Although on the pages that follow I relate much of the ET story from 1983 through 1988, this is not a work of history. My purpose is not to chart every nuance of ET's course or to explore what happened after 1988, when ET, like most programs in the state, was affected by the decline in Massachusetts's economy and the state's budget deficit. Rather, in this book, I seek to uncover from the years 1983–1988 important ideas that can be applied to the management of other welfare, training, and employment programs. States and municipalities can use the specific lessons from ET to manage the JOBS program, which Congress created in 1988, and they can use more generalized lessons about leadership to manage their welfare departments.

But the managerial lessons from ET CHOICES are not only useful for the field of welfare or social services in general. They apply to the management of any public agency—be it a municipal water department or the FBI. Public managers can adapt the concepts of leadership illustrated by ET CHOICES to improve the effectiveness of a multitude of public programs and public agencies. Indeed, ET CHOICES reinforces an important lesson for any executive-branch agency: Leadership counts.

1

The Idea behind
ET CHOICES

Management requires an idea. To produce results, the public manager needs to know *what* results he or she wants to produce and *how* they might be produced. The manager needs a sense of where he is going and a good first guess about how he might get there.

ET CHOICES was based on an idea—an idea about how training and work programs could and should be part of the services delivered by a state welfare department. This idea had eight components, some of which set forth the purposes of the program, others of which suggested how a state welfare department could go about achieving these purposes. Neither the overall idea nor the eight individual concepts were explicitly listed in a master strategic plan of the Massachusetts Department of Public Welfare or even in a definitive speech delivered by the commissioner or the governor. Nevertheless, these eight concepts were repeated frequently and in various ways by the department's publications and people. Together they describe the idea that became ET CHOICES.

Eight Concepts

1. WELFARE RECIPIENTS WANT TO WORK
The "premise" behind ET CHOICES, stated the department, is "that most welfare recipients will choose employment over welfare if given access to quality educational, vocational, job placement and support services such as day care and transportation."[1] This premise is, of course, an assumption. There is some empirical evidence to support it—evidence that indicates that welfare recipients are not distinguishable from the rest of the population (including the working population) in their attitudes toward work.[2] Still, it is an assumption.

This is a sharp contrast to the traditional stereotype of the "lazy" welfare recipient. Not that welfare recipients always want to work; the lives of the people receiving welfare are sufficiently discombobulated that often they do not have employable skills or even know how to find work. Moreover, working is not always a "logical" alternative to welfare—particularly when wages are low or when working causes a family to lose other benefits, particularly medical insurance. Nevertheless, this first concept was that, everything else being equal, enough welfare recipients would prefer to be working and independent over being on welfare and dependent to make it worthwhile to do something about this desire.

Indeed, Massachusetts's leaders offered ET as living proof of this first concept. "With ET, we have destroyed the myth that welfare recipients do not want to work," Governor Michael S. Dukakis stated repeatedly. "The lesson of ET is that when you offer people on public assistance a genuine opportunity, they will choose work over welfare every time."[3]

2. THE DEPARTMENT OF PUBLIC WELFARE SHOULD HELP WELFARE RECIPIENTS FIND "A ROUTE OUT OF POVERTY"

This second concept was not quite as uncontroversial as it might seem. Is the mission of a welfare department to *sustain* people who have no (or little) income? Is its mission to *help* people become self-sufficient? Or is its mission to *force* people to become self-sufficient?

The managers of the Massachusetts Department of Public Welfare chose to emphasize their role in providing dependent families with services that could help them become self-sufficient. As Commissioner Charles M. Atkins wrote in a memo to Barbara Burke-Tatum, the associate commissioner for employment and training, "The ET program's primary goal is to help welfare clients become self-sufficient through employment."[4] Internally, in the department, this mission gave a new sense of purpose to the people who worked there; externally, it presented a new image to the public.

Not that the idea was unique to Massachusetts; state legislators and members of Congress, state welfare commissioners, and county welfare directors have reached the same conclusion (though some argue that those on welfare should be compelled to become self-sufficient). But as with other aspects of ET CHOICES, the leadership of the department publicized and dramatized this concept more than some others have.

The assumption that welfare recipients want to work and the decision that one role of a welfare department is to help them do so (and thus become self-sufficient) provided the philosophical underpinnings of ET CHOICES. The other six concepts were important because they shaped the specifics of the program, but they were all contingent on these first two.

3. TO HELP RECIPIENTS BECOME SELF-SUFFICIENT, THE DEPART-MENT MUST PROVIDE BASIC EDUCATION, JOB-SKILLS TRAINING, AND PLACEMENT SERVICES

Some welfare recipients are ready to work. They have the education and the skills (including the necessary "attitudinal skills") to hold down a job. But they need help in finding a job. They need an understanding of the market for their services and information about specific openings.

Many more, however, are simply not ready for employment. They lack the skills or even the basic education required to get and hold a job. In this case, the department will first have to provide the welfare recipients with general, basic education and specific job skills.

4. RECIPIENTS ALSO NEED SUPPORT SERVICES, PARTICULARLY DAY CARE AND TRANSPORTATION

A training program may be free, but taking advantage of it is not. The welfare recipient confronts the cost of getting to and from the program. And what can a woman do with her young children while she is engaged in a training program? ET covered the transportation expenses of recipients enrolled in training programs and subsidized day care. In fact, ET's day-care support continued for a year after the recipient got a job and left welfare.

Massachusetts provided one other "service": a vigorous effort to obtain child-support payments from delinquent fathers. When a woman obtained a job and sought to leave welfare, these child-support payments provided essential income.

5. TO HAVE A PERMANENT IMPACT, THE DEPARTMENT NEEDS A LONG-TERM PERSPECTIVE

If welfare recipients are to become truly independent they need more than just a job. They need a good job—one that is full-time and generates income (and benefits) that are clearly superior to those offered by welfare. "If a worker works full time all year at the minimum wage," writes David T. Ellwood of Harvard University, "he or she will not earn enough to keep even a two-person family above the poverty line. To support a family of four, one must earn 60 percent above the minimum wage."[5] But such jobs—jobs that support not just an individual but a family—require more than minimal skills and education.

For some welfare, training, and work programs, states and municipalities have given priority to immediate job placements (of any kind) and offered training only if the job-placement effort proved that the individual was not employable. For example, this was true of the Work and Training Program (WTP) of the King administration.[6]

In contrast, the leaders of the Massachusetts Department of Public Welfare sought to identify jobs that could ensure long-term economic stability, and to provide the education and training necessary to obtain and keep one of those jobs. Rather than push welfare recipients into the first available job, the department took a long-term view. It was willing to invest the resources required to get a welfare recipient not just any job but a good job—one that offered a route out of poverty.

6. TO BE EFFECTIVE, ANY WELFARE, TRAINING, AND EMPLOYMENT PROGRAM MUST BE VOLUNTARY

The Department of Public Welfare did require welfare recipients to participate in ET CHOICES. Because ET was the state's version of the federal WIN (Work Incentive) Demonstration program that all states were required to provide, registration was indeed mandatory for all AFDC recipients (except those who were exempt under the federal guidelines). But beyond registration, Massachusetts did not require further involvement. The King administration employed the stick of sanctions—the loss of welfare benefits—to get recipients to participate in WTP. The Dukakis administration employed the carrot of employment—the gain of a job— to get recipients to sign up for active participation in ET. For three reasons, ET's managers decided to make their program voluntary.

First, there was the "Alcoholics-Anonymous assumption." AA believes no treatment will prove effective until the alcoholic explicitly decides that he needs help. Similarly, ET's managers believed that education, training, and job-placement services would have no significant impact until the welfare recipient explicitly decided that she needed it.

Second, ET's managers realized that Massachusetts—even with its low unemployment rate—could not find a job (let alone a well-paying, full-time job that would lead to independence) for every welfare recipient. Nor did the state have the resources to provide education and training for all welfare recipients. There had to be some way to ration the limited state resources that were available for training and employment services. Making the program voluntary was one way to do this.[7]

Third, "sanctions" did not seem to work. Under a mandatory program, a welfare recipient who refuses to participate is "sanctioned": after an often lengthy appeal process, her (but not her children's) benefits are eliminated for a period of several months. But, concluded a special panel created by the National Academy of Public Administration, "sanctions are rarely effective in forcing unmotivated clients to participate and are time consuming for workers."[8] Even Lawrence M. Mead of New York University, who advocates requiring welfare recipients to work, has found that local welfare offices that produce more job placements impose fewer sanctions than do offices that prove less effective.[9]

"Our experience has been you can't club people off the welfare rolls," said Dukakis. "They have to want to do it." Argued the governor: "You can try and mandate anything you want but it won't work without an attractive program."[10] Still, Dukakis's own, personal work ethic was strong. He believed everyone ought to work—including welfare recipients—and he resisted calling his program voluntary. When this word appeared in internal memos about ET, he circled it and sent them back.[11] The voluntary characteristic of ET was clearly its most controversial.

7. EACH RECIPIENT MUST MAKE HER OWN CRITICAL CHOICES

"What makes ET so different from other welfare employment programs?" asked Atkins rhetorically. "The main factor is choice."[12] This concept of *choices* was dramatized in the second word of the program's name: ET CHOICES. There is a similarity between the sixth concept—that the program should be *voluntary*—and this one. But they are distinct.

Each welfare recipient had two choices. First, she had to choose whether or not to participate actively in the ET program. This is the voluntary concept. Second, if she did choose to participate, she had to choose the purpose and nature of that participation. She needed to choose her career objective: did she want to become a secretary, a computer programmer, or a hospital operating-room technician? Next she needed to choose the educational and training programs in which to enroll to get that job. This is the concept of *choices*.

In part, the concept of choices was based on the same Alcoholics-Anonymous assumption that underlay the voluntary concept. If the recipient herself decided that she wanted to become a computer programmer, and decided that she wanted to get her high-school Graduate Equivalency Diploma (GED), then she would be much more committed to seeing the program through. But the concept of choices was also based on two additional assumptions.

The second assumption was that each individual welfare recipient needed her own, individualized "route out of poverty." It would not make sense to attempt to turn all participating recipients into secretaries, or computer programmers, or operating-room technicians.

The third assumption behind the concept of choices was that the individual welfare recipient herself (not her social worker or an outside consultant) was in the best position to make the decisions about her overall objectives and how to achieve them. The department had the responsibility to provide guidance and help—a lot of guidance and help. But the best route out of poverty would be one chosen by the recipient herself.

8. OTHER ORGANIZATIONS ARE BEST ABLE TO PROVIDE EDUCATION, TRAINING, PLACEMENT, AND SUPPORT SERVICES

The King administration, argued Thomas P. Glynn, Atkins's deputy commissioner, had attempted to convert the department into a bank. Its basic responsibility was to determine an individual's eligibility for AFDC and other welfare programs. The job of the employees on the front line, the financial assistance workers (FAWs), was to determine an individual's eligibility for AFDC and other welfare programs. That is, they made sure that the forms were filled out correctly. In fact, numerous clerks were promoted to be FAWs because, after all, the skills required were similar.

Because the job of the department was to process the paperwork properly and mail out the correct checks, it did very little traditional social work. In the last year and a half of the King administration, a part of the agency became involved in education, training, and job search, but those working on WTP were isolated from the workers who determined eligibility. The FAWs knew little about work or training. Thus, in early 1983, the Massachusetts Department of Public Welfare had no distinctive competence in basic education, job training, or employment search.

In government, the natural tendency of an agency's managers is to do all the critical functions in-house. Coordinating anything with other government agencies is a major hassle if not completely impossible. Different agendas, different constituencies, different rules, different expectations, different ethoses all work against effective coordination between agencies. Consequently, in 1983 it would have been natural to predict that if the Massachusetts Department of Public Welfare was going to get into the education, training, and job-search business that it would try to create its own divisions of education, of training, and of job search. After all, the state's employment and placement agency (the Division of Employment Security) had a history of showing a disdain for welfare recipients. Such job seekers were not as easy to place as people not burdened with the stigma of welfare or the despair of dependency. And the state's educational system was even less interested in serving this population.

Nevertheless, Atkins, Glynn, and Burke-Tatum rejected the traditional approach. For most of the services required to make ET work, they decided to rely upon the traditional agencies in state government and to encourage outside organizations to develop additional services to fill specific needs. Rather than undertake the long process of creating these skills within the department, they sought to build relationships with other organizations that already possessed the required capabilities.

The Evolution of the Idea

This, then, was the idea behind ET CHOICES. These eight concepts were not, however, abstract theoretical principles. They reflected the realities of the political climate, organizational culture, and economic circumstances. Nor were any of these eight concepts—or the coherent collection of them—articulated in this form from the beginning. The idea evolved over time, as did the program itself.

Glynn, in fact, observed that there were really two ETs. ET-I was the program for the first three years (from when it was first conceived and implemented in 1983 through the end of the 1986 fiscal year). ET-II was the modification—distinguished primarily by the new emphasis on case management—that began in the spring and summer of 1986. ET-II, explained Glynn, involved "fixing" ET-I.

Over time, the realities and lessons of program management affected the idea behind ET, just as the maturing of the idea affected its management. The result of this evolutionary process was a coherent set of concepts that, though not set forth in a single document, was nevertheless widely understood.

The Mandatory-Voluntary Debate

Throughout the 1980s, welfare reform was on the national political agenda. In October 1988, Congress passed and President Ronald Reagan signed the "Family Support Act of 1988"—a major revision of the nation's welfare laws requiring states to create education, training, and employment programs. In the debate over this legislation, one of the key issues was whether work and training should be voluntary or mandatory. The final bill presented a compromise. If the resources are available to offer educational, training, and job-placement services and child care, all welfare recipients, except those with a child under three years of age, will be required to participate in the new JOBS program.

The debate over whether federal welfare reform should be mandatory or voluntary has been fierce—that is, ideological.[13] Those who advocate mandatory programs emphasize, as has Mead, the obligation of welfare recipients to repay society—through work—for the benefits they have received. Moreover, continues the argument, even if welfare recipients want to work, they will not really do so unless it is required.[14] Others believe that the availability of welfare destroys the individual recipient's initiative[15] and thus should be discouraged. Finally, there is the argument that only a mandatory program will reach the welfare recipients who most need training and employment services. "When you have a voluntary program you skim off the cream," said Drew Altman, then New Jersey's commissioner of human resources. "The people [who are most likely to be served] are just marginally on welfare and can be moved easily into the workforce."[16]

Others are equally vigorous in arguing that any welfare, training, and work program should be voluntary, for reasons already described. Says Glynn: "There are two philosophies of fighting poverty. One is penitence. The other is opportunity."[17]

In reality, the operational differences between ET CHOICES and the mandatory programs in other states have not been as great as implied by the rhetoric. Some programs have been mandatory only for new applicants; others required participation only for the adult males in two-parent AFDC families. At the same time, although ET was nominally voluntary, the department pressured the local welfare offices to produce job placements, and in turn local offices pressured recipients to participate.

Mary Jo Bane of Harvard University has suggested another way to think about whether a welfare, training, and work program should be voluntary or mandatory. The decision might depend on *effectiveness*—"whether one or the other type of program is more effective in achieving what everyone is presumably seeking: the movement of clients from welfare to self-sufficiency."[18] This criterion converts the debate from one over ideology to one about management. Is it easier for a state welfare commissioner and the directors of local welfare offices to produce these results, which both liberals and conservatives desire, using a mandatory program or a voluntary one? To resolve this issue, Bane asked three questions about the relationship between social workers and welfare recipients that are crucial to moving the recipient from welfare to work:

- Given what we know about desired client outcomes and about the broader structure of the welfare system, what kinds of worker-client interactions are most congruent with achieving the goals of successful placement in appropriate jobs?
- What are the elements of an organizational culture and central man-

agement approach that would be most likely to elicit the desired type of worker-client interactions?

- How does a program requirement that participation be mandatory or voluntary affect the likelihood of achieving a supportive organizational culture and successful worker-client interactions?[19]

Bane wants to know whether a mandatory or voluntary program is more likely to produce organizational behavior necessary to deliver the desired result.

Maybe It All Doesn't Depend

An obvious answer to Bane's question is also a common one: It all depends. "The most effective organization depends upon the situation," argues Harvey Sherman. "There is no one 'ideal' or 'best' organization except for a particular agency, at a particular time, with particular people."[20] In the case of welfare reform, for example, whether work and training should be mandatory or voluntary might depend upon the political environment, the source of welfare services (the state or the counties), the skills of the social workers, or the thinking of the chairman of the House Ways and Means Committee. The choice between mandatory and voluntary can depend on many factors.

But maybe it all doesn't depend. Maybe both voluntary and mandatory programs can be made to work. Bane observes that "good programs can be run under either rubric."[21] Judith M. Gueron, president of the Manpower Demonstration Research Corporation (MDRC), which has analyzed numerous employment and training programs, believes that "a number of quite different ways of structuring and targeting these programs will yield effective results." "A key explanation for the successful implementation of these initiatives," concludes Gueron, "may indeed be that states were given an opportunity to experiment and felt more ownership in the programs than they did in the earlier WIN program."[22]

Certainly Atkins, Glynn, and Burke-Tatum "owned" ET. They conceived it and developed it. It was their program. But in many ways it was also the program of everyone in the department. In late 1983, Jolie Bain Pillsbury joined the department as its associate commissioner in charge of the field operations; she played a critical role in implementing each stage of ET and conceiving the next. Pillsbury, too, owned ET.

Atkins, Glynn, Burke-Tatum, and Pillsbury made ET work. The program they developed reflected not only their own beliefs but also the circumstances within which they operated. But they could, I believe, also have produced results with a mandatory program. Had the political environment required one, they could have adapted and developed a set of ideas with the characteristics necessary to make it work. Conversely, managers in other states who have made mandatory programs a success could have done the same with a voluntary program. What is critical is not whether the program is voluntary or mandatory but whether the management strategy selected to implement the chosen approach—and the organizational culture created to support that strategy—meshes well with the approach and with the political and organizational environment within which the program must function.

Leadership Requires an Idea

The eight concepts behind ET CHOICES were not unique. Other states have believed and acted upon similar concepts—though obviously creating programs with different emphases and specifics. Nor was the idea behind ET the key to creating the perfect welfare, training, and work program. Many of the eight concepts on which ET was based have been subject to much debate.

Leadership requires an idea. The eight concepts behind ET not only presented Massachusetts's policies for work, training, and welfare; they also provided the framework for managing these policies. For example, taking the *long-term perspective* obliged the department to provide a wide variety of training services as well as the most basic of educational programs. The reliance on *other organizations* to provide educational, training, and job-search services caused the department to develop a system of performance-based contracts. The *voluntary* nature of the program forced the department to place a heavy emphasis on marketing. The concept of *choices* required that the department provide much personal counseling to individual welfare recipients as well as provide a wide variety of educational, training, and job-search services.

These eight concepts behind ET cannot be automatically transferred to another state. Adaptation is necessary. Conversely, the eight concepts are not the only ones that can produce results. Mandatory programs can work too. So can programs that provide all the necessary services in-house rather than contract for them with outside agencies. What is most important is not which idea the managers adopt, but that they adopt an idea—some idea. It helps if that idea is sound and consistent. But an idea beats no idea every time.

The management of that program should be based on that idea. Other programs based on other concepts have to be managed differently. If, rather than help welfare recipients find a route out of poverty, a welfare, training, and work program were designed to reduce welfare costs, it would be managed differently. The same would be true if the program were designed to ensure that welfare recipients fulfilled their obligation to society. And certainly such a program would be managed quite differently if it were mandatory.

Leadership requires an idea. The public manager needs a general, overarching concept to focus everyone's attention. The exact character of that idea is not as important as that the manager have one—and that it be internally consistent. The nature of the manager's idea, of course, affects the specifics of how he or she manages it. (And some ideas may be easier to manage than others; thus the manager may have to iterate back and forth—adjusting both the idea and the management of it—until he achieves a combination that is internally consistent.) But without an overarching idea, the manager cannot exercise leadership. To lead, the manager has to have a clear idea of *what* he is trying to accomplish and *how* he is going to do it.

The idea must contain a vision—a vision of how the future will be better because of the accomplishments of the organization. Warren Bennis and Burt Nanus echo what many others have observed when they discuss this "universal principle of leadership." The leader's vision, they write, presents "a realistic, credible, attractive future for the organization"—"a clear sense of its purpose, direction, and desired future state"—and thus "provides the all-important bridge from the present to the future."[23]

Atkins's vision was designed to transform the Massachusetts Department of Public Welfare from a bank staffed by clerks who determined eligibility, processed paper, and wrote checks into a social-service agency that helped people get an education, obtain some career training, straighten out their lives, and then find a job that would get them out of poverty, keep them off welfare, and make them self-sufficient for the rest of their lives. Atkins wanted to turn his department into a model for the nation. He, Glynn, Burke-Tatum, and Pillsbury repeated this vision frequently. They wanted everyone in the department to "see themselves," as Bennis and Nanus think should be a leader's objective, "as part of a worthwhile enterprise."[24]

If any welfare, training, and work program is to work, the leaders of the public welfare agency must have a mission. They must be able to convince the organization to pursue aggressively the purpose underlying their work, training, and welfare program. Bane notes that Mead's "description of successful WIN offices (and it is consistent with what we know about successful enterprises more generally) is one of workers and clients with a clear mission—to get clients to work."[25]

The leadership idea must, however, contain more than a vision of the future. In addition to *what* the organization will accomplish, the idea needs to include some concept of *how* this vision will be realized. Not that the leaders at the top need to manage or even understand all the details of implementation. But the vision must mesh with reality. Does the agency have the organizational capability to produce the desired results? How will people be motivated to carry out the necessary tasks? How will the leadership know if it is accomplishing its objectives? The leadership idea must include both a sense of purpose and a sense of how to achieve that purpose.

2

The Birth of
ET CHOICES

In April 1982, the administration of Governor Edward J. King launched its Work and Training Program (WTP) under the authority of the federal Work Incentive Demonstration (or WIN-Demo) Program. WTP was not a traditional "workfare" program. That is, the purpose of WTP was not to ensure that welfare recipients, in return for their monthly check, fulfilled their obligation to society by working at some nonpaying, public-sector job.

Rather, WTP was designed to move employable recipients off welfare by requiring as many as possible to take private-sector jobs. Participants were required to take any job they found if it was at or above the minimum wage and to accept any available child care that met their nominal needs. A recipient who failed to find a job after five weeks could continue the job search (on a group or individual basis), enter a training program, or participate in a "supported work" program.[1] But few training or supported-work positions were available.

AFDC recipients who failed to participate in WTP (and who were not exempt) were vulnerable to "sanctions"—having their monthly welfare check reduced by an amount that reflected their own, but not their children's, portion of the welfare grant. One analysis found that of the 35,100 people participating in WTP during 1982, 5,334 were placed in jobs, and 1,998, or 37 percent, were still in their jobs thirty days later. Another 5,328 recipients were referred for "sanctioning," of whom 1,636 actually had their monthly checks reduced by at least some amount.[2]

The Report of the Work and Welfare Advisory Task Force

In early 1983, Governor Michael Dukakis appointed Manuel Carballo to be his new secretary of human services. On March 4, over two dozen representatives of various social service organizations sent Carballo a letter urging his "immediate attention to several serious problems" with WTP and recommending that he "convene a representative Advisory Task Force to investigate alternative approaches to education, training, work and welfare."[3] The governor was already sending out the word to his departments, recalled Chela Tawa (who then worked for the United Community Planning Corporation), that his second administration would be more open than his first. The new human services secretary, presumably picking up on this theme, invited the group to his office.

At this meeting, on April 15th, Carballo created his Work and Welfare Advisory Task Force and asked the group to develop a new work and training program that met three constraints. The new secretary wanted a program that:

1. Would satisfy federal legislation and regulations under the WIN-Demo program (so that it would be eligible for federal reimbursement);
2. Could be funded by the department's existing state budget for the coming fiscal year (which would begin on July 1); and
3. Would have adequate support in the state legislature.

Recalled Tawa (who became a member of the Task Force), Carballo's charge was, in effect, "If you wanted an ideal program, what would it look like?"

Four weeks later, the Task Force responded with a fifty-page report. Urging "the new Administration to attack the problems of poverty head-on," the thirty-member group proposed "a new work and training program that emphasizes educational programs and training opportunities as necessary steps leading to participants becoming 'primary earners' for their families."[4] The Task Force outlined a program that would:

- Be *voluntary*—"that first priority be given to those showing the most motivation and interest in participating";[5]
- Include a vigorous *outreach* campaign to convince welfare recipients to participate;
- Place *priority* first on volunteers, second on women whose youngest child was 14 to 18 (and who thus would become ineligible for AFDC in the next few years), and third on two-parent families (those who were eligible under AFDC-UP, the AFDC Unemployed Parent program);
- Provide an *individualized assessment* of each participant's social-service needs, educational requirements, and career goals that would result in an "individualized Employment Plan" for the recipient;
- Emphasize *education and training* before any job search;

- *Contract out* many of the assessment and training services;
- Provide *day care* and *transportation* services; and
- Involve active *job development* designed to utilize resources beyond those available through the Department of Public Welfare or the Division of Employment Security and not place the entire burden of finding a job on the recipient herself.

The Task Force's top priority was to change WTP's "punitive approach." The objective of placing recipients in "self-sustaining jobs" will, it argued, "be met far more effectively with a program that is designed to support and motivate, rather than to sanction and punish." Thus, the Task Force emphasized changing the tone of the program so that it would "highlight the positive goals of WTP, meaningful training, education and employment opportunities rather than the negative 'you must do this or else' orientation." In fact, argued the Task Force, a "well-run program . . . need not rely on the sanction to accomplish its goals. Sanctions should be used only as a last resort."[6]

Atkins Appointed Commissioner

Meanwhile, Carballo was looking for a new welfare commissioner. Charles M. Atkins, who had been the undersecretary of human services at the end of Dukakis's first term, had wanted to be the new secretary of human services. (Instead, Dukakis asked him to be the commissioner of mental health, a job that Atkins turned down.) When Carballo was appointed secretary, Atkins (at the urging of Robert Farmer, Dukakis's chief fund-raiser) called Carballo to congratulate him, and occasionally over the next several months, Carballo and Atkins talked.

During one of these conversations, Carballo offered Atkins the job of commissioner of public welfare. Recalled Atkins:

> I took a piece of paper and I said, "Well, Manny, you got me on the hook. What I'd really like to do is do a welfare-to-work program." And we did a back-of-the-envelope calculation about how many people we thought we could place into jobs . . . At the time there were 90,000 families on welfare, and I remember sitting there, and literally on the back of an envelope, we picked a goal of 40,000. I didn't know what I was talking about, but I said, "You know, I bet we could get 40,000 people into jobs." We both got excited talking about: "Wouldn't it be fun to go do that?" And it was just very clear, he and I thought alike on a lot of this stuff . . . Right from the beginning, . . . Manny and I agreed that this was going to be a top priority—placing people in jobs.

On Monday, May 9, Atkins was sworn in as commissioner of public welfare.

For the previous four years, Atkins had worked at Arthur D. Little as a management consultant. Before joining the first Dukakis administration in 1978, he had run Boston's Employment and Economic Policy Administration, which conducted employment and training programs. He had also worked for the Department of Defense, Citibank, and Harvard University. But as a manager, Atkins's formative experience was working for Gordon Chase in New York City.

In 1970, after John V. Lindsay was elected to a second term as mayor, he appointed Chase to head one of his superagencies, the Health Services Administration. Shortly thereafter, Atkins left the Defense Department to run Chase's planning staff. After two years Chase took on a second title as commissioner of the Addiction Services Agency, and Atkins became the deputy commissioner, running the city's efforts to place drug addicts in treatment programs and to find jobs for former addicts.

In his four years as HSA administrator, Chase trained a number of public managers. Chase, noted Atkins, "was just terrific at . . . moving his staff along at the right point in their careers . . . There were literally a hundred of us who he trained and are now spread all over the country." Atkins loved to tell stories about Chase, to talk about what he learned from Chase, and to discuss Chase's principles of management. In fact, Atkins frequently distributed his list of Chase's ten management principles to those who worked in the Massachusetts Department of Public Welfare:

1. Choose carefully what is doable; decide whether you can accomplish something substantial, and then set your goals.
2. If you are unable to meet your goals, change them.
3. Recruit a first-class staff and derive first-class benefits.
4. Understand that it is the output that counts.
5. Be able to quantify results. If you can't find a way, you haven't tried hard enough.
6. Report on your progress to your superiors.
7. Keep yourself well informed on important projects.
8. Schedule periodic meetings with program managers to get results firsthand.
9. Praise your staff.
10. Remember that government has the will and capacity to deliver services efficiently to people in need.[7]

Atkins came to his new job in Massachusetts determined to apply Chase's principles to the general task of running the Department of Public

Welfare—and to the specific assignment of finding employment for welfare recipients.

Developing the Initial Program

Despite the detail of the Task Force report, the welfare department had to convert its recommendations into a working program. Specifically, the welfare department had to obtain federal approval, create the necessary internal structure, establish procedures and distribute them to the field staff, develop or change the relations with contractors, train its own people, bring legislators and constituents on board, communicate a mission, and harness energies.

In 1983, the Massachusetts Department of Public Welfare had five thousand employees, and the contractors through whom it would work had several thousand more. Those associated with WTP had been working with a program designed, in the words of Alan Werner (who became the department's director of research), to "push" recipients off welfare.[8] These employees and the mothers (and occasionally fathers) who were the heads of the 88,000 AFDC cases had been conditioned to this philosophy and to the vigorous use of sanctions.

Now, however, the philosophy was to be reversed. Sanctions were out; marketing was in. The new program would attempt to "pull" recipients off welfare—to attract them to the education and training programs and to the opportunities of meaningful employment. It was a significant managerial task of getting not just one but several large organizations to switch not only their orientation but also their complete direction.

This work began in the Executive Office of Human Services. John Mudd, Carballo's deputy secretary, took the initial responsibility of convening a working group to convert the report into a program. The first group included Ronnie Sanders of Carballo's staff plus two people from the Executive Office of Economic Affairs: Catherine N. Stratton, the new associate secretary who headed the Office of Training and Employment Policy (OTEP, the state's agency for implementing the Job Training Partnership Act, JTPA); and Kristin Demong, Dukakis's finance director during the 1982 campaign and now the new director of the Division of Employment Security (DES). (Demong and Atkins were also wife and husband.)

Soon Atkins began to chair a series of management meetings, which alternated between DES and the welfare department. Like all the other participants, Barbara Burke-Tatum, the new associate commissioner for employment and training, recalled these sessions vividly: "We were meeting on Saturdays and really brainstorming . . . We were charged with coming up with an idea . . . We were going on a lot of guesstimates; there was no research, planning, and evaluation unit. It had been disbanded under the past governor. We were doing a lot of guessing, and [making] a lot of assumptions based on our past experience in employment and training. We didn't know a lot about the caseload."

One Saturday morning that everyone remembers (although they each remember it slightly differently), Atkins sketched out a simple flow chart. "I remember people thinking it through and drawing very complicated flow charts," said Atkins. "At one point, I just got up and took the magic marker with the task-force flow chart in my mind, and just drew what is now written in stone." The exact wording inside the boxes (like everything else about ET) evolved over time; nevertheless, four years later, Atkins's diagram still provided one of the best ways to illustrate and understand the basic operation of ET CHOICES. (See Figure 2.1.)

To manage the process of putting the specifics of the program together, Atkins, Burke-Tatum, and Thomas P. Glynn (the department's new deputy commissioner) developed a detailed workplan that delineated each specific task, the individual(s) responsible for its completion, and the expected date of completion. The initial ET workplan contained tasks such as federal approval, instructions for the field, a procedures handbook, staff training, the distribution of ET's field staff, and marketing. It covered contract monitoring and negotiations with potential contractors, such as DES, OTEP, educational agencies, the Bay State Skills Corporation, and the Commonwealth Service Corps. This workplan also included items concerning assessment, output measurements, and evaluation—work to be done by the re-created office of research, planning, and evaluation.

ET demanded so much time from the top executives in the Department of Public Welfare and other agencies because it was not to be a local pilot project or a regional experiment. Such efforts made little sense to Atkins: "One of Gordon's rules that I've explained to people [and] that I try to follow religiously is: 'Don't come to me with pilot projects. Don't come to me with demonstrations.' Gordon's rule was, [given] the effort that you put into planning and implementing a pilot project or a demonstration project, you might as well do it—in Gordon's case, citywide—you might as well do it statewide." On October 1, ET was going to start, not just in Boston or Worcester, but everywhere—statewide, and all on the same day.

The WIN-Waiver Amendment

First, however, federal approval was needed. So on August 16, the department sent off, to the Department of Health and Human Services (HHS), their proposal to amend the "WIN Waiver" under which WTP had been conducted. The minimum turnaround time for HHS to approve any change in a state's WIN-Demo was forty-five days; thus to begin the new program on October 1, Massachusetts had to submit its paperwork by August 16. (After language and fire, the most important human invention is the deadline.)

This WIN-waiver amendment created "the formidable goal of placing 40,000 individuals into meaningful employment over the next five years."[9] Indeed, it set forth a series of "ambitious but obtainable goals":

- to place 40,000 clients in employment over a five-year period;
- to reduce the size of the AFDC caseload by creating avenues out of poverty through education, training and unsubsidized jobs with upward mobility potential;
- to reduce the average period of AFDC dependency;
- to eliminate welfare recidivism through job and support service stability within available resources;
- to increase welfare clients' employment potential through extensive literacy skill development;
- to break the welfare dependency cycle through early intervention aimed at teenage heads of households and teenage dependent children;
- to reduce, by a significant percentage, the number of AFDC families whose youngest children are 14 or older; and
- to coordinate all public and private employment efforts for which clients are eligible.[10]

The department estimated that "approximately 24,000 AFDC mandatory and voluntary registrants will participate for an estimated 8,000 placements per year."[11]

In the WIN-waiver amendment, the department noted that, although it had "approximately $23 million available to launch ET this year," resources for training and education would be "limited"; consequently, the department proposed to "concentrate its efforts on five selected groups":

- AFDC Principal Earners in two-parent families;
- Volunteers (from any other category of welfare recipients);

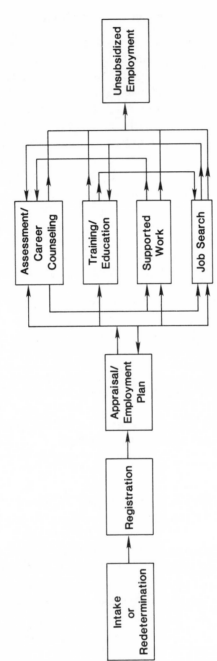

Figure 2.1a   Atkins's original flowchart for ET, June 1983. From the Massachusetts Department of Public Welfare.

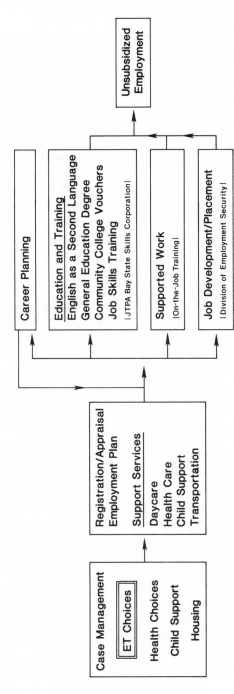

Figure 2.1b   The modified flowchart for ET, 1987. From the Massachusetts Department of Public Welfare.

- Women with Children between ages 14–18;
- Pregnant teenage girls and teenage mothers who volunteer;
- Teenage children of recipients.[12]

Nowhere in the document did the department explicitly state that the program would be voluntary. In fact, it repeatedly emphasized that registration was mandatory. Still, one did not have to read too carefully to understand what was meant by "a program based on positive incentives." For example: "An effective marketing strategy is critical to the success of ET." And: "Self-motivated applicants and recipients who respond to outreach will be placed in active components." Or: "ET has been designed as a positive program which will serve its population and will gain their willing participation. Under such a program failure to participate and imposition of sanctions should be minimal."[13] Only the principal earner in two-parent households (then approximately 8 percent of Massachusetts's AFDC caseload) would really be required to participate.

As described in the WIN-waiver amendment, ET was nearly identical to the proposal set forth by the Task Force. To this coalition of welfare advocates, ET was a major break with the policies of Governor King and with those of Dukakis's first administration. In Massachusetts, previous welfare, training, and work programs had been mandatory with an emphasis (though more in rhetoric than in reality) on sanctions. Now the Department of Public Welfare was about to launch a program that possessed the characteristic the advocates wanted most: it was voluntary.

Such a change was not just happenstance. The advocacy community had influenced the nature of the program. The consultations initiated by Carballo and continued by Atkins and Glynn established a new relationship between the welfare department and those who lobbied on behalf of welfare recipients. A few years later, welfare advocates sued the state using a seventy-year-old law in an attempt to force a doubling of cash payments. And when they annually graded the governor, they usually gave him a mediocre report. Indeed, they continued to fight for increased benefits. But eight years of animosity between the welfare community and the executive branch of state government had dissipated. No longer were the lobbyists for welfare recipients automatically fighting the department in the legislature. Rather, the department's new managers were willing to seek and take advice from welfare advocates, and they could often work in concert. For the department, dealing with the legislature, the press, and the rest of the outside world had become, not easy, but certainly less difficult.

Recruiting the Executive Staff

In 1983, the managerial ranks of the Massachusetts Department of Public Welfare were dominated by white males. "Women were relegated to typewriters when we came here—manual typewriters, no less," noted Burke-Tatum. "I was the only black in the room, and one of very few females." Atkins changed that. "You've seen the picture of the executive staff," he said, "50 percent women and 20 percent minority." Well schooled in the importance of symbols, Atkins had this picture taken and published annually.

The new commissioner not only set out to recruit a different kind of staff. He also wanted his own people:

> One of the lessons I learned the hard way is to recruit your own staff. You wait too long when you walk in here and, for various reasons, you can't get rid of the people you've inherited. You've developed a relationship. It's easier to do when you first come in.
>
> When I first walked in, I said to my executive staff: "No hard feelings. I don't know any of you. I'm posting all your jobs. Nothing personal because I don't know you. Feel free to apply. You don't just get to inherit the job that you were in when I walked through the door."

For Atkins wanted his managers to have a personal loyalty to him: "I was able to . . . say to the staff I inherited, essentially: 'I get to appoint you into this new job, you apply for any job you want.' I told them that, but the message being 'if I appoint you, *I* appointed you and you work for me. You don't have loyalty to the previous guy.'"

And, just in case anyone failed to get the message, Atkins fired the department's legal counsel, Henry Cretella. Four days after Atkins became commissioner, *The Boston Globe* reported on its front page that Mary Badger and her daughter "are homeless today as a direct result of the actions of the state Department of Public Welfare." The *Globe* quoted Cretella as saying, "I don't want to sound callous but housing is not our responsibility."[14] This gave Atkins the perfect opportunity to dramatize his belief that anyone who held "policy views that are not in concert with this administration's commitment to the poor" should not be working for the Massachusetts Department of Public Welfare.[15] It also gave him the perfect opportunity to let everyone know who was now in charge.

In recruiting his own staff, Atkins got a pleasant assist from the King administration: "One of the best things Ed King did was to set up a managerial pay structure that starts at an M1 and goes to an M12." These managers were outside civil service and not members of any union. A person in an M1 management position was paid approximately $20,000 a year; someone who was an M12, such as the commissioner of an agency, received $77,000 per year.

The welfare department had some extra flexibility, as well. Under normal circumstances, reorganizing a Massachusetts department required the consent of the legislature. If Atkins could work quickly, however, he needed only the approval of the Department of Personnel Administration (DPA) in the Executive Office of Administration and Finance. The pay scales for the various M levels were set by the legislature. But before July 1, DPA itself could approve a plan that established for the Department of Public Welfare a whole new set of management positions with new job titles and new management-level classifications (M1 through M12).

Atkins remembered another of Chase's rules: "It's really not the organization chart that counts, it's the people." Nevertheless, he set out to redesign the organization chart. He did not know who would fill the new slots. And once a reorganization was approved it would become permanent. Still, with a new organization and more management positions, Atkins concluded that he would "be able to recruit better people."

At the beginning of 1983, the commissioner was an M12 and the deputy commissioner an M11. There was one M9 (no M10s), and the rest of the executive staff was M8 or below. The directors of all sixty-three local offices reported directly to the assistant commissioner for field operations, who was an M8. "This is crazy," concluded Atkins. "You don't have sixty-three people reporting to one person. No wonder this place is out of control." The assistant commissioner for field operations would bring to Atkins such problems as "a dirty basement in the Waltham office. With sixty-three reports and no middle-management staff, no wonder that's all he knew about. He had no idea what was going on in the field."

The plan that Atkins's staff put together called for four associate commissioners, classified as M10 positions, and seven assistant commissioners, to be classified as M9s. In addition, they created six new "operations managers," M8s, to whom the local-office directors would report and who would, in turn, report to the new associate commissioner for eligibility operations. All this was based on more back-of-the-envelope analysis. Explained Atkins: "I said, 'Well, it seems to be reasonable for one person to supervise ten people, so let's have the sixty-three local offices report to six operations managers.'" This was the "vertical" structure. In addition, Atkins wanted "a horizontal cut by program." Thus he created M7 positions for statewide managers of AFDC, Medicaid, Supplemental Security Income (SSI), and General Relief.

And DPA, recalled Atkins, "gave us *everything* we wanted . . . Tom [Glynn] and I, all of a sudden, had this wealth of high-paying jobs. It enabled us to go recruit the right people . . . especially from the outside." For example, Atkins could say to the assistant commissioner for field operations: "No hard feelings, Duncan. But I'm posting this new job [associate commissioner for eligibility operations], which you think is your job. But it's not. It's a new job." For this and other top executive positions in the department, Atkins recruited aggressively. In fact, few of the people who filled the key jobs had worked in any welfare department before, though many had management experience in some area of human services.

The Leadership Team

It took Atkins six months to assemble his own leadership team. In addition to Glynn and Burke-Tatum, those managers who would have the most direct responsibilities for ET CHOICES included Matthew E. Fishman, assistant commissioner for budget and cost control; Walter E. Holmes, assistant commissioner for administration; Thomas P. Sellers, assistant commissioner for finance; Elizabeth Vorenberg, assistant commissioner for research, planning, and evaluation; and Jolie Bain Pillsbury, associate commissioner for eligibility operations. In November of 1983, when Pillsbury took over eligibility operations, Atkins's top management team was complete.

The associate commissioners had responsibility for "line" operations; the assistant commissioners managed the traditional "staff" units. In most government agencies, the staff units report to the agency head, and the line units report to the deputy. But Atkins's personal proclivities were for direct, line management. So the associate commissioners reported to him, and the assistant commissioners were Glynn's responsibility. In this, and in many other ways, the personal styles of Atkins and Glynn complemented each other well.

During the first Dukakis administration, the welfare department had two commissioners; during King's four years, it had three. Yet Atkins served as Massachusetts's commissioner of public welfare for nearly six years. For his first five years, moreover, there was relatively little turnover in the other top positions in the department. Between late 1983 (when Atkins's top leadership team was finally in place) and the spring of 1988, only one of the four associate commissioners left the department (and her responsibilities were only indirectly related to ET). Over the same period, four of the original seven assistant commissioners left their jobs, but they were replaced internally by people involved with ET from the beginning: Margaret Mulligan, policy and procedures; Carol VanDeusen Lukas, research, planning, and evaluation; Genia Long, budget and cost control; and Howard Waddell, external affairs. Waddell started in the welfare department as a social worker, was promoted to be a WTP supervisor, and then moved to the central office, as director of publications and outreach, to help market ET. Said Waddell, "I'm just as much an ET success story as the clients who've gone through the program."

Not that these were the only people who made ET work. Others on Atkins's executive staff who made significant contributions to ET included Jean Bellow, deputy associate commissioner for eligibility operations; Lee A. Chelminiak, director of communications; Joseph Madison, deputy associate commissioner for employment and training; Dorothy Reneghan, director of management services; and Chela Tawa, director of community affairs.

The five-year continuity of the top leadership in the Massachusetts Department of Public Welfare—at the levels of commissioner plus deputy, associate, and assistant commissioner—is unusual in government. Moreover, the managers working at the next levels were as competent as some working near the top of other government agencies. For five years, ET CHOICES benefited from having an unusually capable cohort of managers who shared a common sense of purpose, a mutual understanding of how the program should work, a realization of what they must do next, and an acquired ability to work together.

There was little doubt who sat at the top of the Massachusetts Department of Public Welfare: Atkins was the leader both in name and in fact. But the development, implementation, evolution, and management of ET CHOICES was the work of a multilayered team of talented public managers.

Getting to Know the Field

Other managers in the department—the operations managers, the directors of each local office, plus their assistant directors for program and for administration—were also important in making ET work. Someone had to counsel recipients, train recipients, and find jobs for recipients. This was the work of the field staff. And Atkins knew nothing about the operation of the state's local welfare offices.

That lack was quickly remedied. During his second week on the job, a worker in Boston's Grove Hall office was assaulted by a welfare recipient. "Apparently it happened quite often," said Atkins, who called Carballo to explain the facts. Carballo's advice, recalled Atkins, was direct: "You better get out there right away. Because what your workers have seen is you beat up on an employee [firing the general counsel]. Now you need to show that you're compassionate toward the worker who got beaten up, physically, by one of the clients." Later that day, at his first meeting of the local-office directors, Carballo introduced Atkins, who explained what was next on his schedule: "We made a big thing out of: 'I'm going to leave this meeting—I'm sorry I can't stay—and Desi Alexander [the director of the office] and I are going to Grove Hall, because I want to meet with the staff right away over this incident of this worker getting beaten up.'" At Grove Hall, Alexander called a meeting and Atkins talked with the workers. "The woman who had been punched out had gone home, and I made a point of calling her and being nice to her."

That worker may have remembered the punch from the welfare recipient more than the phone call from the welfare commissioner, but Atkins clearly remembered his first visit to Grove Hall:

> I'd never ever been to a local welfare office in Massachusetts before . . . It's an old city-owned building that had been left to run down. They had a security guard escort me from the car into the building—maybe twenty yards. They had more security guards than they had clients. Must have been nine security guards going around the building—armed . . . The place was literally an armed camp.
>
> And the waiting room was maybe half the size of this room [or approximately 20 x 20]. And as I stood there, the receptionist would stand up and yell out someone's name for the next client to come forward . . .
>
> It was a shock to see this as the first building. This is the way welfare services were delivered in Massachusetts in 1983!

3

The Structure of
ET CHOICES

On October 1, 1983, the Massachusetts Department of Public Welfare launched its new Employment and Training Program. At that time, 88,236 cases were receiving assistance through Aid to Families with Dependent Children (AFDC). There were 175,000 unemployed people in the state, and the Division of Employment Security (DES) listed 125,000 job orders. The Employment and Training field staff consisted of 104 ET workers, 12 clerks, 2 key entry operators, and 24 supervisors distributed through 44 of the 60 local offices. For the 44 offices with at least one ET worker, the ratio of AFDC cases to ET workers varied from 412:1 to 1163:1. The Grove Hall office in Boston had 3,546 cases and no ET worker.[1]

The Five Programmatic Components of ET CHOICES

From its beginning, ET had five basic components: (1) assessment and career planning; (2) education and training; (3) supported work; (4) job placement; and (5) support services.

1. Assessment and career planning. The ET worker was the primary provider of assessment services, helping the welfare recipient turned ET participant determine what she needed to do to get a job and get off welfare. In some cases, the ET worker would refer the participant to an outside vocational counseling service for an in-depth evaluation of her skills, aptitudes, interests, and needs. For each person, the objective was to develop an "Employment Plan" that included a specific job goal plus the educational, training, placement, and support services needed to achieve it.

2. Education and training. Many recipients required additional education before they could begin any kind of job-training program. Some needed Adult Basic Education (ABE), which was designed to raise the participants' academic skills to the eighth-grade level. Some needed English as a second language (ESL) instruction. Others lacked a high-school degree, while still others wanted to take a couple of courses at a local community college.

In addition, there were a variety of job-training programs conducted by the Office of Training and Employment Policy (OTEP) through the federal Job Training Partnership Act (JTPA) and various nonprofit organizations. Usually, these programs also placed their trainees directly into jobs.

3. Supported work. This program was designed for individuals who had not developed two key characteristics necessary to be competitive in the job market: good work habits and an employment history. A supported-work contractor arranged for such an individual to take an entry-level job with an employer who paid her less than that position's normal wage, provided on-the-job training, and received a subsidy from the welfare department. In addition to the specific job-skills training, the program was designed to "support" the individual—to help her develop the habits and discipline necessary for regular, full-time employment.[2]

4. Job placement. The primary job-placement services were provided by DES. In some cases, the "co-location" of a DES office directly next door to the welfare office facilitated coordination. For example, at the welfare department's Grove Hall office (which was moved from the dingy building owned by the City of Boston to modern and spacious quarters in a renovated supermarket), DES was the only other occupant of the building. A citizen seeking assistance could walk into either office from the outside, but inside there was also a connecting door. Some DES workers actually had their desks in the welfare department's part of the building so that they could take referrals from ET workers and actively recruit welfare recipients for the jobs they had available.

5. Support services. To become independent, welfare recipients often need more than education, training, and a job. Their lives are often complicated by a host of personal crises with which they may be unprepared to cope: An absent father refuses to provide child support. An employer provides no medical insurance, so a mother returns to welfare when her child becomes seriously ill. A day-care program disappears, a mother fails to report for work and is fired. Or the costs of the transportation and clothing make employment less attractive than welfare. Recipients often need specific services and personal support to make the transition from welfare to independence. Thus the department attempted to provide day-care services, transportation and clothing subsidies, transitional health services, assistance in winning child-support payments, and personal counseling.

For recipients who were enrolled in an education or training program, the department contracted for day-care services with the Voucher Day Care Program in the Department of Social Services (DSS). To smooth the transition to employment, a recipient was also eligible for voucher day care for a year after she left welfare. Even after that year was over, DSS's own "contracted day care" program provided a sliding-fee subsidy for many families. The transportation costs to get an ET participant to an education or training program, and to get her children to day care, were also covered by ET. And if DES placed a recipient in a job, it gave her a $100 clothing bonus.

The department's Health Choices program was designed to provide recipients with access to better medical care and, at the same time, to reduce Medicaid costs. Traditionally, a welfare recipient carried a Medicaid card, which some physicians refused to honor, but which could be used to obtain routine services at a hospital emergency room. Under Health Choices, a recipient who was eligible for Medicaid could enroll her family in any of twenty participating health maintenance organizations and community health centers. Under Medicaid, when a recipient's earnings rose to the level that made her no longer eligible for AFDC, she would still receive these health benefits for at least another four months. But Health Choices provided her with "Guaranteed Coverage" for twelve months, the traditional waiting period for new employees under many private health-care programs.

The department also attempted to convince a welfare mother to cooperate in obtaining child-support payments from her children's father. While the mother remained on welfare, these support payments had almost no effect on her family's total income. The recipient received the first $50 a month, but the rest was assigned to the welfare department. After a woman left welfare, however, her family received the child-support checks directly.

These support services may seem trivial compared with finding employment. To get recipients off welfare, asserted one economist, "all they need is more money." The department's view, however, was that the psychological needs of welfare recipients might be at least as great as their economic needs, and their ability to cope with their first major crisis (by some means other than returning to the safety of welfare) might be critical to long-term independence. Thus the department was willing to invest significant resources—employees' time and funding—in providing support that might be necessary to lowering what it called the "barriers to independence."

The Field Operations

In 1980, a new Department of Social Services had been split off from the Department of Public Welfare. Most of the high-paying positions and most of the qualified social workers moved to DSS. This new department did not, however, provide a wide array of social services. It was charged to protect children who were at risk of harm because of family violence and to support and strengthen the state's families, but it focused on protecting children.

The task left for the Department of Public Welfare was to determine the eligibility of families and individuals for AFDC, Food Stamps, Medicaid, and General Relief, and then to process the appropriate checks or other paperwork. Social workers who did financial assistance had their title changed to "financial assistance worker" (FAW). Moreover, the requirements for this position were changed from a college degree to a high school diploma with two years of work in a social services agency. This change did not help morale. Said one of the new FAWs: "I worked hard in college to become a social worker, and I want to stay a social worker."[3] (In March of 1985, in an effort to increase the self-esteem of the department, Commissioner Charles M. Atkins changed the title of his agency's line workers to financial assistance *social* worker, or FASW. "Our workers are professional and compassionate caseworkers and their titles should denote as much," said Deputy Commissioner Thomas P. Glynn.[4])

After DSS was split off, the King administration eliminated the regional structure of the department, thus creating what Atkins called the "crazy" situation. Over sixty local-office directors reported directly to their central-office supervisor, the assistant commissioner for field operations. The executive reorganization that Atkins proposed and that the Division of Personnel Administration approved established the six, new, middle-management positions of operations managers.

Jolie Bain Pillsbury, Atkins's new associate commissioner for eligibility operations, did not, however, re-create the old regional structure. Rather than have the local-office directors report to a regional director, she gave each new operations manager responsibility for a geographically diverse "cluster" of local offices. For example, one cluster included the Roxbury Crossing office in Boston, the office in the adjacent town of Brookline, the office in Worcester (in the middle of the state and its second largest city), and seven other offices in the regionally dispersed small cities and large towns of Athol, Attleboro, Fitchburg, Gardner, Greenfield, Milford, and Norwood.

While Pillsbury had been getting her Ph.D. at Brandeis, she had developed "this whole theory of management." Grouping local offices regionally, she concluded, was "counterproductive—parochialism—never enough sharing." A regional structure did not produce "partnerships; they were much more hierarchial." Pillsbury wanted her cluster groups to be "competitive" but also to focus on "problem solving": "What they are supposed to do is help each other, and figure out the best way to do things, and share ideas and approaches among each other . . . Some of the ops [operations] managers like to rotate [cluster meetings] among offices to give the directors a chance to visit their offices. When we took over, we had directors who had never been in someone else's office. They had only been in their own office for twenty years and had never seen another world." (Once a month, Pillsbury also met with all the local-office directors: "These are our basic management meetings, where we communicate and problem solve.")

Another set of critical structural issues concerned how to organize the delivery of the educational, training, and employment services. The first choice was to provide most of these services through organizations outside of the department. The department decided to "buy," not "make," these services.

But did the individual welfare recipient learn about and come into contact with these services? Under WTP, a small number of the field staff had been designated WTP workers; they, not the FAWs, were responsible for ensuring that recipients fulfilled their obligations under the program. When a woman applied for AFDC, it was the responsibility of the "intake worker" to determine if the recipient was exempt from WTP and, if not, to send her to a WTP worker. Similarly, at each periodic "redetermination" (when the recipient's case was reviewed to ascertain if she was still entitled to assistance), the "ongoing case worker" again checked to see if the recipient should be referred to a WTP worker.

In Boston, there was an additional problem. None of the WTP workers worked in the local offices; they were all in a single office downtown. Burke-Tatum recalls discovering this office and going to her first meeting there:

> I remember coming back and almost being in tears. I went up to Chuck's office and . . . said, "No, you do not believe who I just met with. There is no way we are going to be able to pull this off. We

don't know what we're doing to begin with; now I go up and sit with a bunch of people who are total zombies. They looked at me, they listened to me, there was absolutely no reaction. One guy just fell asleep on me.' I'll never forget he was sitting there; he just went to sleep on me." And that whole feeling about "we'll wear these folks down and they'll just go" was just coming at me. And I said, "If we're going to do employment and training statewide, we've got to get these folks into the local offices."

An AFDC recipient from any of Boston's eight local offices who was referred to WTP had to make another trip to meet with a WTP worker. And given the number of recipients who visited the WTP office and the number of WTP workers located there, Burke-Tatum concluded that "each staff person had the responsibility of two people a week. And I said, 'This makes no sense at all.' "

In the summer of 1983, Atkins, Glynn, and Burke-Tatum decided to keep the same basic internal structure under which WTP had functioned for their new ET program. The regular intake and ongoing caseworkers were responsible for marketing ET: for registering all eligible recipients, explaining the advantages and specifics of the program, and making an appointment with the ET worker if the recipient was interested. Special ET workers were still responsible for helping the AFDC recipients develop and carry out their own ET program. There were, however, two changes.

First, the ET workers were located in every local welfare office. "We dispersed the folks on Tremont Street to the field," said Burke-Tatum. "I don't know if that was my first or second run-in with the union. They went crazy. They were not happy."

Second, all social workers—not just the intake workers, and the ongoing caseworkers, but also all the ET workers—were now the responsibility of the local-office director. The ET worker reported to an ET supervisor, who reported to the office's assistant director for programs, who reported to the director of the office, who reported to an operations manager, who reported to the deputy associate commissioner for eligibility operations (Jean Bellow), who reported to the associate commissioner for eligibility operations (Pillsbury). ET was not run as a separate, renegade operation by the Division of Employment and Training under Burke-Tatum; it functioned through the Division of Eligibility Operations, the regular service-delivery structure of the department under Pillsbury. "If the [local-office] director doesn't have total control of the staff of the office," observed Burke-Tatum, "ET isn't going to work."

It was the responsibility of Burke-Tatum and her people in the central office to ensure that the resources—the choices—were available to each local office. It was the job of Pillsbury and her field staff to use those resources to move recipients from welfare to employment.

The Delivery of ET Services

Although the Massachusetts Department of Public Welfare was organized to provide individual support and guidance to all its ET participants, the actual delivery of services was provided by other state agencies or nonprofit organizations. Education, job-training, supported-work, job-placement, and day-care services were all provided by other organizations under contract with the department. The three largest contracts were with DSS for the voucher day-care program, with DES for job development and placement services, and with the Office of Training and Employment Policy (OTEP) for education and training.[5]

Initially, DES's goal for the first nine months of the ET program was to place 5,000 welfare recipients in jobs with 85 percent of those individuals on the jobs after thirty days. For this, DES received $1,000 for each placement (a number that apparently was not based on any detailed analysis but that seemed reasonable to all concerned).[6]

For fiscal year 1986, the welfare department signed a contract that would pay DES up to $7.08 million for job development and placement services. DES was to attempt to place up to 5,900 of the 11,800 AFDC recipients referred to it by the department. The goals for DES set forth in the contract are shown in Table 3.1 along with the actual results for the year.

For training and education programs, the welfare department con-

Table 3.1   The ET placement record of the Division of Employment Security for FY 1986.

	Goal	Actual
Placements	5,400	5,922
Percentage of placements still on the job after 30 days	85%	85%[a]
Percentage of full-time placements (>30 hours/week)	65%	73%
Average wage of full-time placements	$5.10	$5.40
Percentage of full-time placements with health benefits	65%	75%

Sources: "Interagency Agreement between Massachusetts Division of Employment Security and Massachusetts Department of Public Welfare for AFDC Recipients" for FY 1986, July 1, 1985, and Division of Employment Security, "E.T. CHOICES Performance: July 1, 1985–June 30, 1986," August 21, 1986.

a. Seventy percent were still on the job after six months.

tracted with OTEP, which ran the state's programs under the federal Job Training Partnership Act (JTPA). Joseph Madison, deputy associate commissioner for employment and training, explained that there were three reasons for contracting for such services:

1. The Department of Public Welfare had no expertise operating training programs. "Rather than reinvent the wheel and set up our system, we really approached it by: 'Who does know?'" Madison explained. "Then we try to . . . buy services for our client population through the larger network."
2. The department wanted to "leverage" its funds. Said Madison: "We wanted to not only have an influence on what we bought, but also [on] other services they already deliver for which our clients are eligible."
3. In 1983, JTPA was replacing the old CETA program, and federal funding for employment and training was being cut back significantly. "There was a lot of lost capacity that we could buy back," said Madison. The JTPA organizations "needed the money."

"The first year," recalled Madison, "we were looking to get the program up and running. We were looking for job placements. So at this point we were looking for skills training that would lead immediately to job placements." The welfare department was willing to put $1 million into the JTPA system, but first it wanted to ensure that OTEP did not merely use these funds to continue what it was doing already; the welfare department wanted to establish a maintenance-of-effort agreement for the $60 million that OTEP was already receiving under JTPA. Ten percent of the people served under JTPA were required to be welfare recipients, though in 1983 OTEP had established its own goal of 30 percent and was serving approximately 2,000 welfare recipients annually. Madison's approach was: "What is your [JTPA's] goal for serving welfare recipients? What we want to do is augment that goal. So if you're going to serve 2,000 then what we want to know is what our million will buy on top of the 2,000."

For the first year (FY 1984), the welfare department signed a $1.2 million contract with OTEP. The JTPA system would continue to serve 32 percent of "adult welfare recipients" (of which 90 percent had to be AFDC recipients). It would "provide job training and related services for at least four-hundred-eighty AFDC recipients" and 312 of them (65 percent) would be placed in jobs. This was an average cost per job placement of $3,800. Explained Madison: "We set a performance standard in that program of 65 percent. Sixty-five out of 100 people they serve we expected would get a job. This was way above the national standard and their standard for welfare recipients, which was at that time like 40 to 50 percent."

For the second year (FY 1985), the contract between the welfare department and OTEP was for $1.6 million, "to provide vocational and pre-vocational training to at least 640 ET-registered AFDC recipients," with the average cost per participant set at $2,375. For recipients enrolled in adult basic education, English as a second language, and other pre-vocational programs, 75 percent were required to have a "positive outcome"—that is, to move on to another JTPA training program. For the vocational training programs, the placement rate was still to be 65 percent.

For the third year, the welfare department entered into a new agreement with OTEP that represented a big jump—from $1.6 million for FY 1985 to $4.615 million for the following fifteen months. OTEP was to train 1,405 "ET-registered AFDC recipients," of whom at least 75 percent had to be in vocational training. The other 25 percent could be (but did not have to be) in prevocational training. The performance standard was still a 65 percent placement rate but with an average wage of at least $5.15 per hour; thus OTEP's goal was 913 placements. Because OTEP would receive $4,615 per placement, it would earn $4,215,000 if it made 913 placements. In addition, OTEP could earn up to $400,000 in bonuses.[7]

The Budget

Over the first five years of ET CHOICES, spending on the program nearly quadrupled—from $20 million to $78 million. Originally, the federal government was providing more than 40 percent of the program's expenditures. But federal outlays for WIN decreased significantly so that in ET's fifth year federal funding accounted for only 20 percent of the total. In five years, state expenditures for ET increased six-fold. Over five years, ET expenditures totaled $224 million, of which less than one-third came from the federal government (see Table 3.2).

From almost the beginning, the largest budget component for ET CHOICES was—amazingly—day care. For FY 1988, nearly one-half of the program's expenditures were for day care, with all of this coming from state funds. Over the first five years of ET, the department spent nearly $100 million on day care. The other major expenditures included $35 million for job placement, $28 million for skills training, and $21 million for supported work (see Table 3.3).

Table 3.2 Overall state and federal expenditures for ET CHOICES by fiscal
year (in millions of dollars).

	1984	1985	1986	1987	1988	Total
State funds	$11.8	$15.6	$27.6	$44.1	$61.2	$160.3
Federal funds	$ 8.3	$10.7	$15.0	$13.5	$16.3	$ 63.8
Total expenditures	$20.1	$26.3	$42.6	$57.6	$77.5	$224.1

Source: Massachusetts Department of Public Welfare.

Table 3.3 Fiscal year expenditures for ET CHOICES by category (in millions of dollars).

Category	1984	1985	1986	1987	1988	Total
Job placement	$ 5.1	$ 5.6	$ 7.1	$ 6.9	$ 9.9	$ 34.6
Skills training	$ 2.2	$ 2.6	$ 5.1	$ 7.4	$10.6	$ 27.9
Adult literacy and education	$ 0.4	$ 0.4	$ 1.9	$ 3.6	$ 5.2	$ 11.5
Pregnant teens			$ 0.2	$ 1.0	$ 2.0	$ 3.2
Displaced homemakers	$ 0.3	$ 0.3	$ 0.3	$ 0.3	$ 0.3	$ 1.5
Supported work	$ 3.7	$ 4.4	$ 4.9	$ 4.9	$ 2.8	$ 20.7
Career planning	$ 0.7	$ 1.1	$ 1.1	$ 1.3	$ 1.0	$ 5.2
College vouchers	$ 0.6	$ 0.5	$ 0.8	$ 0.4	$ 0.5	$ 2.8
Support services		$ 0.5	$ 1.7	$ 1.7	$ 3.0	$ 6.9
Program support	$ 2.0	$ 2.6	$ 2.4	$ 2.5	$ 4.9	$ 14.4
Voucher day care	$ 5.1	$ 8.3	$17.1	$27.6	$37.3	$ 95.4
Total expenditures	$20.1	$26.3	$42.6	$57.6	$77.5	$224.1

Source: Massachusetts Department of Public Welfare.

Case Management

The 1983 WIN-waiver amendment stated: "ET will be based on a case management model with the case worker responsible for following the client from point of intake through all phases of participation, including job placement and follow-up . . . Through such a case management system, clients will be tracked through program participation in a sequential fashion, moving from a state of welfare dependency to economic self-sufficiency."[8] This is a description of the traditional model for the delivery of social services: A social worker has a manageable number of specific cases for which he or she is responsible, knows the families on this caseload, and works with them individually to overcome their immediate crises and long-term problems. The job of the FAWs, however, was just to determine eligibility—either at intake or at redetermination. Moreover, FAWs had no specific caseload; they simply worried about the next person who came through the door.

Later, when a case-management system was being established, the limitations of the technology for keeping track of who had what cases meant that each FASW was assigned a particular portion of the alphabet; if there were ten ongoing caseworkers in a local office, each had one-tenth of the total caseload with the first FASW taking the cases with last names beginning, for example, with *Aa* through *Ce*, the second FASW taking cases *Cf* through *Fa,* and so on. When a new applicant named Adams was accepted by the intake worker and joined the office's caseload, she would immediately be assigned to the first FASW. But if too many Adams, Andersons, and Boneparts joined the caseload, some of the Cenaros would be bumped from the first FASW to the second. The technology of the information system was driving who was assigned to whom. If one of the FASWs resigned, the entire pool had to be redivided by nine rather than ten. Thus, although there was a case-management system in name, it never permitted an individual FASW to provide consistent, ongoing, intelligent assistance to a manageable caseload of specific recipients.

For FY 1988, the department undertook to make case management a reality (and the Division of Eligibility Operations was renamed the Case Management Division). In the spring of 1987, at a series of statewide meetings for all FASWs, the leadership of the department explained the specifics of its new case-management system. The department's new *Case Management Guide* described the idea:

> The Massachusetts Department of Public Welfare has adopted the mission of providing clients with a route out of poverty. A case management system provides targeted services to help clients achieve family independence . . . In addition to determining financial eligibility for entitlement programs, the Case Manager and the client plan and secure those services available through the Department necessary to help the client and his or her family become independent . . . The Case Manager is there to support the client to get where the client wants to be—out of poverty . . . Case management is . . . a fundamental change in the focus of the Department's mission—away from helping people subsist in poverty toward helping them find a route out of poverty.[9]

The case-management system was designed to achieve the department's more ambitious mission.

"Like a quarterback calling the plays," said one department publication, the case manager is the central figure in the case-management system. The case manager would have the primary responsibility for helping the recipient to develop her own "Family Independence Plan," which "includes a description of the client's current situation, establishes short and longer term goals, and identifies the barriers that must be overcome to achieve these objectives."[10] In addition, to help develop and implement each recipient's plan, the case manager brought in four specialists to provide advice and assistance: an ET worker, a child-support worker, a Health Choices adviser, and a housing-services worker.

Obviously, to coordinate all these services, there had to be frequent communication between the various members of this "case management team." The case manager had the primary responsibility and was supposed to make appointments—preferably on the same day—for the recipient to see the appropriate specialists. In addition, the "case conference," at which the various workers assigned to a specific case discussed that recipient's Family Independence Plan, was designed to provide that communication. Finally, the case manager's supervisor was supposed to play "a key role in . . . managing the communication between the Case Manager and the other team members."[11]

Coordination and Accountability

The organizational structure of ET CHOICES was quite complex. Within the Department of Public Welfare both Burke-Tatum's Division of Employment and Training and Pillsbury's Division of Eligibility Operations had responsibility for ET. In the local offices, there were both the ET workers and the regular financial assistance social workers. Then there were other state units—DES, OTEP, DSS—plus the private, nonprofit agencies.

For ET to function effectively, all these organizations had to work in concert. Their activities had to be coordinated. It accomplished little for the FAWs to refer an AFDC recipient to her ET worker, if the ET worker failed to provide this recipient with helpful advice or a useful referral. It made little sense for the ET worker to refer a recipient to a training program if, when the recipient arrived, enrollment was closed, the training was ineffective, or there was no follow-up placement. It made no sense for Burke-Tatum's people to arrange for a new training program in Worcester, if Pillsbury's people did not refer recipients to this program or if the program did not mesh with the needs or interests of AFDC recipients in the Worcester region. Given the involvement of so many actors—so many people, so many organizations, and so many units within organizations—getting ET to produce results was a most complicated management task.

Moreover, who, exactly, was supposed to produce those results? The Division of Employment and Training had the primary responsibility for ET, but Burke-Tatum had no control over the field staff who had to do the marketing and make the key referrals. The director of the local office was responsible for achieving a specific number of placements, yet he or she had no control over DES or the other contractors who actually made these placements. Indeed, the local-office director had no control over the contract with DES or over the agencies in the region with which the department would contract for counseling, training, or placement services.

How would all these people work together? How could anyone be held accountable for anything? Who was really responsible for making ET work?

4

Managing for Performance

Charles M. Atkins's successors as commissioner of the Massachusetts Department of Public Welfare are undoubtedly asked, "What are your ten goals?" For, as one departmental employee observed, "Chuck [Atkins] . . . always managed by the ten goals."

Soon after he became commissioner, Atkins established ten goals for the department for FY 1984. (See Table 4.1.) The top goal was to reduce the error rate, which for Aid to Families with Dependent Children (AFDC) stood in January 1983 at 11.4 percent, the third highest rate in the nation. "Implementing ET" was the second item on the list. And for each new fiscal year, Atkins, working with his management team, established a new set of ten goals. (See Tables 4.2 and 4.3.)

Over the years, both the character and the substance of these goals changed. The goals became more specific, priorities were adjusted, and the goals became increasingly central to the management of the department:

- For FY 1984 (and for FY 1985), the top priority was reducing the error rate—the fraction of families on AFDC who were actually ineligible. For FY 1986, ET bumped the error rate to second place, and for FY 1987, the AFDC error-rate goal was down to sixth. After three years, Atkins thought that the department was "doing so well" with the error rate that "I tried to drop it even lower, and my staff gave me a hard time: 'It's too important to drop lower.'"
- For the first year, the initial ET goal was 5,000 job placements. For FY 1985, the ET goal was stated as 8,500 placements—7,000 for AFDC recipients, 1,200 for refugees, and 300 for General Relief (GR). In FY 1986, when ET became the top goal, placements were to total 9,900, with 8,000 for AFDC, 1,000 for refugees, and 900 for GR. For FY 1987, the character of the ET goal changed significantly; the over-

all target was 10,000 job placements (up only 100), but of these 6,000 were to be "priority placements"—full-time jobs paying at least $5.00 per hour after thirty days.

- The appearance of the single page that set forth the department's goals also changed. For FY 1984 and 1985, the goals were typed on the commissioner's letterhead and photocopied. Beginning in FY 1986, the goals were printed in blue ink on bond paper bearing the new logo, a stylized image of two adults and a child with arms upraised, with the wording "Your Department of Public Welfare" underneath.

Over the years, the priorities changed, and the ten goals became much more specific and tougher—with each goal having several subgoals. No longer were the ten goals just the commissioner's; they became the entire department's goals. Atkins recalled saying to his staff: "I've got limited management time. Here's our list of ten. My proposal is you spend 75 percent of your time on this list of ten and 25 percent of your time on everything else."

Achieving the First Year's ET Goals

For ET's first year (FY 1984), the initial goal of 5,000 placements was increased to 6,000. This department-wide goal was divided among fifty-six of the local welfare offices and among the nine months of the fiscal year. (ET started on October 1, 1983; FY 1984 ended on June 30, 1984.) For example, the Adams Street office in Boston had an annual goal of 198 placements and thus nine monthly goals of 22 placements each.[1]

For the first month that ET was in operation, only four of the local offices—Fitchburg, Lowell, Malden, and Pittsfield—achieved their placement goal. (See Table 4.4.) Statewide, the October goal was 654.3 placements, but the department helped only 214 AFDC recipients find jobs.

In November, six local offices made their monthly targets: Fitchburg, Lowell, Malden, Palmer, Waltham, and Woburn. In addition, by the end of November four offices—Fitchburg, Lowell, Malden, and Waltham— were ahead of their year-to-date goals. But statewide, the department was not doing so well: the 346 placements for November were just 53 percent of the monthly goal of 657.8.

At the end of each month, the department's central office collected the data from the local offices and published its "ET Monthly Entered Employment Report," which showed how each office was doing—both for the month and for the year—against its goals. Slowly, these reports

Table 4.1   Management goals for FY 1984, Massachusetts Department
of Public Welfare.

1. Reducing Error Rates (AFDC = 9%, Medicaid = 4%, Food
   Stamps = 10%, GR = 14%)

2. Implementing ET (5,000 job placements)

3. Managing Medicaid (The Health Connection = 12,500 clients and Project
   Good Health = 50,000 clients)

4. Providing Compassionate Client Services and a Better Environment for
   Our Employees

5. Achieving Affirmative Action/Equal Opportunity (new hires = 50%
   women and 20% minorities)

6. Alleviating Homelessness

7. Expanding Refugee Services

8. Increasing Cost Savings/Revenue (Medicaid = $77 million, Child
   Support = $53 million, Finance = $25 million)

9. Developing Computer Systems (MMIS, PMIS, MIDAS, MPACS, etc.)

10. Planning FY85 Budget

began to have a motivational impact. March 1984, the sixth month of
the program, was the first month that over half the local offices met their
monthly goal. March was also the first month that statewide placements
surpassed the statewide goal: 744 placements compared with a goal of
658. Still, through the first six months of the program, only twenty-one
offices had achieved their year-to-date goals. Statewide, the department
was over 500 placements behind; through March 1984 its goal was 3,948
jobs, but it had made only 3,417 placements.

Nevertheless, as the employees of the department—and particularly
the directors of the local offices—began to realize that Atkins was serious
about the ET goals, performance improved. In April, over two-thirds of
the local offices achieved their monthly target, and the number of offices
making their year-to-date goal jumped from twenty-one to thirty-one.
Statewide, the department's placements exceeded its April goal by over
200. In May, placements exceeded the statewide goal by over 300, and
for the first time year-to-date placements actually passed the goal: 5,594
placements compared with a goal of 5,234.

At the end of the fiscal year, ET placements totaled 6,585—safely over
the goal of 6,000. Two-thirds of the local offices had realized their goal.[2]

Table 4.2   Management goals for FY 1986, Massachusetts Department of Public Welfare.

1. ET
   AFDC = 8,000 job placements
   Refugees = 1,000 job placements
   General Relief = 900 job placements

2. Error Rate
   AFDC = 4%
   Medicaid = 3%
   Food Stamps = 5%
   General Relief = 7%

3. Medicaid Cost Savings ($65 million)
   Citibank Management Reports ($15 million)
   Third Party Liability ($20 million)
   Provider Review & Sanction Unit ($10 million)
   Utilization Review ($6 million)
   Coordinated Health ($4 million)
   Smartcard ($2 million)
   Other ($8 million)

4. Homeless
   Shelters (50)
   ET (900 GR)
   EA ($34.4 million)
   GR Medical Services ($18.7 million)
   Housing/707 Certificates (250 certificates)
   Hotel/Motel (350 families)

5. MPACS
   System Development and Implementation
   Office Automation
   Staff Training
   Service Delivery Model (Case Management)

6. Health Choices (Access)
   Coordinated Health: PGH (120,000) and THC (30,000)
   GR Hospital Services (24,000)
   OB/GYN, Dental and Primary Care providers recruited into Medicaid
   Family Planning/Pregnancy Related Services (2,500)

7. Child Support
   Collections ($50 million)
   Savings ($7 million)

8. Revenue
   Finance ($40 million)
   GR to SSI ($1.5 million)
   Federal Reimbursement ($893 million)

Table 4.2   (continued)

9. Productivity
   Incentives and Upgrades
   Training
   Redeployment/Attrition (100)
   Administration Savings
   Office Space/Equipment
   Performance Appraisal (Option II)
   Paper Reduction
10. Affirmative Action
    Women = 53%
    Minorities = 20%

Ten of the local offices had not, however, even achieved 75 percent of their FY 1984 target, and five of these ten offices were in Boston.

That summer, at the forty-eighth annual Welfare Conference, traditionally held on Cape Cod, Governor Michael S. Dukakis personally presented awards to the thirty-seven local offices that had achieved their ET "entered-employment" goals for the year. Calling ET "the most exciting new program in the nation," Dukakis continued: "No department in state government should be prouder of its track record over the last eighteen months."[3]

Increasing the Annual ET Goals

Fiscal year 1985 was the first year for which ET was in operation for the full twelve months, and the job-placement goal was increased first to 7,000, and later to 9,000. The department exceeded this target by over 2,000 placements, and 88 percent of the local offices achieved their goal. (See Table 4.5.) Again, at the annual Welfare Conference, Governor Dukakis presented the awards to the local offices that had met their ET goals. "Now we have proof of what we suspected for the past two years. The Department of Public Welfare is the best," Dukakis told the employees: "The progress that has been made in your Department has been phenomenal. From the drop in the error rate to its lowest level in the history of the Commonwealth, to more than 17,000 ET placements, from increased savings and revenue to increased services to clients, Public Welfare's record is excellent."[4]

Table 4.3   Management goals for FY 1988, Massachusetts Department
of Public Welfare.

---

1. Case Management (Out of Poverty)
   ET = 14,000 quality job placements (AFDC = 12,000, GR = 1,400, FS = 600)
   Non-ET = 14,000 direct job placements
   Child Support = 7,000 quality direct payments
   Health Choices = 30,000 enrollees
   Housing = 2,000 permanent housing placements
   Compassionate Service Delivery to Clients

2. Medicaid Provider Management (Cost-Savings)
   Nursing Home = $549.0M
   Hospital (Inpatient and OPD) = $422.4M
   Chronic Hospital = $164.0M
   Pharmacy = $89.0M
   Physician = $77.5M
   Community Long Term Care = $67.1M
   Mental Health/Mental Retardation = $56.0M
   Dental = $24.3M
   Other Services = $78.1M
   Total = $1,527M

3. Health Care Management
   Long Term Care Plan/Elderly Choices
   Eligibility Redetermination
   Utilization Review
   Privatization Health Insurance Model (Dental, Lab, Pharmacy, DME, Transportation
     Contracts)
   High Risk Population
   AIDS

4. Homeless Management
   350 families in hotel/motels
   Move 250 families from hotel/motels to emergency shelters
   75 shelters
   EA Expenditures ($34M)
   Health Care
   ET

5. Computer Systems Management
   EAS
   MPACS
   Smartcard
   Office Automation
   MMIS
   Maintenance of current systems

Table 4.3   (continued)

6. Contract Management
   Financial Audits (400)
   Programmatic Audits (400)
   LOQC (ET)
   MPACS Lawsuit
   MMIS Rebid

7. Error Rate Management
   AFDC = 3%
   MA = 3%
   FS = 5%
   GR = 5%

8. Personnel Management
   Training (Case Management, ET Contractors, Computers)
   Reduce Central Office Staff (15%)
   Increase Local Office Staff (15%)
   Move 200 "03s" to "02s"
   Implement Career Ladder
   Reduce Sick Leave from 10 to 8 Days per Employee

9. Revenue Management
   Increase Federal revenue (Systems, ET, EA) = $1.1B
   Finance Collections/Savings = $50M

10. Affirmative Action Management
    Women = 53%
    Minorities = 22%
    Vietnam-era Veterans = 5%
    Handicapped = 3.5%

For FY 1986, the ET goal was increased another notch to 10,000 placements. The department easily achieved this goal—exceeding it by over 25 percent. For the first time, every one of the department's fifty-six offices achieved its ET goal.

In January 1986, the department's Office of Research, Planning and Evaluation (RP&E) released a report that examined the workings of ET CHOICES during its first two fiscal years (21 months). Among the numerous conclusions contained in the report was one that related specific aspects of the program's outputs (particularly the wage level) to its real purpose (to help people become economically independent): "If an ET graduate finds a job that pays enough to allow her to close her AFDC

Table 4.4   Placement performance for the first fiscal year of ET CHOICES, October 1983 through June 1984.

Month	Entered employment				Number of local offices meeting goal	
	For month		Year to date			
	Goal	Actual	Goal	Actual	Month	YTD
Oct. 1983	654.3	214	654.3	214	4	4
Nov. 1983	657.8	346	1,315.6	680	6	4
Dec. 1983	658	403	1,974	1,174	11	9
Jan. 1984	657	511	2,628	1,926	20	15
Feb. 1984	658	601	3,290	2,568	20	18
Mar. 1984	658	<u>744</u>	3,948	3,417	30	21
Apr. 1984	658	874	4,576	4,482	39	31
May 1984	658	966	5,234	<u>5,594</u>	39	35
June 1984	658	920	5,892	6,585	39	37

Source: Massachusetts Department of Public Welfare, nine Monthly Entered Employment Reports, October 1983 through June 1984.

Note: Underlined figures indicate the month that the actual first exceeded the goal. Initially the monthly goals for local offices were stated to a tenth of a placement, but that practice ended after two months. For explanation of data presentation, see note 2.

case, chances are excellent that she will stay off welfare. On the other hand, if the job does not pay enough to permit financial independence, the likelihood that the client will eventually return to the grant amount [she had] before ET is much higher."[5] In addition, the RP&E staff developed the following relationship between the starting wage for full-time placements and the percentage of cases that were closed one year later:[6]

	Full-time Starting Wage (per hour)				
	Under $3.51	$3.51– $4.00	$4.01– $4.50	$4.51– $5.00	Over $5.00
Percentage of cases closed after one year	51%	57%	64%	67%	80%

On January 24, 1986, Governor Dukakis announced that the AFDC error rate was down to 3 percent (the level above which the federal government extracts a financial penalty from the state). At last the de-

Table 4.5 ET placement performance for fiscal years 1984–1988.

	1984[a]	1985[b]	1986[c]	1987[d]	1988[e]
ET placements					
Goal	6,000	9,000	10,000	10,000	14,000
Actual	6,040	11,089	12,870	11,719	13,115
Local offices meeting goal	37/56	49/56	56/56	48/58	35,29,33/58
ET ''priority'' placements					
Goal				6,000	14,000
Actual				8,018	13,115
Local offices meeting goal				51/58	35,29,33/58
Direct (non-ET) placements					
Goal				10,000	14,000
Actual				5,275	7,777
Local offices meeting goal				N.A.	N.A.

Source: Massachusetts Department of Public Welfare, Internal Monthly Management Reports for FY 1984, 1985, 1986, 1987, and 1988. N.A. = not available.

a. FY 1984: The program operated for only the last nine months of FY 1984. There were 58 local offices, but only 56 had placement goals, the sum of which was 5,892. The 6,585 placements shown in Tables 4.4 and 4.6 are from reports prepared at the end of FY 1984; later, the department reevaluated all placements made during this fiscal year and concluded that the correct, unduplicated total was 6,040. The department did not, however, reevaluate all the subtotals for either months or local offices.

b. FY 1985: The original goal was 7,000. It was later increased to 9,000. The sum of the AFDC placement goals for the 56 offices was 8,964.

c. FY 1986: The original goal of 8,000 was increased during the year to 10,000. The sum of the AFDC placement goals for 56 offices was 10,008.

d. FY 1987: The ET placement goal for AFDC was combined with a new one for General Relief (GR). The sum of the ET goals for the 58 offices was 10,101 placements. Of the 10,000 placements, 6,000 were to be "priority placements": full-time jobs paying a minimum of $5.00 after thirty days. In addition, there was the goal of another 10,000 "direct placements" into jobs of recipients who did not go through any component of ET.

e. FY 1988: The placement goal for AFDC, GR, and now Food Stamps (FS) was 14,000, all of which were to be "quality placements" (previously called "priority placements"). There was also a goal of 14,000 direct placements that either did not involve an ET component or were not up to the quality-placement standard. The data for local offices meeting their goals are 35/58 for AFDC, 29/58 for GR, and 33/58 for FS.

partment was, in Glynn's words, in the "post-error-rate climate." Having solved the error-rate problem, the department could concentrate on ET.

Thus in the spring of 1986, as the end of ET's third fiscal year approached, the department's leadership began to think carefully about how ET CHOICES could be improved. From the January 1986 "Evaluation" and other data collected and analyzed by RP&E, they decided to

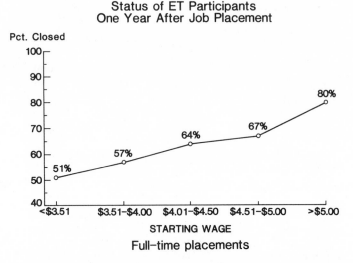

Status of ET Participants
One Year After Job Placement

Figure 4.1   Percentage of ET cases closed, as a function of starting wage. From the Massachusetts Department of Public Welfare.

focus ET's resources on obtaining full-time placements that paid more than $5.00 per hour. The result was what Deputy Commissioner Thomas P. Glynn called "ET-II."

At a meeting of local-office directors, Glynn explained the implications of these data. Using a chart (Figure 4.1) to illustrate the relationship between the starting wage and percentage of cases closed after one year, Glynn drew an imaginary line just to the left of the starting wage over $5.00 and said, "From now on, we're just running ET over here"—to the right of the line. "This part of ET," he continued, pointing to the left of his line, "is now out of business."

The leadership team was unwilling to wait, however, until July 1, 1986, to start the new program. Consequently, at a series of meetings with all the department's Financial Assistance Social Workers, Atkins and Glynn, along with associate commissioners Jolie Bain Pillsbury and Barbara Burke-Tatum, launched "ET Springs Forward." ET-II would start immediately; for the last two months of FY 1986, the ET placement goals would be changed. Both local offices and contractors were asked to concentrate on full-time placements that paid a minimum of $5.00 per hour, and also to obtain a specific number of placements at $6.00 or more an hour. "We sort of galvanized the whole organization in a very focused way to achieve something [more placements] in the short-term," reported Pillsbury. "And it worked. But it didn't make institutional change." That would take much more time.

FY 1986 was the first year that the department's "Internal Management Reports" started listing the average wage of the individuals placed. For all ET placements, this was $5.05 per hour for the year. Average wage was $5.31 for full-time employment and $4.47 for part-time employment. For FY 1986, thirty-five of the fifty-six local offices had an average wage (for both full-time and part-time employment) that was above $5.00 an hour.

The Changing Characteristics of ET's Goals

As a result of the analytical work done in early 1986, the nature of the goals for ET CHOICES changed significantly for FY 1987. The total placement target remained at 10,000 for the year. No longer, however, was the number of job placements alone an adequate measure of the department's—or a local office's—success. Now the focus was on "priority placements"—full-time jobs paying $5.00 an hour or more after thirty days. If the individual was not still employed after thirty days, or was not working full-time (at least 30 hours per week), or was not making (after thirty days) at least $5.00 per hour, the job was not good enough to count as a "priority placement." For FY 1987, 60 percent of the department's placement goal of 10,000 were to be "priority placements." In addition, the FY 1987 goals included another 10,000 "direct job placements" to recipients who had never enrolled in ET.

For FY 1987, the department made 11,719 ET placements—1,700 more than its goal. "Priority placements" totaled 8,018—2,000 more than the priority-placement goal. But the department made only 5,275 direct placements in FY 1987—barely more than half of its direct-placement goal. That year, several local offices had trouble achieving the new targets, as well. Seven offices missed their priority-placement goal and ten did not reach their overall placement objective. Four offices failed to hit either target. (See Table 4.5.) The average full-time wage was up significantly, however, to $6.47 per hour for AFDC and $6.42 for General Relief.

For FY 1988, the goals were again modified. (See Table 4.3.) Now Food Stamp (FS) recipients were also eligible for ET services. And the placement goal was increased significantly, to 14,000. Further, each ET placement had to be a "quality placement" (what had previously been called a "priority placement"). Any other job would, however, count toward the department's second goal of 14,000 direct placements. This second category of non-ET placements included all welfare recipients who obtained a job without enrolling in ET, or who obtained one that did not pay $5.00 per hour, that was less than thirty hours per week, or that did not last for thirty days. Further, ET was not alone at the top of the department's list of ten goals. The new title of the first goal was "Case Management (Out of Poverty)," of which employment and training services were one component. To help welfare recipients find "a route out of poverty," the leadership team concluded, the department additionally needed to provide these women with housing, health care, and child-support payments from the family's missing father.

For FY 1988, the department fell short of its placement goals. Quality placements totaled 13,115—885 less than the goal of 14,000. Actually, the department exceeded its quality-placement goals of 1,400 for GR and 600 for FS. But for AFDC, it missed its 12,000 placement target by over a thousand. The big differential, however, was on the non-ET direct placements; the department had set a goal of 14,000 such placements, but achieved only 7,777. Of the fifty-eight local offices, just thirty-five made their quality-placement goals for AFDC, thirty-three made them for FS, and twenty-nine made them for GR.

Solving the "Boston Problem"

Traditionally, the local offices with the greatest problems had been those in Boston, which had approximately 20 percent of the state's AFDC caseload. The conventional wisdom held that Boston was different—that nothing could be done to improve the operation of the eight Boston offices.

For example, during the first nine months of ET, while two-thirds of the state's fifty-six local offices met their ET-placement goals, only three of the eight Boston offices did so. (See Table 4.6.) The entire department achieved 112 percent of its statewide goal while the Boston offices achieved only 62 percent of theirs. This comparison might be unfair, however. Given that the Boston offices have always been large ones and are obviously located in urban areas, it might be more appropriate to compare them with other large urban offices in the state. Yet even such a comparison put the FY 1984 performance of the Boston offices at the bottom; only two of the other eight largest urban offices (which had over a third of the state's AFDC caseload) failed to achieve their goal, and as a group they achieved 116 percent of the sum of their goals.

By June of 1986, the end of the third fiscal year of ET CHOICES, the seven Boston offices had improved significantly. For FY 1986, all of them achieved their goals, and citywide their placements were 119 percent of their combined goal. During the same year, the eight other largest offices in the state also all met their individual goals and achieved 116 percent of their joint target.

To Atkins, all this was a major accomplishment: "At first ET wasn't

Table 4.6 Placement performance of the local offices in Boston and eight other cities.

Office	Fiscal year 1984[a]			Fiscal year 1986		
	Goal	Actual	Percentage of goal achieved	Goal	Actual	Percentage of goal achieved
Adams Street[b]	198	123	62			
Church Street	117	134	115	204	257	126
East Boston	99	128	129	180	218	121
Grove Hall	234	120	51	348	398	114
Hancock Street[c]	225	118	52	324	400	123
Roslindale	90	42	47	444	537	121
Roxbury Crossing	234	83	35	384	428	111
South Boston	28	50	178	108	135	125
Total (Boston)	1,197	748	62	1,992	2,368	119
Brockton	243	206	85	432	506	117
Fall River	198	217	115	300	347	116
Lawrence	207	310	150	408	481	118
Lowell	198	318	161	372	426	115
Lynn	189	278	147	312	377	121
New Bedford	234	331	141	420	485	115
Springfield	504	428	85	804	908	113
Worcester	306	314	103	504	605	120
Total (8 cities)	2,070	2,402	116	3,552	4,135	116
Statewide Total	5,892	6,585	112	10,008	12,870	129

Source: Massachusetts Department of Public Welfare, Internal Management Reports for FY 1984 and 1986.

a. For fiscal year 1984, ET was in operation for only nine months.

b. In 1985, the Adams Street Office was merged into the Roslindale Office.

c. In 1985, the office at Hancock Street was moved and renamed Bowdoin Park.

working in Boston, but we got it working in the rest of the state. And as soon as we got one Boston office to meet its goals in ET, we broke the back of the old belief around here that nothing could work in Boston because Boston was so difficult." But what, exactly, made the difference?

One explanation was Pillsbury's new cluster system, which Atkins initially opposed. In prior years (before the department's regional structure was disbanded), the Boston offices had always reported to the same regional director, and it seemed impossible to improve them. Indeed, comparing them with each other would do little to help. Would Grove Hall's "accomplishment" of achieving 51 percent of its 1984 goal of 234 placements really inspire Roxbury Crossing, which achieved only 35 percent of its identical 234-placement goal? Under Pillsbury, however, the Boston offices were placed into different clusters reporting to different operations managers. As a result, one operations manager did not compare all the Boston offices with each other; rather, each manager would compare his or her Boston office with the others in the cluster. And each cluster included at least one other large, urban office. Under these circumstances, the inadequacies of the Boston offices simply did not look so impossible to overcome. But the cluster system was not the definitive explanation. Indeed, the managers of one Boston office made it clear that they did not feel compared with other offices in their cluster.

Another explanation could be Pillsbury's decision to fire one of Boston's local-office directors. Atkins had "fully delegated" to Pillsbury the task of appointing and removing local-office directors. "If you're going to run the field correctly, weed out the people who aren't working and I'll back you up on it," Atkins recalled telling Pillsbury. "But it's your decision whom you get rid of, and when and how you do it. Just do it right. Document it so you've got it on paper so it can stand up when people question why we're doing it." That, itself, was a change. Said Pillsbury, "I think only one director in the whole history of the department had ever been demoted or fired for poor performance." It was not surprising that some of the directors Pillsbury inherited were not doing the job.

The first local-office director whom Pillsbury fired—actually, demoted from a management position to a civil-service assignment—was the head of a Boston office who was clearly not doing the job. Indeed, to some of the line managers in the department it was "embarrassing" to have this individual as a colleague. But this director had political connections, and tried to use them. A brother (and former U.S. Senator from a neighboring state) even called Governor Dukakis to get the decision reversed. But the demotion stuck and, said Pillsbury, it "really set the tone—we've been able to go on and do some other things without as much resistance."

To some in the department, this first defrocking of a local-office director was a seminal event—similar to Atkins's early firing of the department's legal counsel—signaling that the rules were now different. Because this local-office director was "literally the worst director in the state," said Pillsbury, "when he was demoted and it stuck, people understood how serious we were."

To others, this demotion was simply logical. "It was something that had to be done," said one office director. Indeed, Pillsbury noted that those "directors who really cared about performance" were already taking the goals and mission "pretty seriously." She thought that the "message" of this first firing "only works for those who are not taking it [performance] seriously." Indeed, some who cared about performance pointed to the later firing of another director of a non-Boston office as having more impact: "Everyone knew that [the Boston director] was bad, but they didn't think that [the non-Boston director] was so bad."

So what did make the difference in the performance of the Boston offices? That is the wrong question. There is no single management "secret"—in this case or any other. Indeed, to look for the sole factor that made "the difference" is to imply that events have singular causes. They do not. The improvement of the Boston offices on ET placements, error-rate reduction, and other indices had many causes: Atkins's system of goals; Pillsbury's clusters plus her decision to demote or fire nonperforming office directors; increased resources; improved technical knowledge (about, for example, how to find jobs for AFDC recipients); and a renewed sense of mission. The lesson is not that Atkins and Pillsbury somehow discovered the hidden "trick" that turned around the Boston offices. Rather, the managerial moral of the story is that the collectivity of the leadership's actions eventually had an impact upon even those offices that everyone had thought were impossible to improve.

The Implicit Contract

One more managerial action contributed to the willingness of local offices in Boston and elsewhere to take the ET goals seriously. Atkins created an implicit contract with his agency: If the local-office directors and line workers could get the error rate down to 3 percent and achieve the ET goals, the department's management would reclassify their jobs to higher levels, reduce the size of the caseload that each social worker had to carry, and renovate the local offices. Although Atkins "was careful not to overpromise," said Glynn, the contract was "very explicit on Chuck's part." The message was: "You produce for us, and we'll produce for you."

Of course, explained Walter E. Holmes, Jr., assistant commissioner for administration, the contract to reclassify the jobs was never binding. What Atkins was really saying, indicated Holmes, was: You get the error rate down and I'll *fight* to get you the upgrading. Changes in job classification required action by the legislature. "The error rate could be 22 percent," observed Holmes. The department could have "an ET program that has placed one person. We wouldn't get [the job reclassification]. The reputation of the agency has a lot to do with achieving" legislative change. Holmes was responsible for winning the upgrades, and he was successful. Between 1983 and 1987, the number of FASW-I jobs stayed constant at 542, the number of FASW-II slots grew from 420 to 494, and the number of FASW-III positions jumped from 178 to 605. As a result, the average caseworker's salary increased from $16,044 to $24,040. "Walter is the best personnel person in state government," said another assistant commissioner. "If you could have anybody, the guy you would have is Walter."

Holmes also had the responsibility of reducing the average FASW's caseload. This meant getting the money to fill additional positions with more social workers. Between 1983 and 1987, the number of caseworkers increased from 1,140 to 1,640—an increase of 44 percent. Over that period, the average worker's caseload dropped from 210 to 134. Such gains, said Glynn, were "the result of the credibility" that the department established by cutting the error rate and making its ET placements.

The third clause in the implicit contract concerned office space. Explained Glynn, "We said to the local offices: 'You get the error rate down, you get ET placements up, and we're going to get you first-class space.'" Further, he continued, "we have tried with mixed success, to sell this in the overhead agencies"—to the Executive Office of Administration and Finance, and the Ways and Means Committees. To them, Glynn's argument was, "Look: If they get the error rate down, they're saving the state $40 million. If we spend $4 million more on rent you guys are $36 million ahead." In four years, the department renovated or moved half of its local offices. For example, in 1987, the notoriously decrepit Grove Hall office was moved into a renovated supermarket building with 23,000 square feet of space; the walls were painted pink, not because the maintenance department had a surfeit of pink paint, but because pink was the color the office's workers voted to have. "Atkins has been a genius at getting the money to upgrade the offices," said one local-office director. "And it has definitely had an impact on morale." Atkins, Glynn, Pillsbury, and Burke-Tatum all believed in and used that old principle of leadership: Fight for your people.

Establishing Goals for Every Unit

The ten annual goals, the statewide ET placement goal, and the ET placement goals for each local office were the most visible aspect of Atkins's use of goals to manage the department. But he did much more. Atkins established goals for every unit in the department. Each unit not only had its ten goals but also some specific "output measures" for those goals.

For example, the Office of Finance, headed by Assistant Commissioner

Thomas P. Sellers, had ten goals—with the first three directly linked to several of the department-wide goals:

1. Collect $47 million in overpayments from Medicaid providers, casualty insurers, estates, and clients. Produce savings of $3 million from contract audits and bill processing edits. Total Finance revenue and savings = $50 million. (Agency Priority #8)
2. Collect $935 million in federal reimbursement, including $5 million in unanticipated reimbursement resulting from special projects. (Agency Priority #8)
3. Conduct 300 contract audits/reviews. (Agency Priority #9)
4. Process 95% of all payments from vouchers, invoices and claims, within 15 work days.
5. Process 95% of all contracts within 5 work days (3 days for approval, 2 days preparation).
6. Develop and implement security and control procedures for agency computer systems.
7. Centralize and automate the replacement of Food Stamp ATPs ["Authorization to Purchase" vouchers] and process 95% of all automated replacements in 1 work day.
8. Ensure client access to a network of 540 Food Stamp issuing agents distributed appropriately statewide and to no-cost check cashing services statewide.
9. Complete development of office automation.
10. Maintain accurate financial accounting systems and flexible processing systems which ensure client access to benefits and support agency goals.

Sellers also established goals for each of his deputies. For example, the FY 1987 objectives for Richard P. Pedroli, the deputy assistant commissioner for the Accounting and Federal Revenue Division, were:

1. Collect $935M in federal reimbursement.
2. Process 95% of payments from payment vouchers, checks and claims within 15 work days.
3. Submit 95% federal reports on time.
4. Maintain network of 540 Food Stamp Issuing Agents with at least 1 location within 3.5 miles in urban areas and within 15 miles in rural areas.
5. Manage within staffing target of 45 FTE.

Sellers's Office of Finance had a general goal to "ensure client access" to the Food Stamp network. For Pedroli's Accounting and Federal Revenue Division, this goal became more specific: "at least 1 location within 3.5 miles in urban areas and within 15 miles in rural areas."

When Sellers sent the final version of each of his division's FY 1987 goals to the corresponding deputy, he wrote that he was attaching: "another copy of the Commissioner's list of FY87 priorities to further reinforce the agenda against which we must manage. You should look to the Commissioner's priorities and to your division objectives as guidelines for decision making. Remember, we should be spending 75% of our time working on these agency goals. Please continue to share these expectations with your managers and your staff." Indeed, to help his staff concentrate on achieving the department's and their unit's goals, Sellers repeatedly reminded them that they should devote at least 75 percent of their time to working directly on achieving these goals.

The process of establishing goals was also used whenever the department took on a major project, such as developing the new ET program, solving the error-rate problem, or creating the case-management system. For each project, the department managers developed a detailed "workplan" that set forth the specific steps needed to complete the project, who was responsible for each of these tasks, a specific date when each was to be completed, and the status of each component. The workplan served as the agenda for periodic meetings—usually chaired by Atkins or Glynn—during which progress on each assignment was reviewed and new assignments and targets set. Then, after such meetings, an updated workplan would be prepared and distributed.

For example, the "Error Rate Reduction Workplan" first developed in late winter of 1984 underwent over a dozen revisions in six months. This workplan was divided into six different "strategies"—"Develop Selective Case Action System," "Improve Local Office Measurements and Accountability," and so on—with a "team leader" responsible for each strategy. For each strategy there were numerous tasks and subtasks, next to which were listed the "responsible person," the "due date," and the "status."

Establishing overall objectives and very specific goals pervaded every operation of the department. At the beginning of one meeting on the ET workplan, Atkins passed around yet another copy of the department's ten goals for the year. Why, someone asked, were these being distributed? Atkins replied that he was "just reminding everyone why we're here—why the taxpayers pay us these wonderful salaries."

Managing for Performance

All this might be described as traditional, textbook management. When a manager—whether in government or business—establishes goals, monitors results, and rewards performance, he or she will accomplish the organization's objectives. In reality, however, the process of managing for performance is not so simple.

After all, the people who usually do the work in a public agency are what Michael Lipsky of Massachusetts Institute of Technology calls "street-level bureaucrats." In their daily work, police officers, teachers, prison guards, and social workers all exercise a lot of discretion. Although they are subject to numerous guidelines and rules, such public employees must interpret these rules, resolve their contradictions, and apply them in situations with ambiguous characteristics. It is difficult for managers to directly observe, let alone supervise, the street-level bureaucrats making these individual judgments. This hinders the ability of the managers of a public agency to influence the behavior of those who actually do the agency's work.[7]

Thus, the management process described above actually has six interrelated but nevertheless distinct aspects:

1. Establish an overall mission for the organization;
2. Set specific goals;
3. Personally monitor results;
4. Reward success;
5. Be vigilant for distortions; and
6. Modify mission, goals, monitoring, or rewards to correct defects.

All the actions taken to implement each component of the process must reflect the unique situation that faces the organization.

1. Establish an Overall Mission
for the Organization

From his very first days as commissioner, Atkins was extremely clear about his—and, as he repeatedly emphasized, Governor Dukakis's—mission for the department. The various documents prepared by the department emphasized—usually in the first sentence—its basic mission. For example, the "WIN Waiver Amendment," submitted in August of 1983, began: "The Dukakis administration is committed to mounting a broad effort that offers real opportunities for welfare recipients to achieve economic self-sufficiency and long-term employment. The new Employment and Training (ET) program proposes to establish a system based on motivating individuals in preparation for long-term, self-sustaining employment."[8]

Atkins also used the department's internal publications to reinforce his message. For example, the in-house newsletter, *Public Welfare News*, often contained a letter from the commissioner. In January 1986, Atkins wrote:

> Jobs, Jobs, Jobs.
> That may sound like a strange message coming from a Welfare Commissioner, but as everyone knows, your Department of Public Welfare is running one of the most successful *employment* programs in the country. That's right. In addition to distributing cash, Food Stamps, and Medicaid cards, we are now in the *jobs* business.[9]

In the Winter 1987 issue, Atkins's letter began: "This year we are facing a new challenge—to move beyond income maintenance and become an effective anti-poverty agency."[10]

Each month, the central office distributed to the field staff a new "policy-issuance package" outlining various changes in policies and procedures. Included was the "Commissioner's Corner"—yet another letter from Atkins. For example, in December 1986, Atkins wrote: "Thanks to your hard work, the Department of Public Welfare has achieved an enviable record in delivering accurate, compassionate and timely services to those in need across the Commonwealth. The next great challenge is for us to build on this record and create an agency that *helps our clients get out of poverty* and become self-sufficient."[11] In April 1987, the department published a new *Case Management Guide* whose first sentence stated: "The Massachusetts Department of Public Welfare has adopted the mission of providing clients with a route out of poverty."[12] The message was straightforward. It was repeated and repeated. No employee could escape from this constant bombardment of the department's basic mission.

But will an agency's mission as defined by its leadership be accepted by the middle managers and line workers who will be responsible for realizing it? Bureaucracies are notoriously unresponsive. The career civil servants see elected officials and political appointees come and go. They have waited out the whims of such people in the past and can certainly do so in the future. In the eight years before Atkins became commissioner, the department had five commissioners. To dramatize his belief that Atkins too would soon be gone, one civil servant refused to use Atkins's name and instead simply called him "commissioner." It was not worth this employee's time, he was saying, to learn the latest boss's name.

How can the leader of an agency expect to develop any followers? The answer depends upon the fit between the leader's mission and what Morton H. Halperin called the "organization's essence . . . the view held by the dominant group in the organization of what the missions and capabilities should be."[13] A leader who wishes to turn a police force into a social services agency or to convert park rangers into an antidrug strike force will inevitably meet with resistance. The police do not view themselves as social workers, nor do park rangers envision fighting drugs as their responsibility. But if the leader of a welfare department wants to help dependent people improve their lives, he will find a large number of people in the agency who share his goal. Given the conventional wisdom, many new public managers are surprised how willing their agencies' career employees are to be led—provided that the leader shares the civil servants' own general sense of their organization's purpose.

Managing for performance requires a mission, a vision, a public purpose that inspires. Explained Tom O'Connor, assistant director of Central Mass. Job Training (an ET contractor in Worcester): "What's made it [ET] work is the dream—that welfare recipients want to work."

2. Set Specific Goals

The next component of this process of managing for performance is to develop very specific goals that give operational meaning to the organization's general mission. How exactly does a department of public welfare help its recipients find a route out of poverty? How does it become an effective antipoverty agency? What does it mean to get into the jobs business? Unless such questions are answered by the organization's leadership in very specific ways, every unit (indeed, every individual) is left to develop a different answer. The result can be contradictions and chaos.

That is why the Massachusetts Department of Public Welfare had job-placement goals for the year, for each local office, and for each month. That is why even the "overhead" units (those that had no direct responsibility for finding jobs for recipients) had specific goals designed to ensure that they would concentrate on the tasks that most directly supported the department's mission. Without specific goals, the most inspiring statement of purpose has little meaning.

Not all goals make equal sense, however. Goals need to be *specific;* people must understand precisely what they mean. Goals need to be *measurable;* people must be able to determine objectively and unambiguously if they have been achieved. In addition, goals need to be *reasonable;* the organization must be able to achieve them. Otherwise people will become discouraged and stop trying. At the beginning, some may view the goals as impossible, but that sentiment can quickly disappear if some parts of the organization begin to achieve success. Also, the goals need to be *simple;* they must be easily understood by those charged with achieving them as well as to all others interested in the agency's mission. In turn, this means that the goals need to be *few* in number. If there are too many goals, people will be confused; what really are they supposed to do? Moreover, the goals need to be *consistent with the mission;* achieving the goals must mean realizing the mission. Finally, the goals must *make sense* to those inside the organization as well as to those on the outside who will be monitoring progress and providing future resources.

It may well be difficult to find goals that possess all these characteristics. Thus the decision about goals may actually come before the choice of a mission. Public managers are expected to produce results. The exact results they are supposed to produce are, however, rarely unambiguous. Usually, the mandate contained in authorizing legislation, the signals sent by legislative committees, the concerns expressed by elected executives, and the pressures received from stakeholders and the public are very contradictory. These provide the manager with some flexibility in the choice of mission and goals. Under such circumstances, the manager may first choose a specific, measurable, achievable, simple, sensible goal and, only then, develop an overarching mission that gives purpose to that goal.

The six aspects of managing for performance are not sequential steps. Rather, the public manager must iterate among them—adjusting mission, goals, monitoring processes, and rewards until they are internally consistent.

3. Personally Monitor Results

After specific goals are developed to give practical meaning to the lofty purposes, progress must be monitored. Indeed, goals contribute little unless the manager is checking to see if they are being achieved. Monitoring the results of the agency's efforts to achieve its goals tells the manager not only whether the organization is realizing these goals but also if it is achieving its mission.

Monitoring, however, is not merely a technological process. It requires more than a management information system to collect and compile data. Someone must gather and organize the information about who is achieving what goals, but the manager must also be personally involved in monitoring these data.

To do this, Atkins again employed lessons learned from Gordon Chase.[14] He used the monthly meetings of the directors of the state's local welfare offices to reemphasize his commitment to the mission of moving welfare recipients from dependence to independence. But in addition to the repeated rhetoric about "a route out of poverty," Atkins used his goals to explain how well the entire department—and its individual offices—were doing against the goals. In part, he did this by distributing the data sheets that compared each local office's monthly and year-to-date placements with its goals. Necessarily, however, these sheets were complicated—many pages filled with lots of numbers. Consequently, Atkins summarized all these data in two lists he distributed at these meetings. One list contained those local offices that had achieved their monthly ET placement goals. The second list contained those that had not.

Naturally, any manager would prefer to be on a list implicitly labeled "the good guys" rather than on a list of nonperformers. Thus, if the goals are as described above—specific, measurable, achievable, simple, and sensible—the manager will try to get his unit to achieve them. Atkins used the monthly meetings—and the monthly lists of good guys and bad guys—to create competition between local-office directors. Observed Pillsbury: "Chuck is very much into competition and measuring results, and holding people accountable—very stringently accountable—for results." Atkins's lists not only dramatized that he was serious about his goals; they also demonstrated—even when originally only four offices were on the list of those meeting the October 1983 placement goals—that it was possible to achieve them. If the peers of a nonperforming director were reaching their ET-placement goals, the nonperformer would go back to his or her office determined to do better next month. And as the list of the good guys grew, it became more embarrassing to be on the other side. Observed one of the department's better local-office managers: "No matter how cynical you are, you want to be part of a winning team." Atkins was determined to convert his department into an organization that thought of itself as a winning team. To be part of that team, you had to achieve your goals.

"Meet periodically with the staff to review their progress" was one of Atkins's "basic management rules." Atkins "defined periodically as monthly," and he held over a dozen such "monthly management meetings."

At meetings with the department's central-office staff, Atkins was very demanding—questioning their analysis, asking why they had not completed a task, pushing them to do a project correctly. At one "ET Workplan" meeting, Atkins's aggressive style kept forty of the department's top staff focused on the agenda: how to improve ET to better reach "hard-to-serve" recipients. Moving through each task that needed to be done next, Atkins gave the responsible individual the opportunity to commit to a deadline. This approach often resulted, I suspect, in people setting more demanding schedules for themselves than Atkins would have done; but when Atkins was unsatisfied with how quickly an individual said he would finish the job, the commissioner exercised his prerogative and demanded a quicker timetable. And he had very specific ideas about what needed to be done and how. To one of his key aides for ET, Atkins said: "Get it out of your system. Report back to us on how you would do it. But also think about doing it my way."

At meetings of the local-office directors, Atkins was less the heavy. He was forever thanking them for their work, asking what they needed to do a job, and promising to try to get it. He sought to be the advocate for both the agency's line workers and its middle managers. Nevertheless, his reputation as a demanding manager preceded him. Many local-office directors were scared of their commissioner.

Atkins also held quarterly meetings to monitor the progress of the outside organizations with whom the department had contracts. And at these meetings he took an even different approach: "These are the heads of the major agencies that are doing ET that don't work for me directly. So no way do I do the kick-in-the-ass routine. This is all praise: 'That's just terrific.' They fight with one another to make their reports to me because they just think, 'Wow, no one tells me that I've done such a good job back where I work.' There's not enough space in the conference room to handle all the people, who just want to get in there." Although he employed a different personal style with the ET contractors, Atkins still used these meetings to get all these organizations to achieve their goals. The first contractor to produce meaningful results was the Division of Employment Security (DES). Atkins explained how the process worked: "Then I could go to other ET contractors and say, 'Look, DES did it,' and then to take it down to the next level and to be able to say to JTPA [the Job Training Partnership Agency], 'Look, Bay State Skills is making it work; you can too,' and then take it to the next level and say to one of the fifteen PICs [Private Industry Councils] that the Boston PIC is making it work and you can too."

Regardless of the group with which Atkins was meeting, his objective and basic approach were the same. He wanted to monitor how individual managers and their units were doing against their goals—dramatizing his personal interest in their progress. He wanted them to be present while the achievements of all the units were reported—exposing each manager to an explicit comparison with his peers. He wanted to create competition between managers and units—motivating them to achieve their units' goals.

4. Reward Success

Why should the people who work for an organization pursue its mission and goals? The traditional answer—often used to explain or excuse the lack of government performance—focuses on the standard financial incentives employed by businesses: large salaries, commissions, perquisites, and bonuses. Yet, argues Frederick Herzberg of Case Western Reserve University, salaries and working conditions are not motivators, though they can undermine employee satisfaction. Among the factors that Herzberg says do motivate are achievement and recognition.[15]

Was Napoleon really the first person, as someone once observed, to discover that men would kill themselves for small pieces of ribbon? Certainly recognition, the public confirmation by others of our own achievements, of our own self-worth, is (and long has been) a powerful motivating force. Thomas J. Peters and Robert H. Waterman, Jr., describe how American companies effectively used public recognition of achievement to motivate performance. Excellent companies, they write, "are full of hoopla" and "actively seek out and pursue endless excuses to give out rewards."[16]

During the first five years of ET, the Massachusetts Department of Public Welfare was full of hoopla. Atkins, Glynn, Pillsbury, and Burke-Tatum actively pursued endless excuses to give out rewards. For example, on August 28, 1986, the department held a ceremony at the State House to "Celebrate the Success of ET CHOICES." Fiscal year 1986 was the first year in which all of the local offices achieved their ET goals, and Governor Dukakis was on hand to present the director of each local office with its ET award—which is displayed in the lobby of the office, just as similar awards are displayed inside any McDonald's. Again, Dukakis took the opportunity to praise ET: "Thanks to your hard work and commitment, ET has succeeded beyond our wildest dreams," said the governor. "You should be very, very proud of having helped make the ET program the best in the country."[17] All the "winners" had their picture taken in front of a big banner saying "Thank You For a Job Well Done" while holding their awards and flanked by Atkins and Dukakis. These pictures made it not only into a frame on the office wall but also, with a little help from Lee Chelminiak, the department's director of communications, into the local newspaper.

Middle managers are inherently risk averse. They see themselves criticized and penalized for their mistakes while rarely benefiting from their successes. Little wonder that so many middle managers, rather than attempt to produce results that are not appreciated, keep their heads down, trying to avoid mistakes and the concomitant punishment. By explicitly acknowledging performance at meetings of the local-office directors and by publicly rewarding performance at periodic award ceremonies, Atkins directly attacked the common lethargy of middle management.

The department's leaders did not, however, honor only their own organization's accomplishments. They were also careful to praise the work of other agencies upon whom they relied to deliver ET's services. They included, for example, other agencies in the August 1986 awards ceremony. Eight local offices of the Department of Public Welfare and the Division of Employment Security were given "The Model ET Team Award," recognizing their "special working relationship." Twenty-five DES "Employment Network" teams received awards for meeting their FY 1986 placement goals. Awards were also presented to three other key contractors: Bay State Skills Corporation; the state Office of Training and Employment Policy; and the Comprehensive Offender Employment Resources System (COERS). The purpose of all such awards was clear: to recognize *everyone* and *every unit* that made a contribution to the department's mission.

5. Be Vigilant for Distortions

Goals, measures of success, and rewards are important to achieving an organization's basic mission. But if an organization is to employ specific goals to measure performance, it needs to ensure that the people pursuing these goals—and the accompanying rewards—do not forget the real purposes behind them. Otherwise, a constant emphasis on goals, measures, and rewards can distort people's behavior. The goals themselves can become the only purpose. As one minister in the Soviet Union said in explaining why that nation's agricultural productivity is so low: "What you've got to understand is how our system works. The minister in charge of making farm equipment is not really measured by who uses it but only . . . [by] meeting his production goals."[18] That problem can arise in any culture—communist or capitalist—and in any organization —public or private.

The mission of any public agency is often grandiloquent and necessarily vague. The mission is a lofty statement of the worthy public purposes the agency seeks to achieve. But the inspirational character of the mission means that it cannot be used to measure progress. For that purpose, something much more concrete is needed. Unfortunately, such goals are inherently narrow. They cannot capture the full meaning of the mission.

This gap between the deliberately expansive and amorphous mission and the necessarily limited and specific goals presents the public manager with a major problem. It is possible, for example, to achieve the mission without actually realizing the goal. More troublesome is the possibility of realizing the goal without actually achieving the mission. Indeed, the incentives created by the goals can so distort the organization's behavior that it fails to achieve its true purpose.

This is why the first aspect of managing for performance—establishing an overall mission—is so important. This is why management must link—repeatedly and directly—the organization's overall mission to the operational goals for achieving that mission. This is why management must repeat and repeat and repeat the organization's basic purposes.

Mere reiteration is not sufficient, however. The organization's leaders must be constantly alert for the equipment minister who cares solely about meeting his production goals. Or for the Soviet nail minister who (according to legend) when measured by the *number* of nails, manufactured millions of tiny nails and, when measured by the *pounds* of the nails, produced a few giant spikes. Any set of specific, measurable goals inevitably creates incentives for distortions.[19]

For example, any welfare, training, and work program that measures success in terms of placements must constantly monitor the quality of those placements. Do the jobs pay enough to achieve the real purpose: converting welfare recipients into self-sufficient citizens? Are people placed (knowingly or unknowingly) into short-term jobs that, although they pay enough, are terminated after a few months, forcing the former recipients to return to welfare? Are welfare recipients placed into jobs that have no future—from which there is no chance to find a route out of poverty? Are local welfare offices and outside contractors, in seeking to achieve their monthly or annual goals, choosing to serve only those people whom they can place most quickly and ignoring the vast majority of the state's poor?

The problem of "creaming" is endemic to social services. Public agencies can choose to skim off the "cream" of people who have risen to the top of the milk bottle of those needing social services, ignore the rest, and publish impressive statistics about the numbers they have helped. Moreover, if a nonprofit contractor receives the identical reimbursement for providing assistance to an easy-to-serve person and a hard-to-serve person, or if a governmental office receives the identical credit for helping the easy-to-serve and the hard-to-serve, they have a major incentive to cream. Agencies seeking to place welfare recipients in jobs must constantly guard against creaming.[20]

Creaming, however, is only the most common distortion. At one meeting of ET contractors, people from these various nonprofit organizations explained specific ideas for training and placing ET recipients. One contractor described how he had "begged" a woman to go on welfare so that she could get ET services. The woman finally agreed, he said—but at this point in the story, a departmental employee turned off the contractor's microphone. The department quickly mobilized to ensure that this did not happen again. "Let's come up with the right criteria," Atkins told his staff. "We'll bounce it off the field. We'll bounce it off the contractors." The incentive was always there for such a distortion; both the indigent woman looking to improve her income and the contractor looking to make its goals would benefit from enrolling the woman in AFDC so that she would be eligible for ET services. Atkins and his key managers wanted to put into place new procedures that would prevent this from happening. But to be sure that these procedures contained the correct incentives, they wanted to check with both their own local offices and with the contractors themselves.

6. Modify Mission, Goals, Monitoring, or Rewards to Correct Defects

Being alert for distortions alone is not enough. Efforts then have to be made to correct these distortions. This requires modifying the mission, the goals, the monitoring process, and/or the reward system. Atkins, Glynn, Pillsbury, and Burke-Tatum were constantly modifying their process for managing ET's performance.

The most obvious example is the changing nature of the goals. For the first year of ET, the placement goal was simple and straightforward: 6,000 placements over nine months. That was just 667 placements per month or, on average, less than a dozen per month per local office. The largest office (Springfield) had a goal of just 42 placements per month. Was this, a priori, a difficult goal? For an organization with little competence in the employment and training business, it might have seemed so. At the same time, precisely because the department had done so little during the previous years, there was creaming to be done. Some women on AFDC (plus many of the men on AFDC-UP) could, with little training, be placed into jobs. The first year's goals were never meant to be the final ones. For the next fiscal year, the department increased its placement goal to 750 per month.

Meanwhile, RP&E was monitoring what was happening—in particular, what the characteristics were of those ET participants who returned to AFDC and of those who did not. It took several years to collect enough data, but in early 1986, the department's management concluded that $5.00 per hour marked the bend in the success curve and thus modified its ET-placement goals significantly. Starting in July 1986, only placements that paid over $5.00 per hour counted toward the goals of the department, its contractors, and its local offices.

In fact, Atkins was constantly thinking about whether and how to change ET's goals. The department's data revealed that women were more likely to remain off welfare if they were placed in jobs with medical insurance. Should the department give credit only for jobs that paid $5.00 per hour *and* had medical coverage (though perhaps also giving credit for placements without medical insurance but with a wage above, say, $5.50 an hour)? This change was never adopted, though the department did introduce its "Health Choices" program, which provided welfare recipients with medical coverage for the first twelve months after their cases were closed.

Of course, modifying the definition of a placement creates its own distortions. For example, only counting jobs paying more than $5.00 per hour provides a further incentive for creaming. It might take at least a year or two of general education and skills training to get a woman who lacks a high-school education to be qualified for any job paying more than $5.00 per hour. Yet women with less education and fewer job skills might, in the long run, benefit more from employment and training services.[21]

Would local offices and their ET workers even attempt to educate, train, and find jobs for women who were not at the top of the AFDC milk bottle? If in October 1983 the program had been launched with a $5.00-per-hour wage criterion and a pool of welfare recipients that contained few women who were easy to serve, many local offices might easily have given up. But because the $5.00-per-hour standard was not introduced until after nearly three years, and because by then the local offices had gained experience and confidence in training welfare recipients and finding them jobs, the task did not appear to be impossible. Some ET workers were willing to begin the process of finding a long route out of poverty for the least-educated recipients. But the department's entered-employment goals were never modified to reflect the harder-to-serve problem.

Daniel Friedlander and David Long of the Manpower Demonstration Research Corporation have suggested a weighted system for measuring performance. Local offices would receive more credit for finding a job for a welfare recipient who had less employment experience. Specifically, they advocated the following weights:[22]

Not employed in the prior year:	4 points per job entry
$1–2,999 in earnings during the prior year:	2 points per job entry
$3,000 or more in earnings in the prior year:	1 point per job entry

Such weights would be useful primarily for internal accounting. The outside world would not be interested in "points." Legislators, journalists, and the public would still ask: "How many welfare recipients got jobs last year?"

Moreover, even assigning different points for different placements does not solve one other problem with the placement goal: job placements are an "output," not an "outcome," measure. Placements reflect a specific output of the Massachusetts welfare department's ET program, but they are not the "out-of-poverty" outcome that the program is really seeking to achieve. To realize that overarching goal, the AFDC recipient must not only possess a job; she must also possess other characteristics necessary to stay off welfare permanently. One way to convert the output measure of placements into something closer to an outcome measure would be to subtract from any month's placements all those former recipients who returned to welfare during the month and who had previously been counted as an ET placement. This would help discourage some of the worst cases of creaming—the easy placement of a woman into a job that has no future—while also encouraging more follow-up with former recipients to ensure that their problems are solved before they worsen enough to force a return to welfare.

Creaming was also a temptation for ET contractors. Contractors were paid for the results of their training programs—for each job placement. They were also paid for education programs—for each "positive termination" or person who graduated from an education program *and* went on to a job-training program.

The contractors had, however, another problem with the system of goals and rewards. Indeed, at one day-long meeting with minority contractors, Atkins and Burke-Tatum repeatedly received one specific complaint, that the reimbursement rate in the department's contracts was set to cover the contractor's costs. Consequently, if a contractor achieved its placement goals, it broke even. But if it came up short on its goals—if the women participating in a specific class did not all find jobs or did not all get "positive terminations"—the contractor did not receive full reimbursement and thus lost money. A contractor had no way to balance out failures with successes. There was no mechanism to make up for a class that had a below-goal placement rate with a class that had a placement rate that was above the goal. To the contractors, the system did not reward them for success; all it did was punish them for failure and encourage them to cream.

Another attack on the creaming problem was the introduction of the "direct placement" goals. For FY 1988, local welfare offices had two placement goals of equal size. One goal was for ET placements (full-time jobs paying $5.00 per hour after thirty days). The second was for non-ET (or "direct") placements. If a local office was doing a lot of creaming to achieve its ET goal, the activity would be revealed by the office's lack of success in achieving its direct-placement goal.

There were other problems with the ET goals to which Atkins chose not to respond. For example, the placement goals for a local office were based solely on that office's caseload. Thus two local offices with the same caseload but located in regions with very different unemployment rates would have the same placement goal. Needless to say, this frustrated the directors of the local offices in communities with high unemployment.

The Value of a Single, Simple Goal

Despite the numerous problems with using any single goal to manage for performance, the selection of a single, simple, specific goal is critical. It is essential, of course, that the goal mesh with the overall mission. But the other characteristics of the goal are not as important. Indeed, there is a distinct advantage of using a very simple goal (e.g., the number of job placements); for once the manager starts making adjustments (e.g., to reflect the characteristics of the person being placed or the characteristics of the region), people will begin quibbling over how large that adjustment should be.[23] And if the manager places primary emphasis on the mission[24] and is constantly alert to the distortions created by the goals, the exact nature of the goals chosen is not as important as is the use of them. It is the simultaneous pursuit of both the mission and the goals that draws the organization together, produces performance, and achieves its public purpose.

For example, part of the Massachusetts Department of Public Welfare was responsible for child support—finding runaway fathers and obtaining court orders requiring them to provide financial support to their children. This has nothing to do with finding jobs for welfare mothers. But it has everything to do with getting them and their families off welfare. To become financially independent—to leave welfare completely behind—may be impossible with only one job, even if that job does pay more than $5.00 an hour. (For a 40-hour work week, a $5.00/hour wage translates to a pretax annual income of $10,400.) Indeed, in the 1980s, most two-adult families came to depend upon two incomes. Thus (until July 1987, when the Department of Revenue took over this responsibility) child support was always on the welfare department's list of ten goals. Though child support rarely got the attention that job placement did, offices that made their child-support goals also received awards and had their pictures distributed to local newspapers. Because of child support's direct link to the department's overall mission, the child-support goals could not be overlooked.

Exactly what form should the child-support goals take? Should they emphasize the number of court orders obtained? The number of dollars collected by the department? The number of dollars going to former welfare recipients? The number of former welfare recipients receiving child support directly due to the department's efforts? The "profit" produced by the child-support bureau? Alone, none of these is ideal. Together, they capture the spirit of the effort. It is necessary, however, to select a single goal for the purpose of establishing a specific target at which individual units can shoot. Indeed, if the indicators are monitored, and the manager is vigilant for distortions, then exactly which specific goal is selected is less important.

What is important is to establish an overall mission, create specific goals, monitor the results, reward performance, be constantly alert for perversions of the basic purpose, and to make the modifications necessary to correct for those inevitable perversions.[25]

Competition against a Goal

This system of managing for performance is designed to create competition among the various units of the organization. But because each unit is competing against its own goal rather than against the other units, the competition is constructive rather than destructive.

Suppose, for example, only one unit—say, one local welfare office—can win the monthly award. That is, a single reward is given to the local office with the largest number of placements (or the largest number of placements divided by its caseload). In this situation, the units have no incentive to cooperate. In fact, if the manager of a local office discovers anything useful about placing welfare recipients in jobs, he or she has a positive incentive not to share that with the other local directors. Next month, some other manager may use that information to win the award.

If, however, every unit is competing to achieve its own goal, every unit can be a winner. Sharing information is not penalized. The director of a successful local office can describe his most effective techniques to his colleagues and still make next month's goal—and thus win next month's award. In fact, the sharing of information becomes yet another way for top management to reward success. Whenever Pillsbury asked a local-office director to explain to his colleagues how he was consistently achieving his monthly goals, she was publicly praising that manager—publicly (if implicitly) telling this local director's colleagues that he had been unusually successful. Simultaneously, all the other directors learned a few tricks that they could employ to meet next month's goals.

In addition, these meetings provided Pillsbury and Atkins with critical information. The reports from the local-office managers revealed what top management had to do to help the local offices achieve their goals. Did the local offices need more resources—such as more job-training slots? Was a particular departmental regulation getting in the way of efforts to place recipients in jobs? With the local offices competing to achieve their monthly goals, the monthly meetings of their directors served to reward the successful directors, to provide very practical information to all these middle managers, and to reveal to Atkins's management team what they needed to do to ensure that the goals were reasonable—that the local offices had the resources to achieve their goals and were free of the bureaucratic roadblocks that could get in the way of even the best units.

Still, competition against a set of goals does create one problem: the hoarding of resources. Local-office directors will seek to obtain the best training and placement slots. And they will want the best people. But this also provides top management with useful information about the value of various resources—particularly people. Because local-office directors are being evaluated in terms of how well they are achieving their placement goals, they will want to recruit the people who are most effective for this task. If several local-office directors were competing for a particular ET supervisor, they would be telling Pillsbury and her operations managers more about how useful this individual really was than any performance-appraisal form could.

Achieving the 50,000-Placement Goal

From October 1, 1983, through June 30, 1988, ET placements totaled 54,833—exceeding the five-year goal of 50,000 placements. In June

1988, Governor Dukakis celebrated the fifty-thousandth ET placement with a major pep rally in the Massachusetts State House. The governor (who was also campaigning for president) declared that 75 percent of ET graduates were still off welfare, that the average ET wage was $6.75 per hour, and that the program had saved the taxpayers $280 million. "We have helped 50,000 families trade their welfare checks for paychecks," declared Dukakis, while standing in front of a banner announcing "ET: 50,000 Success Stories."[26]

The goal of 50,000 placements—along with the annual, monthly, and local-office goals—served to mobilize the department and to give meaning to the work of everyone from the commissioner in the corner office to the FASWs on the line. All had a meaningful target and could track their progress toward it. The goal provided a sense of internal purpose (both for the organization and for the individual) plus a standard against which the outside world could judge them. The periodic celebrations of the achievement of monthly and annual goals provided a reminder to everyone—inside and outside of the agency—of what they were trying to accomplish. Achieving the goals also provided visible evidence of their worth. And it kept everyone focused on the operational definition of the agency's mission to help welfare recipients find a route out of poverty.

The figure of 54,833 placements is, however, despite appearances, hardly a precise number. A diligent auditor would quickly discover that, by the fifth-year standards, many of the earlier placements should be disallowed. Anyone with a pocket calculator can sum the annual placement figures for five years (from Table 4.5) and get a total greater than 50,000. But what is the meaning of this number?

Throughout the first five years of ET CHOICES, the basic mission remained constant. But the characteristics and needs of the welfare recipients changed. The knowledge and information of the department's managers changed. Thus, the program—and the goals—changed.

The repeated modification of the annual ET placement goal is less important for what it says about the sum of the placements (clearly some placements were better than others) than for what it reveals about the department's ability to learn. Five years is a long time in the life of a government program—particularly for one in its infancy. Realizing the department's five-year goal was a managerial accomplishment. But an even better indication of the capabilities of the department's leadership team was its members' determination to monitor constantly the achievement of their goals and their willingness to use that information to modify those goals.

The Massachusetts Department of Public Welfare achieved its goal of 50,000 ET placements. In doing so, it also demonstrated an ability to learn how better to accomplish the real mission behind that goal.

5

An Emphasis on Marketing

"Tonight, thousands of former welfare recipients have job choices and new hope thanks to a state training program," said Jack Williams, anchorman on WBZ-TV's Eyewitness News, on June 27, 1984, as he introduced a story on the state's first public announcement concerning ET CHOICES.[1] The same night WNEV-TV carried Marianne O'Meara, a former welfare recipient who, after receiving some training under ET, had been hired as a secretary at the Braintree headquarters of Bradlees, a department store chain. O'Meara told Channel Seven's audience: "Now the women of this state have choices. We can make career moves. We can choose what we want to do with our lives. We can be in charge of our own future."[2]

Later that evening, on WGBH-TV's Ten O'Clock News, O'Meara explained her views about ET CHOICES to Channel Two's viewers: "We have a chance to make something of ourselves. We earn our own money for ourselves and our families, and we're no longer stuck in a rut which seems to be what happens when you're on welfare. You have no place to go. And now we have choices."[3]

The Framingham Announcement

During the first nine months of the ET program, Commissioner Charles M. Atkins and his leadership team had not talked publicly about what they were doing. Unlike most new public programs, ET had not required a major publicity drive to convince the legislature to enact authorizing legislation. The Massachusetts Department of Public Welfare had simply used existing statutory and budgetary authority to launch ET.

As the end of ET's first fiscal year approached, the department's leadership concluded that they had now established a record of accomplishment that was worth some attention. On the morning of Wednesday, June 27, 1984, Governor Michael S. Dukakis journeyed to the American Optical Corporation's plant in Framingham for a press conference arranged by Lee A. Chelminiak, the department's director of communications. Also in attendance were Atkins, Kristin Demong, director of the Division of Employment Security (DES), Thomas P. Glynn, deputy commissioner of public welfare, and Barbara Burke-Tatum, associate commissioner for employment and training.

The basic facts about ET's first nine months were straightforward enough:

- Beginning on October 1, 1983, the program had placed in jobs over 6,000 Massachusetts AFDC recipients, which Glynn described as "a very big number in this business."[4]
- These jobs were paying, on average, $5.00 per hour; the original target had been an average wage of 50 percent above the average welfare grant, but the result was up 78 percent.[5]
- Eighty percent of those taking jobs were still employed after three months; in contrast, the one-month retention rate for the King program had been only 37 percent.[6]
- In addition to the 6,000 recipients placed in jobs, another 7,000 were involved in education or training programs.[7]

But the Dukakis administration did not recite statistics; it preferred to dramatize the impact of the program on people.

At the press conference, the governor was introduced by Gene E. Lewis, the president of American Optical Corporation, which makes soft contact lenses. Said Lewis: "American Optical is pleased to be the beneficiary of the Commonwealth's progressive efforts to help AFDC recipients find meaningful private sector jobs. More programs like this are needed to lessen the tax bite and keep mature industries in Massachusetts."[8] Dukakis then explained some of the key concepts behind the program—themes that he would continue to repeat for years:

- "The ET program is proving that when welfare recipients are given a genuine opportunity to work, they'll pick wages over welfare every time."
- "ET has become a vehicle to help people out of poverty because it is compassionate, well-managed and has the support of business, labor and state government."
- "The ET program treats welfare recipients with dignity and gives them freedom to make a choice."
- "At the same time, the program provides solutions to the obstacles which have often prevented welfare recipients from becoming self-

sufficient, such as day care, transportation, education, skills training, and counseling."[9]

Other state officials were also quoted by the press. "You won't find employers hiring AFDC people because it feels good," said Demong of DES. "It has to make good business sense."[10]

The stars of the show—particularly for television—were the six women, all former AFDC recipients, whom the ET program had helped find employment. "I wanted out," said Donna Evans, explaining that her new job "makes me feel better toward myself, my life, and my attitude." Evans said she had a dream of "an apartment for my son and myself," and asserted that "I know I'm going to" get one.[11] Marianne O'Meara explained that she and her colleagues "can be out in the real world and feel that we are in command of ourselves finally. The paycheck's not that bad either."[12]

Across the state, editorial writers supported ET. Dukakis's "song of self-satisfaction is justified," stated *The Boston Globe.* The paper concluded that the Dukakis administration had proved that a "voluntary welfare-to-work program can be run without draconian mandates and can get large numbers of people off the welfare rolls and into productive and remunerative employment. That's worth a little fanfare."[13] *The Boston Herald,* traditionally less friendly to Dukakis than the *Globe,* noted that the governor was doing "some boasting" about ET, "and if the numbers are right, he has good reason to . . . We applaud all those who have made the program work thus far."[14] In Springfield, *The Sunday Republican* concluded that "Massachusetts is headed toward national leadership in welfare management." Comparing ET CHOICES with King's WTP program "that flopped," the Springfield paper observed that "the difference is that ET participation is voluntary."[15]

Touring the State

To the governor, to the Department of Public Welfare, to the Division of Employment Security—indeed, to everyone involved—the first effort in June of 1984 to publicize ET CHOICES was a success. In fact, this initial announcement of ET—and of the six ET "success stories"—provided a model that the department repeated and repeated.

One month later, Dukakis visited the Cliftex Corporation in New Bedford to meet with seven former welfare recipients working there. In *The Standard-Times,* the headline was: "New plan has jobs to escape welfare." The lead of the story focused on Lorraine Janusz, a welfare recipient for ten years, who explained why she liked ET: "You have that feeling of being on a sinking ship when you're on welfare, and when you have a chance to jump, you jump." Then the story shifted to Margarita Simas, who said: "I wanted to work and do something for me . . . I wanted to help myself." Finally, in paragraph ten, the governor got to explain the rationale behind ET: "There is a sense of self esteem and self respect because of the program." But Dukakis had no need to worry that he was not mentioned until halfway through the article, for next to it ran a two-column picture of the governor listening intently as Marie Bouchard, a third former welfare recipient, explained her work.[16]

In August, Dukakis was in Springfield, visiting K & M Electronics, Inc., and holding a press conference with women whom *The Morning Union* called "seven success stories." "The good thing about this program was that I was not forced into it," explained Benita Waddy, a mother of two who had been on welfare for three years. "It gave me much more incentive." Explaining that she had already turned down several job offers to leave her employer, the Commercial Union Insurance Company, Waddy said, "The future looks really good." The story ran on page thirteen, but page one featured a picture of Dukakis and K & M manufacturing manager Gerald Fouche watching as Cassandra Frazier, a cable assembler, showed them her work.[17]

Repeat! Repeat! Repeat!

Boston is not only the capital of Massachusetts but also the state's largest city. In any state with this coincidence, many citizens living outside of the dominant metropolitan region believe that state government ignores them and their problems. To combat this feeling, Governor Dukakis took state government on the road. Each summer, he and his top executives moved out to four other regions of the state, set up a temporary state capital in, for example, a community college, held a cabinet meeting, and conducted other state business.[18]

In the summer of 1984 and for several years thereafter, every one of these Capitol-for-a-Day stops included a gubernatorial visit to a local business to promote ET CHOICES. And for each, the basic formula was the same. Lee Chelminiak would make all the arrangements. She would ask departmental employees in the area to identify both manufacturing firms whose executives were enthusiastic about ET and articulate women who had been ET participants and were working in that firm or others.

On the day of the visit, Dukakis would meet the firm's top executives. He also insisted on meeting privately with the half-a-dozen former welfare recipients and ET participants who were part of the program. From these sessions, the governor gained much of his knowledge and confidence in the program. They would all then move to a press conference at which a top executive would praise the firm's ET employees and introduce the governor. Dukakis would explain the key concepts behind ET and introduce the women. One of them would speak, explaining her history on welfare, her experience with ET, and her current job. The governor would also tour the facility and listen to former welfare recipients there explain their jobs, while the press took more notes and snapped more pictures.

The next day's newspaper articles would open with a portrait of one of these women. The typical lead for any ET story seemed to follow a generic three-paragraph format. The first paragraph described the woman's personal history—her unhappy years on welfare. Paragraph two explained how she took a chance on ET and what training and other services, such as child care, she received. The third paragraph described her job, her new outlook on life—independent and confident—and how her children now looked up to her. "Now they [my children] can ask me questions with confidence," both *The Wall Street Journal* and *The Atlanta Journal* quoted Janice Perryman as saying. "Before they would say, 'She don't know.' I'm a different person, so they're different too."[19] The governor's quote would come later in the story, but there was inevitably a picture of him listening intently as a former welfare recipient explained her job.

"One speech is never enough," says U.S. Senator John C. Danforth.[20] Indeed, "Repeat! Repeat! Repeat!" is one of the fundamental rules of governmental communications: "Always repeat the message until you get bored with it, and then repeat it some more."[21] In keeping with this principle, the Department of Public Welfare never stopped explaining the key concepts behind ET CHOICES or dramatizing its success stories. "We have to do repetitive marketing," emphasized Jolie Bain Pillsbury, associate commissioner for eligibility operations. Under Chelminiak, the department's communications office aggressively sought out opportunities to repeat its basic message.

The governor, commissioner, and communications director were not the only ones responsible for marketing the program or repeating the message. Indeed, one of the "Key Features of Case Management," as outlined in the department's *Case Management Guide,* was that all the department's case workers needed to do "Repetitive Marketing." The guide explained the reason for this emphasis: "A principle of teaching and training is that we retain only a small fraction of what we hear and see at any single exposure. For this reason, communications techniques stress the need to repeat and rephrase the same information several times to increase the likelihood of its being understood and remembered. Given the stresses and preoccupation of most public assistance applicants and recipients, the need to restate the features and benefits of services at each point of contact with the client is clear.''[22] The only way to market anything, be it a detergent or a public program, is through repetition. From the governor to the case worker, the marketing of ET CHOICES was characterized by a determination not to get bored with the message—to repeat it, and repeat it, and then repeat it some more.

The Marketing Audience(s)

A ''good rule in business,'' noted Burke-Tatum, is ''when in doubt, market.'' One of the most visible features of ET was aggressive marketing— what John Herbers called in *The New York Times* ''a Madison Avenue type of sales pitch.''[23] When a welfare commissioner from another state was asked to explain the difference between ET and his own welfare, training, and work program, he responded: ''the level of hype.'' Calling ET ''surely the most publicized welfare program in the country,'' one economist wrote: ''This publicity has two targets. One, of course, is the taxpaying public; because of the publicity, Massachusetts is one of the few states where a welfare program seems to be a political asset for state politicians. The other target is dependent adults.''[24]

Aggressive marketing did, indeed, convert ET CHOICES into a political asset. It does not hurt any governor's political standing to be introduced at a press conference by the top executive of a local firm or to be praised by former welfare recipients who now have a job. Nor does it hurt a governor's national political reputation to announce how many women the state's welfare, training, and work program has helped to move off welfare. And it certainly does not hurt a welfare department, when it asks the legislature for more money, if the governor has invited local legislators to various press conferences and singled them out for thanks and praise. The marketing worked in Massachusetts. ''The polls say that 85 percent of the people are in favor of ET, our welfare program,'' said Dukakis's chief of staff, John Sasso, in 1987. ''Can you name another state where 85 percent of the people are in favor of welfare?''[25]

In addition, the ET publicity campaign was designed (at least initially) to sell the program to welfare recipients in the state. The idea was simple enough. Current welfare recipients would read in the newspaper or see on television a former recipient explaining how ET CHOICES was just what she needed: ET provided career counseling, gave her a choice of training programs, paid for transportation, subsidized the necessary day care, found her a job, and continued day care and medical services to smooth the transition to employment and self-sufficiency. Moreover, these former recipients would, without much prompting, explain how much better they felt about themselves—and how their children's attitudes toward them had improved too. Because ET was voluntary— because all an AFDC recipient had to do under the WIN Waiver was to register, not participate—the program depended upon aggressive marketing to attract volunteers.

Marketing did more, however, than boost Dukakis's political reputation or grease the legislative wheels for the next budget. It did more than convince welfare recipients to volunteer for the program. In addition to the "two targets" of (1) "the taxpaying public" and (2) "dependent adults" on welfare, the department had many other audiences for its marketing efforts: (3) business executives, (4) departmental employees, (5) contractors, and even (6) people who worked in other state agencies. Aggressive marketing was a conscious, central component of the management strategy for ET CHOICES.

Marketing to Business

As Dukakis's welfare commissioner, Atkins used knowledge gained in working on employment and training issues for New York City, for Citibank, and for the City of Boston. In Boston, Atkins had had responsibility for providing employment and training services to over 20,000 residents. When, in that job, he had been "asked to take welfare recipients and put them through training programs," Atkins had "refused to do it because, based on my experience in New York, I didn't think putting the hard-core unemployed through training programs was the way to succeed." Explained Atkins: "The experiences I had were essentially all unsuccessful with respect to trying to take 'the hard-core unemployed' and put them to work." If Atkins, who had worked on training and placement programs for the unemployed, was skeptical about their effectiveness for welfare recipients, business executives who knew about such people only through their stereotypes would certainly be dubious.

Thus, Glynn explained, the department's leadership was convinced that they could not sell ET "wholesale." The employers would not believe that it would work, and neither would the equally skeptical welfare recipients. Consequently, for the first nine months of ET CHOICES, the department maintained a conscious policy of not publicizing the program. Moreover, the department's leadership team consciously chose *not* to take the traditional course: have the governor convene a highly publicized meeting of the biggest employers in the state. Rather, believing that they had to sell the program "retail"—individual to individual—they placed the initial burden of marketing on the local offices. During the first nine months of the program, the only marketing material the department produced was a poster that hung in the waiting room of each welfare office.

After the Framingham announcement, however, public marketing of ET CHOICES began. The success stories were designed to market the program to welfare recipients. But these same success stories were also designed to market the program to businesses, for the businesses themselves were part of the success. At the Framingham announcement, the department distributed a long list of "Satisfied Customers: Business," which included many of the largest firms in the state: Bank of Boston, Combustion Engineering, John Hancock Mutual Life Insurance Company, Raytheon, and Wang Laboratories. The subsequent press conferences at various companies continued to promote the program with business.

On November 29, 1985, Dukakis sent a "Dear Fellow CEO" letter "about a real Massachusetts success story" to business executives across the state, which said in part: "During the past two years, I have met many employers who are 'satisfied customers' of E.T. From high technology companies to traditional industries, hospitals to banks, the message from the executives has been the same. On each occasion, they told me that what they need are people who are qualified and want to work, and on each occasion they told me that the E.T. graduates they had hired were among their company's best employees." "For those businesses who haven't tried E.T.," Dukakis enclosed a booklet with no title on its plain, white cover. Instead, there was a single quotation:

> "Since the program's October
> 1983 inception, 170,000 welfare
> recipients have been placed in
> 'unsubsidized' . . . jobs in the
> private sector, saving the state
> an estimated $50 million . . ."
>
> *The Wall Street Journal*
> Friday, July 19, 1985

Inside were individual, full-page photographs of three corporate executives, along with quotations from them in large, red type. For example, Raymond C. Cullen, Jr., senior vice president for marketing services of

Wang Laboratories, was quoted saying: "6,000 Massachusetts businesses have hired E.T. graduates. These are real jobs, not make work. We've got a business to run and we hired Sandra Risner because she was well trained and wanted to work." There was also a picture of Risner with a caption that explained: "After nearly 10 years on welfare, Sandra Risner began a seven month E.T. training program in the field of computer electronics. In December, 1984, Sandra got a job as a customer service engineer for Wang Laboratories, Inc. in Lowell. On call daily to repair Wang computer equipment, Sandra now earns more than three times her welfare grant." The report concluded with a listing of "a sample of E.T. employers" and an 800 number that businesses interested in hiring ET graduates could call.[26]

Internal Marketing

Any marketing effort can have multiple impacts. When Lee Iacocca did his television advertisements—"If you can find a better car, buy it"—he was not just having an effect on the auto-buying public. He was also affecting the attitudes of the local dealers—convincing them that they were indeed selling a quality product. And he was affecting the attitudes of his company's assembly-line workers—convincing them that they were indeed making a quality product of which they should be proud.

Similarly, the efforts to market ET externally also had internal effects. The department's management, said Glynn, "made the positive press work for us inside the institution"; the idea was to promote "institutional self-esteem." Atkins explained how all the publicity over ET CHOICES might appear from the perspective of a financial assistance social worker (FASW):

> I keep hearing, over and over and over again, from this yo-yo who's the commissioner, and even sometimes from the governor, and now even from the president and Congress, [that] the whole country's watching what I'm doing—that we're going to have this thing called national welfare reform and they keep telling me [that it is] because of what I did on ET. And I keep picking up the paper; about once a month, there's a favorable article on my department when three years ago all this department got was bad press to the extent that I wouldn't tell my neighbors that I worked for the welfare department. And now I'm proud where I work. They tell me what I'm doing is great.

Any organization has its cynics, and the Massachusetts Department of Public Welfare has certainly been no exception. But "because of what

Chuck and Tom were able to do," concluded Pillsbury, "our cynicism level is much lower than it was three years ago" (at the beginning of Dukakis's second term). "They were so cynical three years ago, it was amazing," she continued. "It's still there, but it's less."

The department's leadership used the external press, said Glynn, to convince its employees to "become more confident in what we were doing." On September 16, 1986, the Tuesday before ET was featured on the CBS television program "Sunday Morning," Atkins sent a memorandum to "All Employees" urging them to "tune in." When in the spring of 1985 the department won the Public Service Excellence Award from the Public Employees Roundtable, Atkins sent a memo to "All Staff" saying, "Congratulations to all of our staff who have worked so hard to make ET a success and to make us the number one agency in the country!" For all these communications with the department's workers, explained Pillsbury, the implicit message was the same: "You're not just struggling to get this to work. You are on the cutting edge."

Each month, the Policy and Procedures unit of the department would send every worker the "monthly issuance" of details on the latest changes in federal and state policies and the resulting new operating procedures. "It used to be pretty screwed up," explained Atkins. "Tom fixed it so that they come out once a month instead of once a day, and they're in English and the format looks good so workers can understand it. Because, again, if we can't explain it to them, there's no hope for them to do it." The monthly policy-issuance package also helped to repeat some of the department's basic themes. The first page was devoted to the "Commissioner's Corner," Atkins's letter to "fellow employees," in which he congratulated them for another award, thanked them for another accomplishment, informed them of recent developments, and reemphasized basic themes.

The publicity that ET CHOICES received also had an impact on the program's independent contractors—those people who, although they were not employed by the Department of Public Welfare, were nevertheless working on ET and could take pride in being associated with this "national model." Even Dickenson Direct Response, a firm that did much of the early direct-mail work for ET, got caught up in the excitement. Reported Howard Waddell, the head of publications and outreach: "When it [ET] appeared in *Newsweek,* and there was one line about aggressive direct-mail strategy, they called us to tell us it was in there."

Moreover, the marketing had an impact on people who worked in other state agencies—even overhead agencies. Dorothy Reneghan, the welfare department's director of management services, had the responsibility for upgrading the quality of the physical space for the local offices, by either renovating existing space or finding new, better space. She told of the manager in the Division of Capital Planning and Operations who had statewide real-estate responsibilities. The individual dealt with office space all the time, yet he was excited about working with Reneghan on the new Roxbury Crossing office. He did not see himself as moving a welfare office; instead, he was "creating an ET office."

Recruiting Volunteers

Because ET CHOICES was voluntary, it had to function more as a business than a traditional government program. To be successful, ET needed satisfied customers—satisfied businesses and satisfied welfare recipients. Otherwise, it would not have any recipients to participate in training and placement or any firms to hire them.

The decision to make a welfare, training, and work program voluntary not only requires an emphasis on publicity and marketing. Such a decision also requires a welfare department to take an entirely different approach to the program's management. The businesses and recipients involved in the program are very important. What they think counts. To convince a business executive to employ ET participants, training and placement contractors must demonstrate that their applicants are able to do the job. They cannot develop a bad reputation and still meet their placement goals. Similarly, to convince a welfare recipient to volunteer for the program, the welfare department must satisfy her concerns about day care, transportation, health care, and the level of future wages. The social workers in a local office cannot develop a bad reputation and still meet their placement goals. Everyone who works on a voluntary program must pay attention to what the customer thinks.

Much of this could also be said of a mandatory program. Businesses will not hire former welfare recipients who are unqualified—at least not more than once. Moreover, a mandatory program also needs to market its services to welfare recipients. A law requiring welfare recipients to participate in training and employment activities does not guarantee that they will.[27] Somehow, they have to be convinced.

Some argue that a voluntary program is more difficult to operate. A mandatory program not only has the carrot of a job, economic independence, and a better life. It also has the stick of sanctions.[28] For example, Pillsbury argued that social workers prefer a mandatory program because it is easier on them. "They want to be able to say: 'You do this.'" Others would argue that a mandatory program is more difficult to operate because the welfare department will necessarily waste resources counseling and training people who are not really interested in employment. Further, the department must devote resources to tracking down and sanctioning people who refuse to participate. Regardless of which is easier to manage, however, voluntary and mandatory programs are clearly different in their underlying philosophies, operational strategies, and allocations of resources. Certainly, voluntary programs must place a greater emphasis on recruiting volunteers.

During the King administration, Howard Waddell had been the WTP supervisor in the Worcester office. When ET CHOICES replaced WTP, he took on the new program and developed a reputation for marketing it. Waddell explained that, because ET was voluntary, "clients didn't have to come to see us. So there were a number of things that had to change. Number one [was] how we treated people." Under WTP the recipients were required to meet with the WTP workers, who (as a result) "could say anything" to the recipients. Moreover, under WTP, Waddell's workers did "everything by appointment." The attitude of the WTP workers was: "I send out a letter. I expect clients to come to see me. If they don't show up, no big deal." With ET, however, if Waddell's unit mailed out "boring, dry, old 'you have been scheduled for an appointment on' or 'you may continue to be eligible for'" letters, the recipients would not respond. "They didn't have to."

Also under ET, Waddell's unit "had goals. So it was a big deal if they didn't show up. We knew they didn't have to show up. So we really had to change the way we were structured." From being five WTP workers "who maybe had five appointments a day," Waddell's unit became "a revolving, 'take them as they come in' operation—purely walk-in."

First, however, Waddell had to negotiate with Worcester's FASWs to convince them to refer recipients to ET. Once this occurred, the ET workers could not "disappoint" interested recipients by telling them that "someone will contact you in two weeks to see you." Waddell's ET workers would "see them right then—that day—when they're hot, when they're thinking about it." To handle the walk-in volunteers, Waddell "rearranged everything" to accommodate "a steady flow of clients" who were "seen as soon as they came in. That was probably one of the biggest philosophical changes" that he made, said Waddell, and was "what helped us consistently meet our goals."

Still, Waddell "never had quite enough clients coming in." Consequently, he "started getting a little crazy with new ways" to convince recipients to volunteer. Because Waddell already had the names and addresses of every one of his "customers," his first such effort employed direct mail. At first in a very primitive way, Waddell started mailing different ET materials to recipients once a week. In a second effort to recruit recipients, Waddell convinced three ET participants (who were in school half-time) to become "what I jokingly called 'the marketeers.'" They went out "in some cases, in housing authorities door to door, in other cases to groups like Sharing Our Survival, and the parenting teens groups," and talked about ET. "They went to Head Start and did their thing for the parents—just trying to get the word out."

Close to the Customer

Thomas J. Peters and Robert H. Waterman, Jr., attribute to excellent American companies eight specific attributes, one of which is "Close to the Customer." Excellent firms are obsessed with service, quality, and reliability, write Peters and Waterman. Their sales force is trained to be "customer problem solvers." These "excellent companies are better listeners."[29] By being close to their customers, by helping their customers solve their problems, conclude Peters and Waterman, businesses can develop numerous ideas for improving their product.

In February 1985, the Department of Public Welfare created a new Office of Publications and Outreach (P&O) with Waddell as director. The assistant director was Janet Diamond, a former welfare recipient who (reported Waddell) had worked as a "client advocate" for the Coalition of Basic Human Needs fighting the King administration, and who "was brought in by Chuck to humanize the department, to make it more compassionate." It was Terri Bergman, the assistant commissioner for external affairs, recalled Waddell, who "figured Diamond was a great resource for marketing, someone who understands the client's perspective."

During the following summer, Waddell and Diamond initiated a series of two-hour meetings, conducted by Diamond, with six to twelve AFDC recipients. Corporate marketing executives and political consultants frequently use such "focus groups" to understand the thinking of the public—and of particular segments of the public. Sometimes the focus-group participants will be shown several commercials to test their reactions. Sometimes they will be shown speeches by political candidates. Sometimes they will be asked to talk about specific topics, such as the features and quality of American versus imported automobiles, or foreign policy toward the Middle East. Focus groups are not created to provide "statistically significant" tests of public opinion; the sample size is much too small, the questions are open-ended, and the discussions are often rambling. Rather, focus groups are designed to probe beneath the views recorded by public-opinion polls to obtain a more subtle understanding of the attitudes underpinning such views.

Publications and Outreach was responsible for producing materials to market ET CHOICES. Thus, one purpose of the focus-group sessions was to test these materials: What did the welfare recipients think of them? What message did they convey? For example, P&O had a theory that women would be less likely to respond to a letter signed by a man. So Diamond gave one focus group two different letters—one signed by Atkins, the other signed by Burke-Tatum. Said Waddell: "They didn't even notice who it was from. They didn't care. A beautiful theory all shot to hell . . . You can do all the theorizing you want to, but when you talk to the people, it changes your mind."

Diamond and Waddell conducted numerous focus groups for ET participants and nonparticipants, teenage mothers and former teenage mothers, ET graduates and ET reentries (people who left welfare and then returned), public housing residents and rural residents. P&O probed the general thinking of these recipients: "What are you most proud of?" "What do you think of ET?" "Why would you, or wouldn't you, participate?" From these focus groups, they got the surprising news that success stories, which had dominated much of the marketing pitch to recipients, did not sell well. In the newsletters, recalled Waddell, the approach had been: "This is Ruby Sampson. This is how successful she is. Isn't that great? Wouldn't you like to be like her?" From the focus groups, however, Diamond and Waddell learned that the people who "were looking for success as a motivator were the only ones who responded to it. Those people were already registered for ET."

In contrast, continued Waddell, "the people who weren't registered for ET responded very badly" to the success stories: "They almost saw it as an us-and-them kind of situation: 'Why do you have to keep shoving this person in front of me, saying, She's great, and you're still out on welfare?'" To many of the people who had not signed up for ET, the success stories simply dramatized their own failure. The rationalization offered by many recipients was that the people featured in the success stories were somehow lucky—that only special circumstances, such as a grandmother to provide day care, made it possible for them to make it through ET and off welfare. Further, the recipients never truly trusted the written testimonials distributed by the department, for the words could, of course, have been invented. Said Diamond, "They thought these are people we made up."

As a result, P&O altered its marketing strategy. After five issues, the department's newsletter on ET—a "publication for sharing information, ideas, and *success*"—was discontinued.

Multiple Marketing Materials

In Worcester, Waddell had been using direct mail to communicate the concepts of ET to recipients. By the time he became head of P&O, Waddell had concluded that direct mail was the "most effective way" to communicate with the recipients statewide. After all, the department not only knew the names and addresses of its customers; it knew some of their characteristics, as well. Thus, in Waddell's first year, P&O mailed out nine letters to clients and three newsletters. For example, in November 1985, Waddell sent out 109,036 copies of his third newsletter with which he enclosed his first "direct response piece . . . an actual card, prepaid, that went back to a post office box, . . . [so] we could get an idea: Does anybody read this stuff?" He got back 1,388 responses.[30]

Before long, Waddell's direct-mail operation became more extensive and sophisticated. The traditional "check inserts" went into the envelope with each semimonthly welfare check. Each new welfare recipient received a letter about ET, and about a month later a follow-up letter. Between October 15, 1986, and January 20, 1987, Publications and Outreach sent seventeen different direct-mail pieces to 331,804 individuals, of whom 4,975 sent back the enclosed business-reply card, for a (roughly normal) direct-mail response rate of 1.5 percent.[31]

Most of these mailings were simply addressed "Dear Friend" and printed rather than individually typed. Nevertheless, they were all signed by Burke-Tatum and were designed to "develop a public image for Barbara Burke-Tatum which allows clients/consumers of ET to feel that a real person is in control and is safeguarding their interests. It worked for Lee Iacocca and Frank Perdue, and it can work for ET."[32] The response card, too, was addressed to Burke-Tatum, and on the other side, above the space for the respondent's name and address, it said:

Dear Barbara,

( )   Please have an ET Worker contact me.
( )   Please send me the *ET Buyer's Guide.*

Waddell was amazed at the number of personal responses his office received. Recipients would write letters saying: "Dear Barbara, Sorry I haven't written to you sooner. I know you care a lot about what I'm doing. This is what I'm up to." Burke-Tatum even got Christmas cards from welfare recipients.

In January 1987, P&O sent out its first mail-merge letter. Each letter not only contained an individualized inside address and first-name salutation, but also used the first name in a postscript, noted the size of the recipient's monthly grant, and twice mentioned how long she had been on welfare. Three weeks after these letters were mailed, Waddell reported an "overwhelming personal response . . . not all of which has been positive." Some recipients wrote demanding: "What business is it of yours how long I've been on welfare?" Still, said Waddell, "that doesn't dismay us. What we decided is our goal is involvement. Positive or negative, it's still involvement . . . This definitely struck a chord. Not necessarily positive, but it got people involved."

In the waiting rooms of the twenty largest local welfare offices, a series of videos ran continuously featuring women who had used ET to escape welfare. Waddell had discovered from the focus groups that the success stories presented on video did work because "you could see that they weren't scripted." To a generation raised on television, the appearance of a welfare recipient—a woman who looked like a welfare recipient and talked like a welfare recipient—was much more convincing than any written testimonial. "Video transcends the language barrier," observed Waddell; even "most" Spanish-speaking recipients "can understand English television."

Further, P&O discovered an "interesting expressed need . . . for more nuts and bolts materials . . . In order to be willing to take a risk [on ET], a large number of those present in the focus groups wanted to know all the details first."[33] So P&O switched to what Waddell called a "back-to-basics approach" that provided basic information: "This is how ET works. And this is how you can use it to your advantage." One brochure gave "An Introduction to Your Department of Public Welfare," and a series of four colorful fliers emphasized four different aspects of ET: "Your Ticket to the Future is Education & Training," "Finding Good Childcare Isn't Child's Play," "Taking the First Step with Supported Work," and "Your Key to Success Is the Employment Network."

One of the department's most visible publications was the "ET Owner's Manual," which, like other materials, was available in both English and Spanish. Waddell's early research confirmed his belief that many recipients thought they would lose control of many aspects of their lives if they signed up for ET. From this concern evolved the idea for the owner's manual. Waddell explained:

> Terri [Bergman] and I went to McDonald's, and they were introducing the McBLT, and they gave you a little tiny owner's manual with it. I started looking at it and thinking: "That's a way to kind of

empower someone, to tell someone it [ET] really belongs to you." So I went home and pulled out my Hoover vacuum cleaner owner's manual. This [ET owner's manual] is patterned almost exactly on that.

This piece has actually been the most successful thing we've produced. I think that the reason for it is—number one—it's a little lighthearted. It doesn't look programmatic. The second thing is, in fact, it does make a commitment that the program belongs to them. It has everything: from giving the opportunity to the client to fill in stuff so they know who their worker is, what the telephone number is; [to] a warranty card that they can send to us that says the program belongs to them. It also gives us some collateral information on how they found out about it.

"My Mom and ET"

From the focus groups, Waddell, Diamond, and others obtained additional ideas that they used to modify their overall marketing strategy. Specifically, Waddell started to think about sending out direct mail signed by the child of an ET graduate "who talks about his mother and says: 'I'm sure you've got kids and they'd probably feel the same way if you were to work.'" This idea emerged from an important discovery: The major source of self-esteem for many welfare recipients was their children. When the women in the focus groups were asked, "What are you most proud of?" a typical response was "my kids."

From this discovery, the department moved to replace the success-story approach with a new marketing theme: "My Mom and ET." Building on the idea that the focus of a welfare recipient's life is her children, Waddell's office prepared a number of materials for this campaign.

The first item, the "ET CHOICES Activity Book," was designed to be interactive. In addition to pictures to color, it contained activities for the mother and child to do together. Each activity included an explicit ET message for the mother. One page featured a woman—presumably a former welfare recipient and ET participant—as an auto mechanic; opposite it were pictures of a wrench, starter cables, and a jack.

Soon, Waddell had a drawing that became the My-Mom-and-ET logo. It was featured, for example, as the cover of the "My Mom and ET Calendar," which, like the activity book, was designed to be interactive. For some months, there was a puzzle (with answers in the back). For others, there was simply a picture to be colored, though the caption always had a message:

- One young boy to another: "Tomorrow is Career Day at my school. My mom is coming to talk about her work."
- Four kids playing basketball: "Since my mom works, I go to the after-school center and do things with my friends. Sometimes we play basketball, sometimes football. How many sports can you think of that use a ball?" This was followed by a message to the mother: "ET pays for full-time daycare and after-school care for children up to 14 years old. ET will pay almost all the cost of your child care for up to one year after you start work."
- Several adults in a classroom: "My mom goes to school every day and takes the bus just like me." Again, this page also included direct information on ET: "ET will pay your travel costs in getting to and from your ET activity. Whether it's going to skills training, getting your GED, or looking for a job, ET will pay it until you start work."
- At a party, one girl to two friends: "This Halloween I dressed up like my mom. She works in a hospital operating room. She even let me wear her mask."

For ET CHOICES, the market message was no longer: Enroll in ET to make yourself a success. The new message had become: You owe it to your children.

The Marketing Mix

The classic definition of business marketing includes the four components of the marketing mix: *product, price, distribution,* and *communication.*[34] Marketing is not just advertisements and commercials. It also includes the decisions about what product to sell, what price to sell it at, and how to distribute it.

For ET CHOICES, top management made many of the marketing decisions very early. The *product* was to be an entire series of products: everything from English as a second language for immigrants who were a long way from entering the job market to direct placement for recipients who were ready for jobs. The *price* was to be very low: day care and transportation—the big costs of participating in any training—were to be subsidized; and the price of moving off welfare and into employment would also be reduced through a continuation of the subsidies for day care and medical insurance. The *distribution* of most of the product was to be primarily through outside contractors. And, initially, *communication* was to be through word of mouth.

For a business firm, being close to the customer means more than advertising people who understand their customers' whims. It means more than a sales force that is in close contact with individual customers.

It is more than an admonition from corporate leadership. Being close to the customer means everyone in the firm is involved in the sale, improvement, and design of the product.

Being "close to the customer" helped the Massachusetts Department of Public Welfare to improve ET—to modify the various elements of its marketing mix. Being close to the customer helped the department modify its *product*—to broaden its product line significantly, as local offices reported to Burke-Tatum and her deputy, Joseph W. Madison, what kind of contractor services they needed. Being close to the customer convinced the department that it had to lower even further the implicit *price* of the program by extending Medicaid coverage after AFDC from four to twelve months through the Health Choices program and by providing an initial $100 placement bonus from DES's "Employment Network" to cover such things as new clothes for work. Being close to the customer meant improving the *distribution* of the product by, for example, "co-locating" DES offices inside local welfare offices, so the ET worker could walk a recipient over and introduce her to a DES worker. And, of course, being close to the customer helped the department learn how to improve its *communications* with its customers.

Everyone Does Marketing

One general conclusion that emerged from the focus groups organized by Waddell and Diamond was that: "Brochures and posters are 'not enough' . . . Dialogue, a chance to ask questions and express fears, is needed. For this, we need a worker acting as marketer/salesperson. That worker need not always be the FASW, but the FASW, as case leader, must either provide the information in adequate amounts or make a positive referral—escorting the client to a waiting ET worker if necessary."[35]

Marketing means attempting to get your ideas across in any way you can. Marketing ET CHOICES involved Dukakis's participation, delivering speeches, giving interviews, introducing success stories. And Atkins was always happy to have the governor delivering this message of success. For example, at the beginning of his third term, when the AFDC error rate had dropped to 2.1 percent (from 11.6 percent four years before), the governor, not the commissioner, held the press conference to make the announcement.[36] Atkins learned well one of Gordon Chase's rules concerning "The Care and Feeding of Bosses and Chief Elected Officials": "Give the good press to the chief and accept the fact that there will be precious little left over for you."[37]

Not that this hurt Atkins. Dukakis's repeated appearances with yet another group of former welfare recipients generated much more exposure for ET CHOICES than would have such appearances by any welfare commissioner. Atkins was willing to have his governor make all the announcements about the success of ET not merely because his mentor said that was how to play the game; he did it because it was best for his department, best for his program, and best for himself. An announcement that ET was doing good things was newsworthy and helpful. An announcement *by the governor* that ET was doing good things was much more newsworthy and thus much more helpful.

But Dukakis's marketing efforts were not limited to holding press conferences. In May 1987, while attending the inauguration of the president of Bridgewater State College, the governor described ET to the president of the Massachusetts College for the Arts, Robert O'Neal. O'Neal observed that he was having trouble filling two secretarial positions, and Dukakis responded that he should call Atkins and David A. Haley (head of the Department of Personnel Administration, which had a contract to place ET participants in state jobs). In addition, the governor had his secretary follow up with both Atkins and Haley to make sure that the jobs indeed got filled.

Atkins, too, was involved in marketing the program directly to employers. Standing in the check-out line at a Boston department store, he observed the manager "going crazy" because he did not have enough clerks to handle the customers. So Atkins asked how much the store paid its clerks—$6.00 per hour—and how many it needed—twenty. Said Atkins: "You'll have them tomorrow. Here's my card." Later, Atkins told his staff: "I reported to the governor on how proud I was of finding twenty jobs. Now he's holding me responsible and asking for periodic reports."

Placing welfare recipients, however, was not easy. Although the store manager told Atkins he paid $6.00 an hour, actual offers were only $4.25. Of the first twenty-eight people whom DES sent over, only two (one white male and one white female) were hired. "It really opened my eyes to how tough it is out there for our contractors," Atkins told his staff. There was always the problem of discrimination: "The manager of the store, who wants to maximize his profit, is trying to keep the bidding down as low as possible . . . Here's a woman, probably young, so they'll pay $4.25. The males, they will pay higher." Being directly involved with the customers gave Atkins an "insight into the difficulties of getting that wage up out there in the field. And more credit to those folks, the ET contractors, that are getting an average wage up to $13,000 a year. It ain't that easy is what I'm learning first hand."

Nevertheless, the department's contractors were out there marketing jobs to recipients and recipients to jobs. The welfare office at Grove Hall shared its building with a branch of the Division of Employment Security. Nine DES employees were there, including five ET "job developers" who actually worked in the welfare department's part of the building. Every morning, one of these DES employees, Roosevelt Cole, would make several trips out to the waiting room to market the idea of employment to the welfare recipients waiting to see their FASW. There was a yellow poster on the bulletin board announcing in red letters "This Week's HOT JOBS," and Cole would hand out a flier listing about ten additional jobs (all paying over $5.00 per hour) and make a pitch for them. "Usually at least five or six people come back with me," he reported one morning. "On Monday, I got eleven people to come back." This day, however, not a single AFDC recipient was interested. But one man, who was only in the waiting room because he was accompanying a welfare recipient, found some of the jobs of interest. The man was not eligible for placement through ET, but Cole quickly escorted him over to the DES side of the building where he could indeed get assistance in finding a job.

6

Making Government More Businesslike

"We really do have the best employment and training program in the nation," Jolie Bain Pillsbury, associate commissioner for eligibility operations, told several hundred social workers in April 1987. For several years, the Massachusetts Department of Public Welfare conducted a dozen all-day meetings across the state. Every local-office director, assistant director, supervisor, and social worker attended one of these conferences, which were officially titled "Partners in Professionalism." Everyone called them PIPs.

One objective of these meetings was to thank everyone for the prior year's efforts. "We don't do it enough unless we set a day aside to say 'thank you,'" Deputy Commissioner Thomas P. Glynn told the audience at one PIP.

A second purpose of the PIPs was to focus attention within the department on its own accomplishments. For example, Glynn noted that during the previous year the department had placed 3,000 homeless welfare recipients in permanent housing. "The experts at Harvard said it couldn't be done," observed Glynn, "but we did it." Using a slide displaying the department's "97% Perfect" button, Glynn also talked about how, in four years, the department had gone from having the third highest error rate in the country to being well under the 3-percent federal target. Celebrating past successes served a third purpose: to pump up the department's adrenalin and generate enthusiasm for tackling the next set of projects.

A fourth purpose was to set out the program for the coming year—to reinforce the fundamental, underlying purposes of the department, and to explain the specific steps to be taken to achieve those purposes. The invitation to the 1986 PIPs, which was sent individually to each financial assistance social worker, stated:

> The theme of this year's conference will be
> the critical role of the professional social
> worker in helping clients move towards
> self-sufficiency by participation in the ET
> CHOICES Program:
>
> - Agents of Change: How Do We
>   Break the Welfare Cycle?
> - Focusing on the Potential of
>   Every Individual
> - Teamwork at the Local Level: How
>   to Build Bridges to Success
>
> Your role is paramount in turning the welfare
> experience into positive opportunities for
> our clients.

With her usual humor and enthusiasm, Pillsbury told the local-office directors that "with the distribution of the invitation, we begin the build-up of positive feelings that will reach its height on the day of the PIP."

Partners in Professionalism

A local-office director (chosen by his or her colleagues) hosted each PIP and, as Pillsbury put it, introduced "the mucky-mucks." In 1987, each PIP began with the "Commissioner's Perspective"—a slide presentation, with Glynn occasionally substituting for Commissioner Charles M. Atkins.

Next Pillsbury made her own presentation, entitled "Case Management: A Route Out of Poverty." Stressing that the department was no longer merely in the income-maintenance business, Pillsbury explained to the state's social workers what she called their "new" and "radical" mission. The department had to move beyond merely "delivering accurate, compassionate, and timely services," she said. "Our new mission is to help people out of poverty."

Also on the agenda for the 1987 PIPs was a video on case management. With a drama student playing the role of a welfare recipient and departmental employees anxiously assuming the others, the video was designed, Pillsbury said, to illustrate how case management might work. One feature of the case-management system was to be the case conference—a periodic meeting of a team of social workers (ET, Health Choices, housing, and child-support workers) to review a recipient's progress and discuss future steps. At the beginning of the video's case conference, the case supervisor distributed to each person on her case-management team a t-shirt with the appropriate imprint: "ET CHOICES," "HEALTH CHOICES," and so on. When the video was first viewed in the commissioner's conference room, key managers laughed nervously at this scene. It seemed too hokey. Indeed, at the PIP, the scene generated similar giggles. But by the annual Welfare Conference that June, everyone was demanding t-shirts, and the department was rushing to ensure that it would have an adequate supply.

In the afternoon, those attending the PIP were divided into small groups to discuss specific aspects of case management. But the highlight of each PIP was a panel on "Case Management in Practice."

The Case-Management Panel

The panel on case management presented not a theoretical description of this new process but a real-life success story. At one PIP, Joseph Madison, the deputy associate commissioner for employment and training, introduced panelists who had all made a contribution to helping Laurie Millett move from welfare to work. This panel included four individuals from the Somerville welfare office: the ongoing-payments supervisor, the child-support supervisor, the ET worker, and the health-choices adviser. Also on the panel were the contractor who gave Millett her computer training and her employer in the city's office of human services. All of these individuals briefly explained their role in helping move Millett from welfare to work.

Then it was Millett's turn to speak. Prior to the PIPs, Pillsbury had told the office directors that the case-management panel "is the center of the day, because the client is the center of the case-management system." Indeed, Millett was the star. She was obviously nervous, as all the members of the panel had been; none of them had ever addressed this large an audience. Yet as Millett explained her odyssey from welfare to work, her nervousness created an empathy in her audience. At the end of Millett's presentation, everyone—from social workers to executive staff— gave her a standing ovation. As usual, Pillsbury led the applause.

By itself, the case-management panel was effective in achieving the three objectives of the PIPs. Asking people to be on this panel was a most effective way of thanking them for their work. Indeed, for each PIP there was a different panel, thus distributing the praise (while ensuring that each presentation was original and fresh). At the same time, the mere existence of these panels celebrated the concrete accomplishments of the department's staff and created enthusiasm. Finally, the panel dramatized the department's new mission (in a way that no speech or memo could) and provided some specifics about how to make it work.

After the case-management panel, Barbara Burke-Tatum, associate commissioner for employment and training, took a microphone and wandered around the room doing what one departmental employee called "her Oprah Winfrey thing." The objective was to encourage social workers to ask questions about the case just described by the panel or to raise issues that had been troubling them about the case management. Burke-Tatum would either let the panel respond to the question, field it herself, direct it to another member of the leadership team, or solicit responses from the audience.

One social worker asked whether the department would help a former welfare recipient go back to court when the father of her child stopped paying child support. It may well have been in the state's long-run financial interest to support the former recipient's claim to continued child support. (If child-support payments stop, even a single mother with a job may be forced to return to welfare.) Yet neither federal nor state laws authorized expenditures to support child-support litigation by former recipients. Like other questions about a policy dilemma that the department had yet to resolve, this one produced no definitive response.

A similar question-and-answer session followed the case-management video, this time with Pillsbury as moderator. In the video, when the case worker asked the recipient where she wanted to be in six months, the young woman with her first baby responded with an optimistic view of her future. But one social worker asked Pillsbury how she could go about changing the attitude of recipients who had been on welfare for a long time: "If you ask them 'Where do you expect to be in six months?,' you know full well that they expect to be on welfare."

These discussions did more, however, than raise policy dilemmas or provide useful technical information. They also involved the department's line workers. Although most were unwilling to take the microphone before several hundred of their colleagues, some did seize the opportunity. And they did not just ask questions. Social workers delivered short speeches, offered arguments or points they had been waiting for months to express, and presented inspirational stories. These question-and-answer sessions rarely produced a complete resolution of issues troubling the field staff, but they did give everyone an opportunity to air their ideas and opinions.

Continuous Praise and Reinforcement

The annual PIPs were not the only time that the department's leadership team thanked the field for its efforts, celebrated its successes, pumped up enthusiasm, and reinforced the basic mission. Before the 1987 PIPs, every field supervisor attended a case-management conference to discuss the department's new mission (a route out of poverty) and its new system (case management). After the PIPs, Pillsbury expected all her local-office managers to hold a meeting of their office staff and give their own version of her speech on case management. The Welfare Conference on Cape Cod served similar purposes, as did the department's numerous publications.

At the beginning of 1987, the department distributed a large (22" by 18") calendar. At the bottom was a brief message from the commissioner:

Case Management—A Route Out of Poverty

Our mission is not only to provide the basics of food, clothing, and shelter. Our ultimate goal is to provide our clients with a route out of poverty. This is accomplished by a variety of means, most notably the ET CHOICES program. Each of us, by performing our duties to the best of our ability, contributes to this goal and shares in our achievements along the way.

The department's annual report for 1985 was titled "Milestones: Twenty-one Days from the 1985 Calendar." These dates were grouped into five programmatic categories—the error rate, child support, homeless shelter, Medicaid, and ET. And with each there was an illustration—occasionally a graph, often a picture of some employees or a recipient. For example:

- November 30. "Somerville welfare office tops child support collections goals." The photograph pictured four members of the Somerville Child-Support Enforcement Unit.
- December 31. "More than 31 local welfare offices were better than 97% perfect." Accompanying this were two photographs of caseworkers, one from Grove Hall, the other from Holyoke.
- October 1. "After fourteen years on welfare, Ruby Sampson became a surgical technician." Sampson was pictured in, naturally, her surgical gown.

The 1986 annual report, emphasizing "A Route out of Poverty," also featured employee photos. Next to a full-page picture of Camella Despres, a head clerk at the Fall River welfare office and a Peformance Recognition Award winner, was this quote: "It just makes you feel good to be recognized after 26 years of work. It makes me feel proud of the work I've done all these years, and happy to be working for a Department that appreciates its employees."

In June 1986, the department's newsletter, *Public Welfare News,* contained the front-page headline: "ET Number One Priority for Coming Year." But the newsletter also reflected management's early drive to reduce the error rate: "AFDC Error Rate Lowest in History" (May 1985); "Error Rate Drops to 4%" (September 1985), and "Error Rate Hits All Time Low" (March 1986). Like any in-house newsletter, *Public Welfare News* celebrated the accomplishments of individuals and units: "31 Forms Junked" (November 1984); "MMIS [Medicaid Management Information System] Saves $56 Million" (December 1984); "Massachusetts Leads States in Welfare Caseload Decline due to ET" (January 1986); "Child Support Collections Up, Somerville Leads the Way" (March 1986). Accompanied by pictures of supervisors and social workers, such articles usually concluded with "special thanks" for individual efforts.

Atkins personally led this reinforcement effort. Whenever he conducted a meeting, no matter how large or small, he would always remind the employees in attendance of their mission. He was not particularly eloquent. Indeed, before a large audience he often appeared nervous; no one would ever accuse Chuck Atkins of being silver-tongued. But for Atkins, reciting his agency's mission was not a reflexive but an intellectual act. He well understood that this was an essential responsibility of leadership—the head of any public agency must personally and continually remind all employees of their basic purpose—and he was determined to fulfill it. It did not make any difference whether he enjoyed doing it or was even good at it. Atkins knew he had to do it—and he did.

Publicizing the Awards

Public Welfare News also reminded everyone who received the latest awards. In addition to the Employment and Training Awards for those offices that met their ET goals, the department distributed many other annual awards:

- "Child Support Awards" to those units in local offices that realized their child-support goals.
- "Excellence in Attainment Awards" to other units that met their own, specific goals.
- "Compassion Awards" to fifty employees who performed unusual acts of compassion and provided services "above and beyond the call of duty."
- "Performance Recognition Awards" to about a dozen individuals and units for "exemplary work performance and contribution to meeting Department of Public Welfare goals."

In the lobby of the department's central office hung poster-size photos of the Performance Recognition Award winners, who were also the department's nominees for the state's Manuel Carballo Award for Excellence in Public Service and who received the "Commonwealth Citation for Outstanding Performance." The department's 1987 calendar listed the 1986 winners of the Commonwealth Citation, the Operations Manager Award, the Massachusetts Public Welfare Administrator's Association Recognition Award, the Child Support Award, the Excellence in Attainment Award, and the Commissioner's Compassion Award.

Further, whenever employees were honored, the department's press office notified their local newspapers. "Welfare office cited for excellence," announced the *Salem Evening News* on July 31, 1986. At the annual Welfare Conference the previous month, the Salem office had received the Employment and Training award for placing 188 recipients. "You have much to be proud of," the paper quoted Atkins as saying. "You have helped welfare recipients find a way out of poverty and have given them hope for the future. You did this by offering them training, education and real jobs." That same quote appeared in other stories on local winners; many newspapers ran the department's press release verbatim. Accompanying the article in the *Salem Evening News* was a photograph (also provided by the department) showing Florence Skarmos, a caseworker in the Salem office, accepting the award from Atkins and David A. Haley, the state's personnel administrator. In the background of every such picture hung a banner saying "Thank You for a Job Well Done, Your Department of Public Welfare."

Similar publicity efforts accompanied other awards. "Local welfare office receives award for child support efforts" announced the *Chelsea Record* on July 30, 1986, after Chelsea's unit exceeded its $760,000 collection goal. Accompanying the article was another picture: William Dineen of the staff of the Chelsea child-enforcement unit receiving the award from Atkins and Robert Anastas, the department's director of child support enforcement. In late July 1986, pictures of caseworkers, Atkins, Haley, and Anastas graced the pages of many of the state's newspapers.

Cynicism and Politics

Awards will be widely accepted as fair if they possess two characteristics: (1) they are based on achieving a predetermined goal, and (2) that goal is derived from a reasonably equitable formula. For example, to receive the ET award or the child-support award, a local office had to attain a standard and objective level of performance. Either an office made its quota, or it did not. There was little basis for controversy.

In contrast, awards that lack these two characteristics can easily become controversial. For example, decisions about who would receive

Compassion Awards and Performance Recognition Awards were clearly human judgments. The selection committee had to use very imperfect information in choosing from a long list of nominees. Moreover, the final decision involved factors other than pure merit. The winners would have to be balanced along numerous demographic dimensions. They could not all be white males or all be black females; they could not all come from the executive staff or from local offices in Boston. Thus, the ten nominees who just missed getting one of the Performance Recognition Awards would be as deserving as many who won. Anyone could complain: My friend Sally should have won but did not because of this person or that factor. Some people in the department grumbled that such awards were based on "politics."

While watching an awards ceremony, one social worker complained about a variety of problems in the Massachusetts Department of Public Welfare. ET was, said this FASW, "baloney"—a "production line" that simply got people jobs no matter how long they lasted. Nostalgically, this departmental veteran remembered the old days, when social workers did real social work. Such social work was still needed, the FASW continued, but unfortunately it was not "cost effective"; twenty years before (when the real social work was done) a social worker would work with only twenty-five people per year.

This social worker also did not like the department's awards. The people who won the Compassion Awards were "brown-nosers," and the person from this social worker's office who won the award was "a screamer"—that is, someone who screams at welfare recipients. And yet, as did everyone else, this social worker clapped enthusiastically whenever a friend won an award.

When there is no objective and equitable standard for any kind of award or reward, anyone who does not win and does not have any friends who win always has a convenient and simple explanation: politics.

The Massachusetts Civic Interest Council

Others had different complaints about the department's management. In January 1987, the Massachusetts Civil Interest Council reported that the department had "wasted" over the previous two years "thousands of dollars to dine, entertain and lodge department employees."[1] MCIC's report focused on expenditures for three activities: the PIPs, a series of training seminars for child-support workers, and a 1986 incentive program for ET Springs Forward.

The 1985 and 1986 PIPs, said the MCIC report, "were held at some of the finest hotels and function rooms in the state including the Hyatt Regency Cambridge, the Sheraton Rolling Green Andover, and the Boston Park Plaza." The report noted that the cost for 30 PIPs was $92,081, that "the cost per person ranged up to $21.75," that 5,264 banquet dinners were served, that the luncheon at the Park Plaza "itself cost $12.50 per person," and that a bill at the Sheraton Rolling Green "included a $250 charge for the rental of crystal and silver." Concluded the report: "While the homeless rummage for scraps in dumpsters in the alleys below, welfare employees are being served steak dinners in the Grand Ballroom of the Park Plaza."

Six three-day training seminars for child-enforcement workers cost the state $29,734, said the report, of which $14,376 was for meals. But MCIC focused its criticism on the $8,803 spent for the 155 state employees who, even though "there were no evening sessions," spent two nights at the hotel where the seminar was held. Moreover, continued the report, "most of the employees who stayed overnight actually worked at local offices that were only a short distance from the hotel."

For meeting the ET Springs Forward goals at the end of fiscal year 1986, the department "rewarded" each local office with a $10-per-employee bonus that could be used for plants, pictures, an office party, or whatever. All the offices used all or part of their money for a party of some sort. The MCIC report listed some of these expenditures:

- The Gardner Office had 35 roast beef dinners catered from DBA Crystal Catering at $9.95 per person.
- The Worcester Office enjoyed a $950 luncheon buffet from the Wall Street Deli along with $275 worth of pizza from Dean Park Pizza. They topped it off with Do-It-Yourself Sundaes for 200 people from The Broadway, at a cost of $290 . . .
- The Chicopee Office dined on the $10 per person smorgasbord from Lena's Catering of Holyoke. It included lobster newburg, roast beef, lasagna and golompkes for $470.

"You'd think the Welfare Department could find better ways of spending working people's tax dollars," said an MCIC spokesman. Concluded the report: "Although the Department has told MCIC that these expenditures saved thousands of dollars, or were a reward for past savings, there is no factual evidence to prove these expenditures lead to any savings. In fact, Department employees interviewed by MCIC said the events provided little in the way of meaningful training and were really just a nice day away from the office."

ET and the Press

On January 15, 1987, the MCIC report generated headlines across the state. "Watchdog group slams welfare department," declared the Lynn *Daily Evening Item. The Boston Herald* announced: "It's party hearty time at Welfare."

All this press coverage was quite predictable. Robert M. Entman of Northwestern University has written that journalists possess not an ideological bias but three important "production biases that spring from the economic market." Editors need to generate stories that sell advertising in newspapers, on radio, and on television. The production biases, writes Entman, "grow out of the need to manufacture news to attract and retain mass audiences."

Entman's first bias is the "simplification bias." Reporters and editors prefer "stories that are simple to report—convenient and inexpensive, and safe, rather than inconvenient, risky, and costly." They "also prefer stories that are simple [for the public] to understand." "Journalism conveys a simple message more readily and accurately than a complicated one," writes Entman, "and it deems simple messages more accessible and attractive to audiences."

The second of Entman's production biases is the "personalization bias." Again, "to encourage audience interest and identification," editors and reporters devote less attention to "institutional, historical, or other abstract forces," and instead focus on personalities. "Journalists tend to explain events by reference to the actions of individuals," writes Entman: "To lend drama and provide a concrete narrative framework, journalists favor news that clearly involves well known individuals in conflict. If the story takes an archetypal form (David vs. Goliath, Good vs. Evil), so much the better."

The last of Entman's three production biases is the "symbolization bias." Journalists prefer stories with a symbol provided by "a dramatic action, intriguing personality, or stirring slogan." Symbols help journalists manufacture their product because they "condense widely-shared, familiar meanings and carry broad political connotations." This bias is also derived, argues Entman, from what editors and reporters believe their audiences want. Symbols, he says, "can stand for a familiar stereotype or shared public understanding of the subject covered in the story," or they can "connote a wider cultural value or archetype, such as patriotism or individualism."[2]

U.S. Senator William Proxmire discovered all this when he started giving out his monthly "Golden Fleece Award" for wasteful federal expenditures. What generated the most attention were the smaller expenditures—items that were easy to understand, focused on individuals, and symbolized governmental prodigality.

In July 1987, Proxmire gave his award to the Commerce Department for "a 'see no evil' policy permitting local authorities to so mismanage a federally-funded revolving loan program that the local economy was hurt rather than helped and $1.3 million—over 90 percent of the money—was lost."[3] In the jargon of journalism, such wording can produce a severe case of MEGO—"my eyes glaze over." What exactly does this program do? Did it really not do any good? What's a revolving loan fund? How much is $1.3 million really? Was 90 percent truly "lost"? A complicated program is difficult to explain in the first sentence of a press release.

Contrast this with Proxmire's January 1977 award to the Department of Agriculture "for spending nearly $46,000 to find out how long it takes to cook breakfast." The following month, the Law Enforcement Assistance Administration won the Golden Fleece "for spending nearly $27,000 to determine why inmates want to escape from prison."[4] Both awards were easy to understand. Both government activities looked flagrantly silly. And the amount spent on these programs fell within everyone's personal experience. Every taxpayer could easily comprehend $27,000 or $46,000—and what he or she would do with it, were it not wasted on some ridiculous government study.

Similarly, although newspaper articles about the MCIC report dutifully included the total expenditure of $143,000, what really generated attention were specific expenditures, such as $250 to rent silver and crystal. Newspapers often reported how much the welfare offices in their area spent from their ET Springs Forward award on a party or luncheon. One newspaper even printed the names of the employees who stayed overnight in the region's Holiday Inn.[5] Regardless of the local angle, however, almost every journalist picked up on the $290 the Worcester office spent for do-it-yourself ice-cream sundaes. Such expenditures were simple to understand, involved local individuals, and symbolized the familiar stereotype of government waste.

Of course, the simplification, personalization, and symbolization biases of the press had also been a major benefit to ET. Indeed, beginning with its original, June 1984 Framingham press conference, the department repeatedly and skillfully exploited Entman's three production biases.

The success stories were simple to report. The department's press staff did all the work; they found articulate women, set up the press conference, provided a tour of the plant, and created photo opportunities. The success stories were simple to comprehend: by working hard and with the help of ET, welfare recipients escaped poverty and became productive citizens.

Second, the stories were dramatically personal—the individual triumph of a determined woman. Deserted by her children's father, trapped in poverty, and burdened by a lack of education and training, the woman had, through hard work and determination, overcome adversity and converted failure into success. Each woman—each success story—was an intriguing personality. Each former welfare recipient told her own personal, and very moving, story of how she escaped from welfare.

Finally, these success stories had symbolic content—concrete action, stirring slogans, familiar stereotypes, and cultural values. The department always held the press conferences at a production facility, where it was possible to see, photograph, and film a former welfare recipient doing something. (Women who worked as secretaries or computer operators might be asked to join the press conference, but the tour would be not to an office desk but to a laboratory or manufacturing workbench.) And there was always the extra-terrestrial slogan: ET.

Stories about welfare recipients can often reinforce the familiar stereotype of the lazy welfare queen who collects more than she is due. But the symbolism in the ET success stories tells a different American tale, of the struggling, impoverished individual who through hard work (and a little outside help) has managed to pull herself up by her bootstraps and become a contributing member of society. The real symbol behind each ET success story was one of our most widely shared cultural values: the American Dream.

Bringing Business Management to Government

In response to the MCIC report, Atkins defended his department's employees. He called the report "an insult to the workers of this department, who I think have done an outstanding job."[6] "I very much resent [the report]," said Atkins; "it's aimed at 5,000 of the best employees in state government."[7] "This was money well spent," he argued. "We gave some employees a free lunch to say 'thank you.' Yes, we rented silverware for $250. Did you think they were going to eat with their fingers?"[8]

Atkins's response went beyond a defense of his employees' hard work. He emphasized that, in addition to saying "thank you," the expenditures were designed to train and motivate. The meals, he argued, were "a terribly important approach in motivating employees of this department to do excellent work."[9] "It was not $143,000 spent on entertainment and lodging. It was $143,000 to train and motivate people to continue to do the kind of good job that they've been doing out there without a lot of thanks."[10] Atkins linked the training seminars for child-support enforcement with the progress his department had made: "We're getting 25 percent more in child support payments than three years ago and now take in $53 million." He also emphasized the drop in the error rate from 11 to 2.5 percent and the placement of 30,000 ET participants. "Using these training conferences and motivation workshops, we got workers to be more accurate on the job and we avoided $40 million in federal penalties," he argued.[11] "We did it by bringing people in, training them, motivating them and rewarding them with a free lunch," he continued. "What's wrong with that?"[12]

Finally, Atkins argued that his department was only doing what was standard managerial practice in business: "Government should not be afraid to reward and motivate its employees. The private sector does it all the time. And it works."[13] "We've tried to borrow lessons from the private sector," said the commissioner. "What we cannot do is give government employees extra money. The only thing we can do to say thank you to an employee is give them a free meal, give them a certificate, get them out of the office for a training session for a day or two."[14]

Not everyone in the state, however, bought the argument that public management ought to imitate business management. In an editorial titled "Who says no free lunch?" the *Marlboro Enterprise* declared:

> Welfare Commissioner Charles Atkins says the practice of rewarding employees is taken from a page out of private industry.
> That is where this type of reward should stay. Atkins should realize that private industry has a budget for such expenditures and may pass the cost to customers who have the option of not buying the service or product. But taxpayers do not have that option. We pay anyway.[15]

Similar editorial sentiments were expressed by *The Patriot Ledger* of Quincy: "This is one practice that should be left to the private sector, where it can be written off as a business expense. The tab for the welfare employees' meals was picked up by the taxpayers, and that's not right . . .

Governor Dukakis used to be famous for inviting people to brown-bag lunch meetings in his office. That is a lesson the Welfare Department should borrow."[16]

Ironically, when private industry writes off this part of its budget as a business expense, taxpayers again have no option. Such write-offs either raise taxes, decrease services, or increase debt-service costs. But that is not the issue. Apparently there exists, somewhere in our collective subconscious, a feeling that certain practices, while quite acceptable in business, are simply forbidden in government. This sentiment involves not a question of ethics but of propriety. When the welfare department produced its multicolored brochure "My Mom and ET," several members of an advisory committee—friends, not antagonists, of the department's mission and programs—thought it was "too good" for government.

For the first PIPs in 1985, Pillsbury "said to the people arranging it, 'I want pink chandeliers,' meaning I wanted it elegant to convey this message" that both the conferences and the participants were special. "So they went all out," Pillsbury observed. "And it wasn't that expensive." In 1987, after the MCIC report, the Massachusetts Department of Public Welfare held its third round of PIPs at, for example, the Teachers' Union Hall in Dorchester rather than at a downtown hotel. Observed Pillsbury: "We're only saving a couple thousand dollars. But the Boston Teachers Union is not the Colonnade [Hotel]. There are no chandeliers. It's this code word: No parties, and no chandeliers."

Simultaneous Loose-Tight Properties

In the concluding chapter of *In Search of Excellence,* Thomas J. Peters and Robert H. Waterman, Jr., discuss the eighth characteristic they attribute to excellent American companies: "Simultaneous Loose-Tight Properties." These firms are "loose"; corporate leadership permits—indeed, exhorts—individual units to be autonomous, entrepreneurial, and innovative. "They encourage the entrepreneurial spirit among their people, because they push autonomy remarkably far down the line." At the same time, these firms are "tight"; corporate leaders insist on a few key values that define the firm's mission. They develop an organizational culture that supports and reinforces those values, and carefully monitor how well the various units are doing at realizing them. "The excellent companies are measurement-happy and performance-oriented." These firms are, conclude Peters and Waterman, extremely "tight" about their mission but very "loose" about how their subunits should go about accomplishing that mission.

Corporate leadership can be "loose" about implementation, Peters and Waterman argue, because the existence of tight, stable values disciplines the behavior of units and individuals. At the same time, these values give "people confidence (to experiment, for instance) stemming from stable expectations about what really counts." Excellent companies, argue Peters and Waterman, exercise control not through rules that constrain negative behavior but through values that reinforce positive behavior.[17]

Unfortunately, management as practiced in government often takes the inverse approach. All too frequently, public management has *tight-loose* properties. Government is tight about implementation, but loose about mission. In part, such a characteristic may be inherent to government, reflecting underlying differences between public and private organizations. But it also reflects our cultural attitudes toward government.

Government is "tight" in that its leadership tells its agencies exactly how they should do every little thing. Such rules inevitably curb autonomy, entrepreneurship, and innovation. When it comes to purpose, however, government is very "loose." The central values of an agency are rarely defined with clarity; legislative majorities and governing coalitions are put together by obfuscating purposes rather than by resolving them. And even if a leader does choose to articulate a clear set of values, there is no guarantee that he or she will maintain influence for long. Given that elected officials, appointed executives, and legislative majorities can quickly disappear, does a civil servant want to bet a career on the permanence of the values articulated by any particular leader? Yet without a clear set of values—without a sense of what the mission is—such officials, executives, and legislatures need some way to discipline the behavior of the civil servants. The result is a complex set of very tight rules that constrain the negative but do little to reinforce the positive.

The management of the Massachusetts Department of Public Welfare was, however, characterized by many simultaneous loose-tight properties. Atkins, Glynn, Pillsbury, and Burke-Tatum all shared a common set of values. There was no dissent within the management team about the department's mission. From his first week as commissioner, when he fired the department's legal counsel, Atkins repeatedly emphasized a few values. And consistently at the very top of his list were two important ideas: compassion for all welfare recipients; and assistance to help them find a route out of poverty. The marketing campaigns as well as the individual efforts of Atkins and his executive staff were designed to articulate, dramatize, repeat, and reinforce these key values. The PIPs, awards, publications, press, and reports all did this. So did the decisions that each executive made about how to spend his or her time; their presence and active participation at a meeting or event sent clear, unmistakable signals about what they thought was important.

Because government is commonly characterized by inverse *tight-loose* properties, the staff agencies—those units that control budget, personnel, contracting, and procurement—often control the line agencies. Through the creation, interpretation, manipulation, and enforcement of the tight rules on implementation, the staff units—or what Gordon Chase liked to call perjoratively the "overhead agencies"[18]—run the government.

The line units, the people who are actually responsible for delivering government's services, can challenge these rules. But such a challenge can only be effective when it is based on a clear set of values. If the line can argue that the rules are interfering with their ability to achieve a clearly stated and accepted mission, then they have a firm basis on which to appeal the rules to the top executive (who was the one, after all, who established the mission). Without a clear sense of purpose, however, the staff units and their rules will inevitably win.

At the Massachusetts Department of Public Welfare the organization chart dramatized that the expressed responsibility of the staff units was to serve the line. The associate commissioners, who ran the line units, reported to Commissioner Atkins; the assistant commissioners, who ran the staff units, reported to Deputy Commissioner Glynn. In part, this reflected Atkins's own personal predilection for hands-on, operations management. In part, however, it reflected the efforts of Atkins and Glynn to make sure that the staff served the line. And Glynn did not have an easy job, for example, convincing the staff unit responsible for policies and procedures that their job was not to dictate new regulations for the line workers to follow but rather to help those on the line do their job. But in June 1987, at the executive staff's annual strategic planning meeting, Glynn was able to say: "The service units understand that they are service units, and the operating units haven't complained about them in a long time."

Atkins, Glynn, Pillsbury, and Burke-Tatum delegated to the local-office directors, supervisors, and social workers the responsibility for achieving their goals. While stating clearly the values for the department, the management team also admitted that it had very little detailed knowledge about how to realize them. At one meeting of the local-office directors Pillsbury said, "There is no right answer" to the question of how to implement case management. "You'll be inventing unique solutions that will help each other."

For the traditional income-maintenance function of a welfare department, standard operating procedures are essential. Who is to receive welfare payments and how much cannot be decided by individual social workers. The overriding concern for equity requires that the same eligibility rules be applied to everyone (although obviously the "street-level bureaucrats" who apply the rules inevitably exercise discretion[19]). For the distribution of financial assistance, it makes little sense for the managers to articulate general values and then monitor the eligibility and payment decisions of the social workers to see if they are doing a good job. For the writing of welfare checks, government's traditional tight-loose system has some merit.

Nevertheless, articulating the agency's mission can help the street-level bureaucrats exercise the discretion that the standard operating procedures cannot eliminate. During Atkins's first week on the job, when *The Boston Globe* reported Mary Badger and her daughter were "homeless today as a direct result of the actions" of his department, the new commissioner emphasized that a legalistic interpretation of the rules could not justify failing to fulfill the department's basic responsibilities: "Workers, most of them overworked and sincere, sometimes take a very narrow view of things. If a situation isn't in the manual, they say there is nothing they can do. I have no excuse. They take their signal from the top and until I got here there was no leadership. Things are going to change."[20] When he fired the department's legal counsel, Atkins made it clear that he would like the department's employees to exercise discretion and initiative: "If housing isn't our direct responsibility, helping her [Badger] find housing is. If we can't do it, we should find the proper people who can."[21]

Finding jobs for welfare recipients is a qualitatively different chore from determining eligibility and writing checks. Standard operating procedures make little sense for an employment and training program with the philosophy of ET CHOICES. Each individual needs different training and different services. There is some concern for equity. But there is an even bigger concern for effectiveness. And if everyone receives the identical training and identical services, they will inevitably be appropriate for almost no one. Thus, though a tight-loose approach may make sense for the income-maintenance function of a welfare department, loose-tight management is essential for a welfare, training, and work program.

Forcing Decisions and Responsibility
Down into the Organization

Establishing and articulating the overarching mission of the department was the easy part. Getting the local-office directors and individual line workers to take responsibility for performance was much more difficult, for this was a major change from the standard operating philosophy of the department and, indeed, of most government agencies.

Not that the change from the tight-loose properties for eligibility and payments to loose-tight management for ET was appreciated throughout the department. "The introduction of permission to be creative at the line level was not welcomed," observed Janet Diamond, the former welfare recipient who went to work for the department. "Workers were angry and confused, and, above all, distrustful." Having grown accustomed to using the department's standard operating procedures as both helpful guidelines and a dependable crutch, some people found it hard to take responsibility for results. But through repetition of the message and changes in personnel, the department management team's philosophy began to have an impact.

Pillsbury, whose Division of Eligibility Operations was responsible for delivering ET services through nearly sixty local offices, explained that "from the very beginning," there were two components to the approach: "very direct accountability but with some flexibility." Pillsbury's message to each local-office director was, "You're responsible and we're holding you accountable for the ultimate output" of job placements. "We didn't say to the director, 'You will follow these eighteen steps to get a job placement,'" continued Pillsbury. "We said, 'Here are some resources, here are some guidelines (and you always have these procedures and these computer systems). We're going to measure you very tightly every month. It's up to you to figure out how to make it work.'"

This approach created some controversy. The local-office directors complained, recalled Pillsbury: "How can you hold us responsible for things we don't control? I don't make the job placements. You've given me all these contracts that I didn't play a role in choosing. You can't hold me responsible." Pillsbury's response was simple: "That's management." And, she continued, "because the pressure of having to achieve to a carefully measured outcome was put at the local level, they solved their own problems."

"The necessity to market ET and other programs," noted Diamond, "has forced change." As the result, she said, "some ET supervisors are finding ways to get their own personal computers so that they can more effectively adapt local programs to client needs and to monitor their own progress." When forced to, "the field learned to play the game."

Still, the local offices needed resources. That was the responsibility of Barbara Burke-Tatum and the Division of Employment and Training. Burke-Tatum's division provided the contractors from inside and outside state government to provide education, training, day-care, and job-placement services. Pillsbury's division made use of these resources to achieve their placement goals: "My responsibility was managing people—the clients and the workers. Barbara's responsibility was managing the services, i.e., buying the contracts. They come together at the local level." At that point, explained Pillsbury, the local-office directors had to solve a variety of problems including "how to motivate people in a voluntary program."

Forcing responsibility down into the organization—to the local offices, the ET supervisors, and the individual ET workers—was, concluded Diamond, an essential characteristic of ET: "It takes a lot more than believing in the mission and wringing one's hands about the poor. It takes creative solutions and risk-taking action at the local level . . . The real change is not in throwing a good Employment and Training program together. The real change is in tapping into the creative intelligence of 2,500 plus employees. This is only accomplished by building long-term trust and consistently adhering to one central idea—the mission. When the end is this clear, the means will surface."

The system for managing ET "worked," argued Pillsbury, "because it was very clear from the beginning what the mission was. Then, we created a set of measures that would tell us what would happen. And, we held people accountable, but told them their job was to figure out the problem. They couldn't wait for us to design the perfect system." Tight on the mission, with an emphasis on values. Loose in implementation, with an emphasis on autonomy, entrepreneurship, and innovation. Excellent public agencies are also "measurement-happy and performance-oriented."

Throughout the spring of 1987, Pillsbury was sending an unmistakable message to her field staff. Case management was extremely important—not just to her, but to Atkins, Glynn, and Burke-Tatum, too. By concentrating directors' meetings, assistant directors' meetings, and PIPs on this single topic, she made her message very clear. At the same time, the leadership team in the central office did not know exactly how the new system would work. The local-office directors, the supervisors, and the individual social workers would have to figure that out.

But if an agency's top leadership does not tell the field what to do, what does it do? In this case, the leadership team peformed four important functions. First, it set the values and the overall mission of the department—to help welfare recipients find a route out of poverty. Second, it developed a general approach (case management) and offered some initial guidance—tentative suggestions and potentially useful ideas.

Third, the agency's leadership generated resources for use by the local offices—contractors to educate, train, and find jobs for ET participants. Fourth, it provided a vehicle for technological transfer—watching carefully what the field was doing, figuring out what produced results, and then enabling these experts to tell everyone else how and why their ideas worked.

Transferring Technologies

Disseminating local technologies is not easy. It may not be at all obvious what aspects of a local innovation make it work, and even if they are obvious, they may be difficult to explain on paper or to a large audience. The welfare department's leadership chose to have the innovators present their ideas to their colleagues; thus, at the meetings of the executive staff, of local-office directors, and of assistant directors, it was the members of a team from a local office who explained the latest idea that they, themselves, had developed.

This approach had a great impact on morale. Most members of the team had never been asked to make a presentation, and inevitably they were nervous. But by delivering the presentation personally, these innovators received substantial credit from their colleagues for their ideas. Moreover, because the people who made the idea work were the ones who actually described it, their message was much more credible. It was not the folks from the central office telling the field how to do something; it was the people in the field who were explaining how they did it.

But this approach also has a disadvantage. Critical details may be forgotten, not really understood, or inadequately explained. The field staff may be motivated to try an idea developed by some of their colleagues, but do they have the technical knowledge necessary to make the idea work? In fact, at one point, Pillsbury confessed that "the technical side hasn't caught up yet." The department did a much better job of explaining the mission of ET than of providing technical information on how to make it work. For example, at one of the PIPs, an ET worker pointed out that the Department of Social Services had a housing specialist "that nobody knows about."

Another example involved day-care services to ET graduates. Massachusetts actually had two day-care programs: voucher day care and contracted day care. By switching from vouchers to the contracted program, a former welfare recipient could receive a day-care subsidy long after she had graduated from ET and left welfare. Thus, for a former welfare recipient, eligibility for a day-care subsidy depended not upon the number of months since her case had closed (as did eligibility for Medicaid) but on the level of her income. In FY 1988, a Massachusetts mother with three children was eligible for a sliding-scale subsidy for contracted day care until her annual income exceeded $22,750. Yet discussions at various meetings revealed that few in the department really understood how the two day-care programs meshed. Commissioner Atkins, Associate Commissioner Burke-Tatum, and many financial assistance social workers talked about the state's day-care subsidy as if it expired at the end of twelve months—revealing a lack of technical knowledge about how these two programs really worked.

Still, the department consciously opted for a loose-tight operation. The role of the Policy and Procedures unit in the central office, for example, was not to write rules that constrained the field but to help the field. Each year, the Massachusetts Public Welfare Administrators Association, which is composed of the directors and assistant directors of the local offices, gave its Recognition Award to "an individual who has made a major contribution to improving local office operations." In June 1988, when presenting this award to Jeff McCue, the department's director of administration, Atkins commented: "Supporting the field—that's what the job of the central office is all about." At one of the PIPs, Pillsbury observed that social workers are accustomed to being given very specific instructions by the central office. But, she explained, "You can't do case management that way. You have to be more flexible. You can't do it by the cookbook."

The Role of Rewards in Government

In their chapter "Productivity through People," Peters and Waterman write of the role of "Hoopla, Celebration, and Verve." They describe "the hoopla, razzle-dazzle, and constantly changing menu of prizes, awards, and other incentives" employed by different corporations: "The systems in the excellent companies are not only designed to produce lots of winners; they are constructed to celebrate the winning once it occurs. Their systems make extraordinary use of non-monetary incentives." At Hewlett-Packard, "top management's explicit criterion for picking managers is their ability to engender excitement."[22]

Similarly, in *A Passion for Excellence*, Peters and Nancy Austin discuss "a subject that is most conspicuously absent from management textbooks: Fun, Zest, Enthusiasm." Despite their enthusiasm for enthusiasm, however, Peters and Austin feel compelled to raise and respond to a common question about motivational expenditures:

How do I convince my boss that we ought to spend possibly hundreds of thousands of dollars on a single bash for, say, our salesforce?

Beats us! No short-term cost/benefit analysis will provide justification. You simply must believe in people and believe that people like to be around one another and share one another's successes. Sorry. We have never had a shred of luck with our clients on this. We think that if you could smuggle that reluctant dragon into an IBM or Limited [Stores] celebration, you could make a believer out of him or her. Short of that, we're stymied, too.[23]

Atkins claimed that the $143,000 criticized by MCIC motivated his department's employees—that it helped the department continue to place ET recipients, cut the error rate, collect more child support. His benefit-cost calculation indicated that an expenditure of thousands produced results and saved millions. MCIC, however, found that "there is no factual evidence to prove these expenditures lead to any savings." And that, of course, was true. Whether or not the $143,000 motivated people to work more effectively, it is impossible to prove such a linkage.

Yet why is a practice so common in business viewed by many as unacceptable in government? Is this because, to prevent waste, government has an unwritten rule (which is more stringent than its counterpart in business) saying that before a public manager can spend money, he must somehow prove that it will produce results? Hardly; silly spending does not seem to be less common in government than in business. Is it simply because taxpayers rather than customers are paying the cost? Perhaps; but any private-sector activity that can be written off as a business expense also costs the taxpayers in terms of higher taxes, reduced services, or higher interest rates. Certainly, there is an important difference between the taxpayer caught in a monopoly and the customer who can vote with his pocketbook. Nevertheless, the taxpayer is paying the public employee a salary to produce results. Why not pay for a few balloons, bells, and whistles if that will help produce those results? Why are millions for salaries acceptable, but thousands for hoopla not?

The answer to this political riddle may lie in the all too common inverse tight-loose attitude toward government. When everyone knows exactly what an organization is trying to produce, it makes perfect sense to encourage autonomy in management; in this situation, management and staff can be trusted to concentrate on producing those results. When people cannot agree on the mission of a government agency, however, there are no corresponding results on which to concentrate. Indeed, without an agreement on basic purposes, thinking about government management inevitably focuses on the inputs. How much was spent?

How many people are employed? Is this up or down from last year? If your social responsibility is to produce some significant results—to help despondent and dependent women become financially independent and socially productive—an expenditure of $143,000 is not all that significant. But if all you can think about is controlling costs, $143,000 looms as very important.

Not that controlling costs is unimportant, or that private firms ignore it. Yet profitable businesses "seem to focus especially on the revenue-generation side," report Peters and Waterman; "we find high-performing companies in different industries to be mainly oriented to the value, rather than the cost side of the profitability equation." Peters and Waterman insist that "the quality versus cost trade-off" does not really exist: "There is nothing like quality. It is the most important word in these companies. Quality leads to a focus on innovativeness—to doing the best one can for every customer on every product; hence it is a goad to productivity."[24] Indeed, the real issue is productivity—the ratio of results to costs. Everyone wants the numerator to go up and the denominator to go down. The argument from *In Search of Excellence* is that concentrating on the numerator of results, rather than on the denominator of costs, is the best path to increasing the ratio of productivity.

The loose-tight management approach taken by Atkins, Glynn, Burke-Tatum, and Pillsbury was possible because they had a very clear sense of what their department's mission was. They knew what results they wanted, and they concentrated on producing them. But for those who had not devoted as much time to thinking through precisely what the department should accomplish, the costs loomed much larger.

7

Management by
Groping Along

On October 1, 1983, just six months after Charles M. Atkins became welfare commissioner, ET began operating statewide. Literally, of course, this was not true. How could it be? Many local offices did not yet have a single ET worker. Many offices had only a few contractors available to provide training. Many offices did not even know the people in the Division of Employment Security (DES) with whom they would have to work. ET was a statewide program only on paper.

Nevertheless, ET was designed to operate statewide from day one. It was not a pilot project to be tested in a few, select offices. It was a real program, designed to produce very specific results in nine months. These initial demands for results were, of course, modest, but in subsequent years the goals would necessarily be increased. Thus the question was not *whether* the program would work. The question was *how* to make it work. Atkins's managerial philosophy was clear: "Get it up and running, and then fix it."

The Many Stages of ET CHOICES

From its conception in the spring of 1983 through its fifty thousandth placement five years later, ET CHOICES constantly evolved. Deputy Commissioner Thomas P. Glynn divided the program into two distinct phases, ET-I and ET-II, and further subdivided each phase by year:

ET-I	1983–84	Get the program up and running
	1984–85	Develop the system of contractors
	1985–86	Develop the field staff
ET-II	1986–87	Focus on the hard-to-serve
	1987–88	Implement the system of case management

The shift from ET-I to ET-II was marked by the department's revision of the definition of a job "placement." Starting July 1, 1986, a placement only counted if: (1) the job was full-time, (2) the wage was $5.00 an hour, and (3) the job lasted thirty days. All this was explained at a quarterly meeting of the ET contractors. Recalled Glynn: "For every contractor sitting in the room, half of their job placements were less than $5.00 per hour. The average was $5.00. We made the average into the floor. So that was kind of threatening . . . We would not reimburse for part-time placements. We said: 'That's what we've learned from the [January 1986] evaluation: It really makes a difference to our clients to give them full-time jobs paying $5.00 an hour or more.'" In response, Jane Tuoey, who managed ET for DES, observed that the program should now be called ET-II. Said Glynn: "It wasn't the next increment. It was a different program. The quality was really going to now be the dominant variable rather than getting the assembly line to run right, which was sort of the dominant thing in ET-I."

To Glynn, ET-II was "really trying to go back and fix it." Moreover, he concluded, "Fixing ET is a lot harder than putting it up."

Do the Doable First

In 1983, even "putting it up" did not appear all that easy. The Massachusetts Department of Public Welfare is a very large organization. Despite Governor King's Work and Training Program (WTP), the department had little expertise in helping welfare recipients find jobs; nor had it exhibited much desire to do so. Atkins and Glynn had to create capabilities where few existed.

From the conversations that Atkins had with Manuel Carballo, secretary of human services, before he became commissioner, Atkins knew where he wanted to go. But he did not know how to get there. Neither Atkins nor Glynn had any experience managing welfare. Yet they did not create a planning division to design the perfect ET. Rather, the department's leadership team started ET using their experience and hunches. For example, Atkins (remembering another admonition of Gordon Chase) eschewed the pilot-program strategy: "Instead we said, 'Let's put it up across the whole state, and get it up and running, know that it's going to work better in some areas than others, and then fix it.' I think it scared people at first, but it worked."

Getting it up and running was the first task. This required getting some people in some offices—and then some people in every office—working on ET. This required getting some of the training programs created by

the Job Training Partnership Act (JTPA) to do some work for ET participants. It required getting some DES offices to place welfare recipients in
jobs. But it did not require anything very fancy. For example, the department made no effort to create, in the first year, a case-management
system. The ET of year one was an extremely primitive program compared with the case-management system developed for year five.

In the first year, ET had to concentrate on the doable. Thus, the placement goal was low: only 6,000 for nine months. Moreover, the definition
of a job placement was not very strict: any job—full-time or part-time—
at any wage level would count. In early 1983, Carballo had suspended
WTP; thus, when ET started in October 1983, the department had not
been pushing recipients to find work for over six months. Consequently,
there existed a pool of recipients who could be motivated, trained, and
placed. Indeed, the recipients attracted to ET during its first year were
more job-ready than the average; 32 percent of all those on AFDC had
worked during the previous two years, compared with 69 percent—more
than twice the AFDC percentage—for those participating in ET.[1] So even
though few employees in the department had any experience with training or work programs, and even though the placement goal of 6,000
looked formidable, the objective for that first six months was quite doable. After all, in the first nine months of WTP, the department had found
jobs for 5,334 welfare recipients.[2]

For the first year of any welfare, training, and employment program,
focusing on job-ready recipients makes a lot of sense. It permits the
agency to make a number of placements while, at the same time, developing experience, identifying problems, and learning what to do next.
Such a focus will be criticized as "creaming." From a management perspective, however, this is the logical way to start any employment and
training program. Even if the program's design is copied directly from a
nearly identical state, the people who will run it have no idea how to
make it work. They will need experience. The program design may not
start from zero, but the managers and staff do. Consequently, it makes
sense to start off with the most job-ready recipients, so that the entire
organization can make progress while groping along.

Nevertheless, a complete get-it-up-and-running-and-then-fix-it strategy requires a little audacity, and even the most intrepid manager can
have second thoughts. Barbara Burke-Tatum, the associate commissioner
for employment and training, recalled the launching of ET: "Chuck [At-
kins] got nervous around September and he said, 'Maybe we ought to
wait and not start in October.' And I said to him, 'Chuck, there is so
much we haven't thought about. There's so much we won't know

about.' Because it was not like we had this elaborate resource bank when we did this planning, because we didn't. I said to him, 'We'll get it up and we'll fix it as we go along.' So that was my cry: 'We'll fix it as we go along. If it's broken now, we'll fix it.' And essentially that's what we have been doing with this program.''

The strategy adopted by ET's leadership for the first year was clear: First, do the doable. Set a reasonable goal. Achieve it. In the process, convince others that this program is doable. Also, in the process, learn both what is doable next year and how to do it. Learn what is broken. Then fix it.

Fixing ET CHOICES

The change in the definition of a job placement was only one of the many broken components of ET that was fixed. The marketing strategy was modified significantly when Howard Waddell and Janet Diamond, in Publications and Outreach, discovered that success stories did not sell. The types of training contractors changed particularly as refugees, who needed English as a Second Language programs, became a larger portion of the caseload. And the department struggled with how to provide day care to another growing segment of the caseload—Hispanics, who traditionally have been unwilling to leave their children with strangers.

ET also changed as more and more people began working on the program. To get DES employees actively involved required locating their offices next to the welfare department's. Because relocation could only happen when leases on office space expired, this requirement was not completed until year four. In addition, the leadership team was constantly exploring how to motivate the financial assistance social workers—the FASWs, whose primary function was to determine eligibility—to recruit recipients to participate in ET, to refer them to the ET workers, and to follow up on their progress.

Atkins, Glynn, and Burke-Tatum talked about "fixing" things that were "broken." Jolie Bain Pillsbury, associate commissioner for eligibility operations, used a different vocabulary; her key words were "evolution" and "iterative." But they described the same managerial approach: "We're constantly evolving in how this is going to work," said Pillsbury. Constant evolution is "an underlying concept of management that we have. I wandered around the first year and taught everyone in the field one word: 'iterative.' I thought that 5,000 people had to know that word iterative so that they could understand." Echoed Burke-Tatum: "Now we've learned basically how to do ET. We've learned that we have the capability and the ability to fix it as we go along."

Mistakes, Feedback, and Flexibility

Fixing anything requires feedback. To correct the inevitable mistakes, someone must first report those mistakes. For ET CHOICES, this feedback came from several directions. Obviously, the focus groups conducted by Diamond and Waddell provided feedback. So did the data collected and analyzed by the department's Office of Research, Planning and Evaluation. The innumerable formal meetings and informal discussions that the executive staff held with local-office directors and their staffs provided more information and warnings. Atkins argued that not only did he try to correct problems with ET, but he was "being public about" it: "We know there are problems with the program and we're determined to fix them. We are not afraid to acknowledge those facts."

But could those in top management, sheltered in headquarters, ever get any real feedback from the field? Did they hear about the truly critical problems? Or did they learn about them only when they became big enough to make it into the newspapers? Atkins had "always been terrified" that he would not hear the bad news. "Given my management style," which he described as "if you don't make your goal, you lose your job," Atkins worried that the field would not tell him when the department was making a major mistake.

Thus Atkins "tried to bend over backwards to encourage" those working in his agency to report problems. His message, he said, was: "Look, we're in this together. If we can identify the problems early on, we can get you some help to fix them. And I don't shoot the messenger. We do have bottom-line goals, but we really all ought to support one another to make it happen." This approach, concluded Atkins, "has mostly worked." Nevertheless, "I do have a few people who work for me who don't want to tell me when things go wrong, and that's the downside of that management style."

Learning about things going wrong is not enough, however. Management also needs to analyze these mistakes and then fix them. This requires flexibility—the ability to make the necessary changes in the organization. Martin A. Levin of Brandeis University and Barbara Ferman of the Illinois Institute of Technology see "implementation as error correction . . . The test of a good policy or good program is not the absence of error but the ability to detect errors and correct them."[3]

In part, flexibility is a question of program design. Has the program been put together in a way that is not susceptible to modifications? Is it impossible to fix one problem without redesigning the entire program?

In part, however, flexibility is a question of mental outlook. Do the program's managers think—"know"—that they got the program right the first time? Was the original program so oversold that it is impossible to make changes without a major embarrassment? Or has everyone— from top management to line workers—known from the beginning that they were not working with the perfect program? Have they understood all along that they would have to fix it? If so, the need to make changes will not be so surprising nor will the task of doing so appear so massive. Managers who grope along understand and explain from the beginning that the program will require numerous and periodic changes, modifications, and improvements. Atkins told his agency: "Don't be afraid or ashamed if you discover that something is wrong with the program. Let's approach it with this management style: . . . Get it up and running, and then fix it."

The Campaign Speech

The value of a succinct statement of mission to the overall management of a business firm[4] or public agency[5] is widely recognized. Often this is summarized in a clever phrase: "IBM Means Service." Ray Kroc's theme for McDonald's was: "Q.S.C. & V.," or "Quality, Service, Cleanliness, and Value." Yet rarely does a public agency have a clear one-paragraph (or even one-page) statement of purpose, let alone a clever phrase to summarize it. By contrast, over the first five years of ET, the Massachusetts Department of Public Welfare had several: "Accuracy, Compassion, Timeliness"; "A Route Out of Poverty"; "Family Independence Plan."

A succinct summary of an agency's mission does not, however, emerge from some single, brilliant insight. It evolves, much as "the speech" of a political candidate evolves during a campaign. The candidate has a sense of the message to be communicated but not which words will achieve that purpose. Thus the candidate gropes along, testing different ideas before different audiences and gauging the reaction to each. Then the candidate tries different combinations and permutations until finally the words and phrases that work best take hold.

"Accuracy, Compassion, Timeliness," recalled Pillsbury, "were the first code words" for conveying a sense of purpose: "We invented that on purpose, and it kind of evolved nicely in that I focused on the mission and felt that it had to consciously be conveyed. And very definitely, I invented with [Deputy Associate Commissioner] Jean Bellow's help, the word ACT. In other words, I was coming up with the first ACTion plan for error reduction, and we came up with ACT." Then, in 1986, Pillsbury "started thinking about the fact that our mission had to change, and that we didn't have any way of saying it. And I tried a number of things." (Pillsbury noted that "I keep saying 'I,' but it was through group discussions and thinking.") The department began to experiment with case management—and to train the line workers in case management—but it did not have a succinct way to summarize the new mission; "we were really struggling," admitted Pillsbury. Then, John O'Sullivan, director of training, and his staff came up with "the case management arrow and out of poverty." Still, continued Pillsbury, "He hadn't gotten it down to it's a 'route out of poverty.' And I came up with something that didn't fly. It was H_2O: Hope, Help, and Opportunity—H_2O. That didn't fly. So we just kept working at it until—almost group think—we discovered the words 'route out of poverty.'"

"Groping along" accurately describes the process by which any organization creates the sentences, phrases, and words it uses to describe its purposes. Conversely, this managerial search for words provides a useful metaphor for describing the process of management: "Management by Groping Along," or MBGA.

Most Managers Grope—a Lot

An effective manager has an excellent sense of his or her objectives but lacks a precise idea about how to realize them. Nevertheless, the manager does possess some ideas—some deduced from theory, some adapted from past experiences, some coming strictly from hunches—about how to achieve these objectives. Unfortunately, neither the general theories nor the specific techniques in any manager's repertoire are derived from situations precisely like the current one. From the numerous "lessons" that the manager has learned from the past, he must not only choose those that appear to be most appropriate; he must also adapt them to the new, unique task he now faces.

Thus, despite years of experience and study, even the best manager must grope along. He must test different ideas and gauge the results of each. Then he tries different combinations and permutations of the more productive ideas. Rather than develop a detailed strategy to be followed unswervingly, a good manager establishes a specific direction—a very clear objective—and then gropes his way toward it. He knows where he is trying to go but is not sure how to get there. So he tries a lot of different things. Some work. Some do not. Some are partially productive and are modified to see if they can be improved. Finally, what works best begins to take hold. This is "management by groping along."

Some might call it "management through experimentation." Indeed, good managers do experiment a lot. But the verb "to experiment" gives the wrong impression. "Experimentation" suggests that the process is scientific, which it is not.

Admittedly, "to grope" is not exactly the right verb either. The diction-ary's definition is "to feel or search about blindly, hesitantly, or uncer-tainly." The manager is not blind. Off in the distance, he can see clearly the top of the mountain. But between the trailhead and the summit are many paths obscured by trees, ledges, and clouds. The manager is uncer-tain about which trail will get him there—or whether he should bush-whack. He has a compass, which he has learned to use through study and experience. Unfortunately, however, no one has prepared an up-to-date map of the region, though the manager can easily pick out some of its prominent landmarks, and he has learned from experience the subtle-ties of detecting some of the less obvious but perhaps even more critical features. He has also tried to pick up the folklore of the mountain from some of the old-timers. But no one has ever climbed this mountain before (and, indeed, most of the old-timers are telling him it is foolish to try). So although the manager can hire a guide who has experience on similar terrain and who can help keep him from falling into a deadly crevice, he will still have to grope his way towards the top. He will not do this blindly, but he will not be very scientific either.

Significantly, however, the experienced manager will not set off imme-diately for the summit. Rather, he will do the doable first. The manager will pick out a nearby plateau—one with a good view—and set out with his team to conquer it. This approach has several purposes. For one, the manager and his organization are now closer to their ultimate goal. Sec-ond, while achieving this intermediate goal, they develop their capabilities—ones they will need to reach the summit. Third, the man-ager and his organization learn a lot—about themselves as a team and about the additional capabilities they will need. Finally, reaching this first plateau provides a sense of accomplishment. The climb may have been hard but the view (if the manager picked this initial goal cleverly) is gorgeous. The summit may still be a long way off—and still obscured in the clouds—but it no longer appears to be unattainable. Moreover, the naysayers are not quite as vocal, and some additional sponsors and work-ers have "signed up"[6] with the expedition.

Karl E. Weick, of Cornell University, has advocated such "a strategy

of small wins'': "A small win is a concrete, complete, implemented outcome of moderate importance. By itself, one small win may seem unimportant. A series of wins at small but significant tasks, however, reveals
a pattern that may attract allies, deter opponents, and lower resistance
to subsequent proposals. Small wins are controllable opportunities that
produce visible results . . . Once a small win has been accomplished,
forces are set in motion that favor another small win." To follow a strategy of small wins, the manager gropes along, from one plateau to the
next, building on the lessons from the previous climb to decide what
additional capabilities are needed and what the next target should be.
"Small wins provide information that facilitates learning and adaptation," writes Weick; "feedback is immediate and can be used to revise
theories." Moreover, each new plateau provides a base for the next ascent. "Small wins are stable building blocks," he argues. "They preserve
gains."[7]

Finally, "the psychology of small wins" reduces the risk involved in
undertaking the next ascent. Indeed, a subsequent target can be chosen
that will almost guarantee success. And even if an organization does not
attain the next plateau, the failure is not fatal. The impact of all the
previous wins still overwhelms this latest loss. (At the gambling tables in
Las Vegas, almost everyone tends to pay more attention to the infrequent
wins than to the much more frequent losses.) Moreover, observed Weick,
the optimal sequence of small wins cannot be planned in advance: "the
next solvable problem seldom coincides with the next 'logical' step as
judged by a detached observer. Small wins do not combine in a neat,
linear, serial form . . . More common is the circumstance where small
wins are scattered and cohere only in the sense that they move in the
same general direction . . . Careful plotting of a series of wins to achieve a
major change is impossible, because conditions do not remain constant."[8]
After the next plateau is reached, the manager may discover that the
view is nothing special or that this target is no closer to the summit. He
must keep groping along toward his ultimate goal.

How the nation's governors describe their own approach to management illustrates the process. "We try a number of things, some work and
some don't," Governor Lamar Alexander observed when he was governor of Tennessee.[9] As governor of Utah, the late Scott Matheson would
talk about his "flounder system." Although to some of his advisers this
phrase "connotes the process of acting clumsily or ineffectively," to
Matheson "it represents the natural struggle of government—to move
forward and obtain footing in a constantly changing organizational and
political climate."[10]

Good managers grope along. But they grope intelligently. They understand their goal and design their groping to move them toward that goal. For the manager who has "a bias for action," Thomas J. Peters and Robert H. Waterman, Jr., offer the slogan "Ready, Fire, Aim."[11] But that phrase misses the mark. A more accurate sequence for the three words is "Aim, Fire, Ready."

Getting *ready* is not the initial chore. The businesses that Peters and Waterman studied rarely prepared so carefully. Rather, the first task is to decide upon the goal—to take *aim*. The manager has to understand what his target is. Even then, rather than get everything *ready* for a single, big shot, the manager quickly *aims* in the general direction of the target and *fires* off an initial round. Based on what this first shot produces, he then gets his organization *ready* for the next round (perhaps improving the sight, perhaps getting a new gun or a new marksman, perhaps moving into a better position, perhaps even modifying the goal), *aims,* and *fires* again. The slogan should be "Aim, Fire, Ready. Aim, Fire, Ready. Aim, Fire, Ready . . . " Or perhaps just MBGA.

Atkins's leadership team knew its objective. There was no ambiguity about it. They wanted to move welfare recipients from dependency to self-sufficiency. They knew exactly at what they were aiming. But to hit this target, they did not know how to fire the gun—or even which guns to fire, or whether they needed to design completely new guns. Nevertheless, rather than get completely ready before firing, they shot off year one's ET. When they saw where that first shot went, they got a little more ready and shot off another program for year two. Indeed, even after four years, the leadership team made it clear to the field that it did not know precisely how year five's ET would work. Still, they were prepared to learn from the experience and then fire off year six's program.

Management by Wandering Around

One of the most important contributions that Peters and Waterman have made to the literature on management is the concept of "Management by Wandering Around."[12] "MBWA" was derived from observations of how managers in successful companies behave. Peters and Waterman adopted a simple research design. They selected a number of U.S. firms for their superior financial performance and record of innovation; then they sent the McKinsey research team out to interview and observe the forty-three companies that they defined as "excellent."[13] The result, their book *In Search of Excellence,* with its emphasis on corporate culture and the leadership's values (rather than on management information systems or quantitative marketing research) spawned other books that some now call the "excellence literature."[14]

MBWA is not important because it offers some great, new theory of human or organizational behavior. It is not important because it finally settles through original and creative empirical analysis some fundamental debate among the intellectual giants of the field. MBWA is not important by any of the standard criteria of social science. In fact, Peters and Waterman didn't even coin the phrase; they learned it from one of their excellent companies, Hewlett-Packard. Nevertheless, the idea of management by wandering around is important for both its descriptive and its prescriptive power.

The concept of MBWA is important for its descriptive value. It explains what managers—at least the managers of large, successful firms—do with a good portion of their time. Like the research of Henry Mintzberg of McGill University, it helps us understand what managers really do.

In *The Nature of Managerial Work,* Mintzberg observes that the work of a manager is "characterized by brevity, variety, and fragmentation."[15] Peters and Waterman say that the manager's work is characterized by a lot of wandering around. Of course, the writing of Peters and Waterman does not look as scientific as Mintzberg's. For example, *In Search of Excellence* contains few graphs; by contrast, one graph in *The Nature of Managerial Work,* entitled "Frequency Distribution of Managerial Activities by Duration (in hours)," shows that desk work averages 15 minutes in duration, telephone calls 6 minutes, scheduled meetings 68 minutes, unscheduled meetings 12 minutes, and tours 11 minutes.[16] Peters and Waterman write simply: "The name of the successful game is rich, informal communication."[17] Mintzberg reports: "The job of managing does not develop reflective planners; rather it breeds adaptive information manipulators who prefer a stimulus-response milieu."[18] Peters and Waterman conclude that managers of excellent companies have "a bias for action."[19] The literary style is quite different, but the two descriptions of what managers do are quite similar.

The concept of MBWA is also important for its prescriptive value. It tells a manager something he can do to be more successful: Spend time with your customers, your suppliers, and your employees. Find out what they are thinking, what problems they confront, what ideas they have. Praise them; reward them; make them feel wanted, respected, and valued.

The concept of MBWA also implies what managers ought not to do. They should not spend all their time behind their desks. They should not spend all their time reading and dictating memos. They should not spend all their time in meetings with their immediate staff and direct subordinates. Managers need to get information more personally and directly from the people most affected by their decisions. They need to convey their ideas personally and directly to the people upon whom their organization is most dependent.

Mintzberg's work was primarily descriptive, though he did offer some prescriptions. The major purpose of Peters and Waterman was prescriptive, though their prescriptions were derived from their descriptions of what managers in their "excellent" companies did. These somewhat different perspectives appear to lead to somewhat different conclusions. Mintzberg's five chief executives spent 59 percent of their time in scheduled meetings, 22 percent on desk work, 10 percent in unscheduled meetings, 6 percent on telephone calls, and 3 percent on tours. One of Mintzberg's "propositions about managerial work characteristics" is: "Tours provide the manager with the opportunity to observe activity informally without prearrangement. But the manager spends little of his time in open-ended touring."[20] Peters and Waterman would be quick to argue that Mintzberg's five managers do not wander around enough, and Mintzberg, in fact, reached a similar conclusion: "The surprising feature about this powerful tool [the tour] is that it was used so infrequently."[21]

As a prescription, management by wandering around is not meant to be taken literally. The manager is not supposed to open the dictionary and discover that the first definition of the verb "to wander" is "to move or go about aimlessly." Nor did Peters and Waterman recommend a militaristically rigorous regime—between 1:30 and 3:15 each day the manager should wander—although they do believe that the wandering should be conscious, purposeful, and organized.

Peters and Waterman did not discover that 41.5 percent of the variability in business productivity can be explained by wandering around. Rather, the prescriptive value of management by wandering around lies in the host of managerial concepts captured and implied by the phrase. MBWA means that managers need to know what their people— customers, employees, and vendors—are doing and thinking. Peters and Waterman found that their excellent companies were "close to the customer," and that MBWA is one way to establish and maintain this personal rapport. MBWA means that managers should treat people as humans—that they should go out of their way to listen to them and to praise them. Management by wandering around suggests that the people are more important than the numbers.

The Value of MBWA

All of this, of course, sounds so obvious—so obvious that it could not possibly be dignified with some academic-sounding phrase. Yet management by wandering around is an important concept precisely because it captures an obvious idea: managers can learn a lot and motivate a lot just by wandering around. And yet, given the actual behavior of many managers, it is clear that the idea is not all that obvious.

Paying attention to the obvious is important. And capturing an obvious and helpful concept in a catchy four-word phrase is valuable indeed. Most management concepts (no matter how fancy their window dressing) are simple. And, to have any impact, these simple management ideas must be expressible in some pithy phrase. Peters and Waterman were not the first to say that managers wander around a lot. But the wandering that others describe is more abstract and conceptual, less vivid and physical. MBWA is important because it is clever in its wording and compelling in its symbolism. These four words are a contribution because they capture not just one but an entire collection of important managerial ideas.

Moreover, MBWA debunks a durable managerial myth. Our stereotype of the manager is reflected in the cartoons in *The New Yorker*. Sitting in a big room behind his large and empty desk wearing his coat, the manager pushes a button and demands: "Ms. Jones. Send me some decisions to make." Peters and Waterman, however, implicitly argue that good managers do not and should not sit waiting for people to come to them. Excellent managers get out from behind their desks. They wander off to talk with people—lots of people. They search out customers. They wander to where their employees work. They visit their suppliers.[22]

In government, management by wandering around does not have the same reputation that Peters and Waterman gave it in business. When a government manager visits a district office, a journalist is apt to call it a "junket." Travel funds are frequently cut because travel is considered a nonessential activity. When senators and representatives return to their districts to learn what their "customers" are thinking, they are criticized for goofing off. House Speaker Thomas P. O'Neill took to calling congressional recesses "district work days," but that only gave journalists more opportunities to poke fun. Perhaps O'Neill should have called the recesses management by wandering around.

It is possible to go through the motions of wandering around without realizing the benefits of the process. There is no value in the wandering itself. Wandering around is important only because it is a good way to accomplish other, real objectives. Among other things, MBWA helps provide the feedback necessary for MBGA.

A manager can try to obtain such feedback in other ways. Often a top manager will hold a series of luncheon meetings with lower-level employees in a special dining room. The purpose, to give the manager an opportunity to hear what the employees are thinking, is laudable. But the environment is all wrong. The setting reinforces the differential in status and hardly conveys a desire for give and take between equals. The manager has not wandered anywhere. He has summoned the flunkies to his turf. The phrase "management by wandering around" is not at all subtle on this point: the benefits come from the manager's wandering off to visit customers, employees, and suppliers, not by making them come to him.

The concept of management by wandering around is important for one more reason. It gives managers who are already wandering around (but who are not sure that they should be doing so) a license to keep doing it. Neither the cartoons in *The New Yorker* nor the traditional management literature has suggested that managers *ought* to wander around a lot. Managers do strategic planning. They develop information systems. But wander? MBWA is important because it has helped some managers be more analytical and purposeful about what they already did naturally.

The Value of MBGA

Not only do managers wander. They also grope. "MBGA" does not offer, any more than does MBWA, a new theory of organizational behavior or settle a fundamental debate about management. Neither can the importance of MBGA be ascertained by applying the standard procedures of social science. Nevertheless, the idea of management by groping along is a powerful idea, both descriptively and prescriptively.

The concept of management by groping along has descriptive value. It explains what managers of large, successful organizations do with much of their time. While they are wandering around, they are also groping along. Good managers have a good sense of where they are going—or at least of where they are trying to go. They are constantly looking for ideas about how to get there. They know that they have no monopoly on good ideas about how to accomplish their purposes. Thus, given their bias for action, they spend less time analyzing these ideas than experimenting with them. Analysis as well as intuition can be very helpful in eliminating ideas that are way off target. Neither, however, is very helpful in determining, a priori, which of several good ideas will work best[23] (though analysis can be helpful, a posteriori, in sorting out which did).

The concept of MBGA is also important for its prescriptive value. It tells managers something they can do to be more successful: Establish a goal and some intermediate targets. Then get some ideas and try them out. Some will work and some won't. See which ideas move you toward your goals. You will never know which ones are productive until you experiment with them.

MBGA also implies what managers ought not to do: Don't spend all your time attempting to plot out your exact course. You can never possibly get it right. In fact, you can be sure that, no matter how carefully you plan, things will not work out as you think. Murphy lurks everywhere.[24]

As a prescription, management by groping along is not meant to be taken literally; managers are not supposed to "search about blindly." MBGA means that managers need a clear sense of their objectives, but will necessarily be in the dark about how to get there. MBGA means that managers have to try lots of different approaches—indeed, that the only way that they will learn how to realize their objectives is through much experimentation. Moreover, MBGA means that managers— especially successful managers—will make mistakes. Groping means taking risks. Groping means making mistakes.

Groping Along and the Myth of Managerial Prescience

MBGA directly contradicts another stereotype of management. The stereotypical manager (now at his club) who confesses that he is just groping along is the butt of the jokes from his more confident, all-knowing colleagues. "The rewriting of corporate history," which Rosabeth Moss Kanter, of the Harvard Business School, argues "is often part of the innovation-and-change process," can mean that "accidents, uncertainties, and muddle-headed confusions disappear into clear-sighted strategies."[25] Managers are not supposed to grope along, but they do.

When any management story is told, the emphasis is on premeditated and purposeful action rather than on groping.[26] The manager hardly wants to portray himself as merely having stumbled onto success. Observed Nietzsche, "No victor believes in chance."[27] And yet, writes Kanter, "There is a long philosophic tradition arguing that action precedes thought; a 'reconstructed logic' helps us make sense out of events, and they always sound more strategic and less accidental or fortuitous later."[28] The historian may serve as a co-conspirator in the manager's effort to redefine stumbling as strategy. Many chroniclers, whether journalists or scholars, look for interesting lessons—lessons that can be found in the manager's intelligent and flawless (or misguided and inept) forecasts, decisions, and actions. How can there be a story if all the manager did was grope along?

In government, there is an additional reason why a manager will not admit to groping along. To convince all those who control the numerous checks and balances involved in authorizing a new policy, the public manager has to oversell the idea as very, very good. But if the idea is so good, why should we merely experiment with it? How can we deny anyone the benefits of this wonderful new idea? Thus we enact legislation or adopt regulations to ensure that the policy applies to everyone. Tomorrow. If having some "model cities" in a few urban areas is a good idea, every city ought to be a "model city."

The Legislator's Conceit is that the idea itself—the policy—is all that matters. Implementation is a mere detail. If the legislature gets the idea right, the tasks of motivating people, designing systems, and building capabilities will be trivial. But the bargaining inherent in the legislative process (to say nothing of the absence of human prescience) ensures that the policy never comes out "right." The legislation is full of ambiguities, contradictions, and unknowns. Often it will be unclear which summit the manager is supposed to climb—or whether he is supposed to dam the valley instead. Yet given the durability of the delusion that we can separate management from policy, few recognize the need for the manager to grope along. The political dynamics of initiating policy ideas is biased against such experimentation.[29]

The concept of management by groping along, like that of wandering around, is important for one more reason. It too gives managers who sense that they are really just groping along a license to keep on groping. Neither the management literature nor cartoons in *The New Yorker* suggest that managers *ought* to grope along. Managers develop strategic plans. Why? Because they will work. Why else? Who ever heard of a manager who just groped along? MBGA is important because it can help some managers be more analytical, purposeful, and unashamed about what they already do naturally.

Groping Along versus Strategic Planning

Management by groping along sounds so idiosyncratic. —The concept runs counter to our evaluation of our own intellectual abilities—contradicting our desire to plan carefully for the future and degrading our yearning to be rational. Strategic planning is a much more attractive concept. It suggests that we know where we are going and that we have a clear notion of how we are going to get there.

The strategic-planning approach to management is an effort to make management more systematic—more scientific. Borrowing from the concept of dynamic programming,[30] strategic planners work backwards from where they want their organization to be at some time in the future to where it is now; the objective is to develop a policy, an "optimal path," that tells the manager how to get from here to there. Implicit in this thinking is the belief that the manager can determine such an optical path from an analysis of the organization's resources and capabilities and its political, cultural, and economic environment. Having developed the strategic plan, the manager can follow it to get precisely where he wants to be.

Ironically, while business is becoming disenchanted with strategic planning, government is becoming mesmerized by it. "Strategic planning, as practiced by most American companies, is not working very well," writes Robert H. Hayes of the Harvard Business School. This, he argues, is because American companies have a "'strategic leap' mentality" rather than one that seeks "continual incremental improvements." Comparing international business competition to guerrilla warfare that is taking place in "a swamp whose topography is constantly changing," Hayes described American business as "a bunch of hares trained in conventional warfare and equipped with road maps [strategic plans]" while the Japanese and Germans are "a bunch of tortoises that are expert in guerrilla tactics and armed with compasses."[31]

Hayes's metaphor of a swamp dramatizes (in a way that my metaphor of climbing a mountain does not) that the political, economic, and social environment of both a business firm and a government agency is constantly changing. But the metaphor of guerrilla warfare is not quite right for government. A business firm is, indeed, trying to defeat its competitors—to win a bigger market share. A government agency is trying to achieve public purposes. Although the political rhetoric emphasizes climbing mountains (e.g., the "strategic leap" of eradicating poverty), the real goals are more modest (finding jobs for some welfare recipients). A better metaphor for government management might be climbing sand dunes. The topography is changing constantly, and the footing never very sure. The objective is not to defeat others at guerrilla warfare but to scale some modest but still significant heights.

As governor of New Hampshire, John Sununu argued that it is difficult, impossible, and, in fact, a mistake to develop a comprehensive plan for the future: "You can think you know more about the system than you really do." Further, Sununu argued, long-range planning creates "long-range commitments" that possess "tremendous inertia, sometimes, in allocating resources." Drawing upon his engineering training, Sununu used the concept of feedback in a simple control system[32] to illustrate the kind of policy mechanism he thought worked best: "It's a little like being in the shower. It gets a little too hot, you turn the cold water on. It gets a little too cold, you turn the hot water on. [You do that] instead of trying to design a system that with one setting of the dials would always deliver exactly the right temperature; that is a very difficult task." Sununu applied this concept to public management: "What you may want to do is create a mechanism that is lean and dynamic and responsive as you go along in order to accommodate the response of the system to changes and inputs that you have either no control over or, in fact, can't identify . . . You develop a system that allows you to respond to changing environments, changing needs and changing times. You cannot lay out, today, the script. But you can build the mechanism that is able to adapt, and respond, and reform, and allocate resources, and focus energies. That's all you can do."[33] That is, public managers need to design systems that permit them to manage by groping along.

Groping Along and Muddling Through

In his classic article "The Science of Muddling Through," Charles E. Lindblom of Yale University argues that, both descriptively and prescriptively, "the method of successive limited comparisons" is superior to "the rational-comprehensive method."[34] True strategic planning is impossible, he writes, because the necessary "means-ends analysis" cannot be done. Lindblom argues that the "limits of human intellectual capacities and on available information set definite limits to man's capacity to be comprehensive." Thus "every administrator," he continues, "must find ways drastically to simplify." To do this, the administrator relies upon a "comparative analysis of incremental changes."

Such an approach is also necessary because administrators are "unable to formulate the relevant values first and then choose among policies to achieve them." Consequently, "one chooses among values and among policies at one and the same time." Public policies are selected, Lindblom emphasizes, not by comprehensive analysis but through bargaining among differing interests and different philosophical perspectives.

In Hayes's swamp of business competition, those who are muddling through would appear to have no compass or even any real objective. This month they might be trying to stave off an attack; next month, they might attempt to build a fortress; the following month, because a scout discovered an enemy outpost, they might decide to attack it. With no real sense of purpose, they bargain (fight?) with each other for this month's policy.

In contrast, those managers who are groping along—not groping *around*, but groping *along*—not only possess a good compass. They also know in which azimuth they are headed. Along the way, they may learn some things about swamps in general, about this particular swamp, about the technology of bateaus, about the ecology of quagmires, and about the principles of navigation. The manager may be groping along, but he has no trouble specifying the utility of his new knowledge: it is valuable if it helps him get where he and his organization are going. Such knowledge may also be valuable in helping the manager to modify his azimuth—to clarify what his objectives should be.

Lindblom's "muddling through" concerns public policy-making—the formulation of policies by analysts and the bargaining over policies by interests. "Groping along" focuses on public management—the leadership of government agencies by their top managers.[35] Lindblom is concerned with how a lost patrol in the desert selects the routes it will consider taking, compares the prospects and pitfalls of these different routes, and bargains to decide which one it will try first. I am concerned with how the captain leads this lost patrol back to its fortress.

Indeed, both strategic planning and muddling through are more concerned with policy-making than management. Both emphasize the choice of a policy rather than the management of one; they seem to imply that once the correct policy is established—either through analysis and strategic planning or through bargaining and muddling through—the management of this policy is a relatively trivial exercise. The tasks of mobilizing resources, motivating people, modifying goals, and building organizational capacity are not addressed.

The *policy* of ET CHOICES was established through a process that could well be described as muddling through. In fact, Lindblom's approach of "successive-limited comparisons" describes well how the policy of ET CHOICES was developed. Goals were not chosen first and then alternatives analyzed to see which one best achieved those goals; rather the complete package of placement ends and of training and job-search means was developed simultaneously. Analysis of the policy and its alternatives was drastically limited; there was neither the time nor the resources to examine all the possibilities. Yet the final policy was acceptable to liberal advocates for the welfare recipients, to Governor Michael S. Dukakis (who often took liberal positions on social policy but conservative ones on fiscal issues), and to the conservatives in the Reagan administration's Department of Health and Human Services.

The history of ET can be divided into policy and management phases. First, a policy that would establish both the ends and the means of ET had to be developed. Through a process of muddling through quickly, this phase was done in less than four months. Then, an organization that would use the available means to achieve the stated ends of ET had to be led and managed. Through a process of management by groping along, this phase went on for over five years.

Survival, Purpose, and Adaptation

MBGA is a sequential process of adaptation in pursuit of a goal. The manager tries some approaches, achieves some successes, adapts the more successful approaches, and continues to pursue his goal.

Scholars of business management have written profusely on adaptation as strategy.[36] Their emphasis, however, is on coping with the external environment to ensure survival. If the organization is a business firm, it makes sense to emphasize the managerial goal of survival. It makes empirical sense: the firm's manager is, in fact, attempting to ensure the continued survival of the firm. This is in the interest of not only the top executive but also the stockholders and the company's other employees (unless the situation has become so disastrous that survival requires firing half of them). In addition, the survival of the firm is socially useful. Assuming that the firm is not imposing too many of its own costs on its physical or social environment, the continued existence of the firm in a free market is (by definition, according to the values of economics) good for society. People are freely paying for the goods or services that the firm produces, a process that itself establishes the value of the firm's efforts. Thus, as long as the firm is willing to play by the rules that society establishes for the marketplace, we want it to strive for survival.

For government agencies, however, the objective should be different. Many public agencies are created precisely because the market cannot provide its services efficiently (e.g., national defense) or because there exists no such market at all (e.g., for welfare). For such government agencies mere survival is not good enough. Indeed, the Massachusetts Department of Public Welfare could have continued for decades to determine eligibility and process checks, and Atkins, Glynn, Burke-Tatum, and Pillsbury were not motivated by the need to ensure their agency's survival. Rather, they practiced MBGA—their management strategy of adaptation—because they had a very specific social vision for their agency. They wanted to convert welfare recipients into productive citizens. They wanted to be running what Atkins called "one of the most successful employment programs in the country."[37]

A business executive can have a vision too—indeed, possessing a vision is a characteristic of many successful firms.[38] But because it is not constrained to be in a particular line of business, a firm can quickly switch its product lines—and its vision. It can move from buggy whips to brake pads. The R. J. Reynolds Tobacco Company can diversify into RJR Industries, and then swallow Nabisco Brands to become RJR/Nabisco. The firm did not have to live or die with cigarette consumption; it could become a diversified food-products company. Indeed, Hayes argues that a business should start not by establishing ends but by creating means: "a company should begin by investing in the development of its capabilities along a broad front . . . as these capabilities develop and as technological and market opportunities appear, the company should encourage managers well down in the organization to exploit matches wherever they occur . . . Top management's job, then, is to facilitate this kind of entrepreneurial activity . . . Do not develop plans and then seek capabilities; instead, build capabilities and then encourage the development of plans for exploiting them."[39] For a firm concerned with its survival, encouraging the creative and entrepreneurial use of its existing capabilities makes perfect sense.

For a government agency, however, this kind of entrepreneurship (deriving strategy from capabilities) has limitations. Atkins could take his department into the "jobs business" not only because no one else in Massachusetts was in the business of finding jobs for welfare recipients but also because this activity fit within the overall public mission of his organization. But as commissioner of public welfare, he could not take on the mission of cleaning up pollution in Boston Harbor or acquire the city of Springfield. He could not even seize the opportunity created by his newly acquired job-training and job-placement capabilities to provide these services to welfare recipients in Rhode Island or even to the general public in Massachusetts.

Because Atkins, Glynn, Burke-Tatum, and Pillsbury were groping toward very specific policy objectives, their processes of adaptation differed from those for business.[40] They were not just adapting their organization to changes in its environment. Nor were they merely anticipating environmental changes, prospecting continuously for new market opportunities, or attempting to shape their environment and forcing their competitors to respond. They were interested in more than survival. They had a very specific mission for their organization, and they were aggressively groping their way toward it.

Luck and the Manager's Repertoire

Of course, the reason organizations survive or goals are achieved may have nothing to do with brilliant strategic planning, or effective bargaining among interests, or intelligent groping along. It may simply be dumb luck. The success of some public managers in achieving public purposes may be largely a matter of luck.

Atkins did not start off groping, however, because he knew nothing about management or nothing about employment and training. He had held numerous managerial positions in business and government (including several in the employment and training field), and he had studied public management. Yet rather than using this knowledge to develop a multiyear strategic plan, he started off groping along. He recognized that he knew little about his new agency, about welfare recipients, and about the Massachusetts political environment of 1983. Moreover, he understood that no strategic plan—no matter how brilliant—would bring along his senior staff, middle managers, and line workers. They all had to grope along together, while Atkins motivated them with a series of small wins.

But Atkins did have a large managerial repertoire—much of it developed during his years with Chase: establish goals, measure results, and reward performance; report frequently to your political superiors on your activities and accomplishments; keep on top of every major project in your agency.[41] Atkins used his entire repertoire. He was groping along, but he was not doing it blindly. He knew where he wanted to go and had some good ideas about how to get there.

At any one time, a good manager is groping in a number of different directions. The better managers—those with the largest and most applicable repertoires—may begin groping in better directions. But they are still groping. They do not know precisely how to proceed, though experience and study makes them better at selecting initial directions.

But a more important distinction between good and bad managers may be how quickly they learn from their groping. Managers with larger and more diverse repertoires may be better at recognizing critical patterns and specific lessons (just as a general with more battlefield experience will be better at understanding the flow of the battle, coping with exigencies, and recognizing opportunities). Moreover, recognizing a success is relatively simple. The truly difficult task—the one that may best distin-guish between good and poor managers—is the ability to read the ambig-uous results of any particular undertaking, to recognize when an initial guess is wrong, and to terminate, curtail, or modify the undertaking before it consumes too many resources. Even good managers may start out groping in the wrong direction. They may not make fewer mistakes, but they do recognize a mistake more quickly and act appropriately to prevent it from becoming a calamity.

Engineers and Laws: Managers and Principles

An engineer's professional repertoire contains thousands of physical laws: $F = m \times a$. $E = m \times C^2$. $E = I \times R$.[42] The engineer knows all the major laws, and remembers enough about the minor ones to know how to look them up. Which physical laws the engineer employs de-pends upon the particular problem he faces. All of the laws are correct. The task is to determine which ones are relevant and how they can be applied to the problem at hand. Thus the engineer's repertoire contains not just the equations for these laws but also an understanding of how and under what circumstances each law is useful. At the beginning, an engineer never knows precisely how he will solve a particular problem. He can make some guesses derived from his engineering repertoire. But he does not know for sure. So he experiments with different approaches to see how the physical laws he knows work in this current situation. The engineer must grope along.

The same is true for management. Like the engineer, the manager has a large professional repertoire.[43] There are thousands of managerial principles:

- "Stick to the Knitting."[44]
- "The degree to which the opportunity to use power effectively is granted to or withheld from individuals is one operative difference between those companies which stagnate and those which in-novate."[45]
- "Giving people a role in shaping decisions secures their com-mitment."[46]
- "Influence adheres to those who sense what it is made of."[47]

As with the laws of physics, these rules are both prescriptive and descrip-tive. $F = m \times a$ not only describes the relationship between force, mass, and acceleration; it also prescribes how many newtons of force you need to apply to accelerate a body with a mass of 50 kilograms at the rate of 50 meters per second squared. Similarly, "stick to the knitting" describes what "excellent" companies do, and prescribes how to become an excellent company.

Unfortunately, the manager must cope with two complications that the engineer does not have. First, the principles of management are less precise. "Stick to the knitting" leaves ambiguous precisely what each firm's (or agency's) knitting is. The mass and acceleration of a physical body are very well defined. The knitting of a firm is not. Second, with the singular exception of the first nanosecond of the Big Bang, the laws of physics apply everywhere and at all times. In contrast, as Herbert A. Simon of Carnegie-Mellon University observes, the principles of management are often contradictory.[48] Peters and Waterman advocate "simple form, lean staff."[49] But Kanter demurs: "to produce innovation, more complexity is essential; more relationships, more sources of information, more angles on the problem, more ways to pull in human and material resources, more freedom to walk around and across the organization."[50]

So how does the manager make use of the various principles in his managerial repertoire? Is "stick to the knitting" the principle that most applies in this situation? How narrowly should a firm's knitting be defined? And is there some other managerial principle—such as "be alert to new opportunities"—that points in a contradictory direction?

Which principles the manager applies depends upon the particular problem he faces. All of the management principles are correct. Some are applicable in some situations; some in others. The manager's task is to determine which ones are relevant, and how they can be adapted to attack the problem at hand. At the beginning, a manager never knows precisely how he will solve a particular problem. He has some ideas— based on the thousands of managerial principles in his repertoire. But he does not know for sure. So he experiments to see how the principles he knows work in the current situation. Like Atkins, Glynn, Burke-Tatum, and Pillsbury, any manager must grope along.

8

Managing and Evaluating Social Programs

During the 1960s and 1970s, the United States conducted a series of "social experiments" to determine what would happen if the nation's welfare system was replaced with a negative income tax. In a 1987 analysis of these experiments, Alicia H. Munnell, vice president of the Federal Reserve Bank of Boston, emphasized that one "lesson" to emerge was "the merits of random assignment." This lesson, she argued, would become

> important if Congress endorses the [Reagan] Administration's proposal to embark on a series of state experiments in welfare reform. If these experiments are to help in improving the welfare system, they must assign participants randomly to control and treatment groups. Only this approach avoids self-selection bias, a phenomenon for which no statistical method can compensate. Nowhere are the difficulties of evaluating programs without random assignment more apparent than in Massachusetts. Encouraging results have been claimed for the state's Employment and Training (ET) Choices program, but the lack of a control group makes it impossible to separate the effects of the training program from the impact of an economy operating with very low levels of unemployment.[1]

Indeed, the Massachusetts Department of Public Welfare was frequently criticized for failing to evaluate ET CHOICES with a policy experiment that included the random assignment of some welfare recipients to a treatment group that received ET services and other recipients to a control group that received no such services.

A Surfeit of Alternative Explanations

Any phenomenon has alternative explanations. George Bush was elected president because of the economy. Or he won because his staff produced more effective television ads. Or because he was a better speaker. He was taller. The nation's voters were more Republican. He was more conservative. He had a better strategy. He executed his strategy better. The voters agreed with him on the issues.

Similarly, if an employment and training program places welfare recipients in jobs, there exists a surfeit of alternative explanations for this phenomenon: The women in the program had already learned the required skills. They possessed the necessary attitudes toward work. They were more motivated to get a job. The state's economy was improving. The unemployment rate was low. New industries were looking for entry-level employees. Or it could be that the content of the employment and training program changed these women in such a way that they were able to find jobs. But there are many explanations that have absolutely nothing to do with the program.

Of course, none of these explanations may be correct; the real cause may be something that has occurred to no one. Conversely, all of them may have contributed something to the success of these women in finding jobs. If so, how much did each explanation contribute? Specifically, the public-policy question is: How much did the program contribute above and beyond the other explanations?

Which alternative explanation is correct? How much did each factor contribute? Research design and statistical analysis can help answer such questions. But any statistical method is only as good as the data. What data is collected and how it is collected can have a significant impact on the ability of statistics to discard alternative explanations and sort out relative contributions. And the best way for statisticians to produce the kind of data that they need to eliminate alternative explanations and to determine the net contribution of different factors is to conduct a policy experiment.

Control Groups and Random Assignment

The concept behind such a policy experiment is relatively simple. The objective is to determine the "net impact" of the policy. To do this, it is necessary to *compare* what happened with the policy in effect with what happened (or would have happened) without the policy. (What would have happened without the policy is often called the "counterfactual state.") The best way to do this is to create two groups: the "treatment group" receives the "benefits" of the policy; the "control group" is denied these "benefits." To prevent unseen bias from affecting this comparison, people are assigned randomly to one of these two groups. Then, if the difference in the consequences for these two groups is large enough—if it is "statistically significant"—that difference can be attributed to the treatment. The treatment had an impact—a *net* impact. If, however, the difference is so small that it could simply have been a random result, then it is not possible to attribute any impact to the treatment. In such a situation, other factors—but not the policy—explain the results.

Medical researchers continually conduct such experiments to test the efficacy of various drugs and other treatments. And in the past two decades, dozens of public-policy experiments have been conducted in the United States.[2] Of all these, perhaps the two most famous are the 1954 polio-vaccine experiment and the negative-income-tax experiments.[3]

To test the ability of the Salk vaccine to prevent polio, the National Foundation for Infantile Paralysis randomly assigned children to either the treatment group, which received the Salk vaccine, or the control group, which was injected with a sugar solution of similar appearance. The experiment was "double blind"; neither the participants themselves nor the medical personnel who administered the injections and tested the participants knew who received the vaccine or the sugar solution. Such a double-blind experiment is designed to eliminate the "placebo effect": If patient and physician are told that a new medicine is amazingly effective, this patient may show improvement—in his or her own eyes and in the eyes of the physician—even though all the patient received was a sugar solution. Thus, if both treatment and control groups are given the apparently identical treatment, so that both groups get the same placebo benefit, any difference in polio cases between the two groups can be attributed to the effect of the treatment itself rather than to any placebo effect. The polio experiment revealed that the Salk vaccine cut the probability of catching polio in half and the probability of contracting paralytic polio by over two-thirds.[4]

The negative-income-tax experiments were designed to test an economic rather than a biological phenomenon. Economic theory suggests that giving people welfare checks will reduce the number of hours they work.[5] But by how much?[6] To answer this question, families were randomly assigned to two groups. The control group continued to receive the welfare checks for which they were eligible under Aid to Families with Dependent Children (AFDC). The treatment group received a monthly check based on a specific negative-income-tax formula.[7]

This social experiment cannot be double blind. The participants have to know how much they are receiving, as do the people who write the checks and collect the data. But this is not a real impediment. After all, the purpose is to determine how the size of the welfare check and the rate at which earnings are "taxed" affects families' decisions to work. The key to determining the impact of welfare payments on work effort is to have both a treatment group that receives the special negative-income-tax payments, and a control group that receives "nothing" (which in this case means regular AFDC payments) *and* to assign people randomly to these two groups.

The purpose of random assignment is to ensure that both groups are identical with only one exception—whether or not they receive the treatment. If the experimenter makes these assignments, he or she may subconsciously introduce some bias. For example, the experimenter might implicitly judge certain families to be "worthy" of extra assistance and assign them to the treatment group. The only way to prevent some unseen bias from sneaking into the assignment of participants to treatment and control groups is to have this done by an arbitrary, random mechanism—such as flipping a coin. With potential biases thus eliminated, the true, net impact of the treatment can be determined by measuring the outcomes (incidence of polio, or hours worked) for the treatment group and comparing this with the outcomes for the control group.

This concept of policy evaluation—random assignment to treatment and control groups—is easy to understand. Indeed, the concepts have diffused from the arcane world of social science even to popular culture. One fledgling rock band even called itself "The Control Group."

The Demonstration of State Work/Welfare Initiatives

In 1982, the Manpower Demonstration Research Corporation (MDRC) undertook a five-year, eight-state policy experiment concerning welfare and work. MDRC's objective was to evaluate the net impact of various state programs that added different kinds of work components to AFDC. To do this, MDRC conducted experiments in large cities (Baltimore, Chicago, San Diego), in multicounty regions that included both rural and urban areas (Arkansas, New Jersey, Virginia, West Virginia), and statewide (Maine). In Maine and New Jersey, the program was voluntary; in the six other states, it was mandatory. Some of the mandatory programs (Arkansas, Chicago, Baltimore, Virginia) required participation by all AFDC recipients. But San Diego's program was mandatory only for new applicants, and West Virginia's concentrated primarily on AFDC-UP (unemployed parent) cases. For many programs, the dominant activity was "job search"—simply looking for a job—followed (if no job was found) by some work experience. But Maine provided prevocational training, Baltimore offered education and training, and New Jersey focused on on-the-job training.

These differences in the programs reflected different purposes: San Diego's and Chicago's programs were designed to move welfare recipients off the rolls as quickly as possible. Baltimore, Arkansas, and Virginia focused on the longer-term benefits of work experience. West Virginia operated a traditional "workfare" program; with a high unemployment rate, the state's goal was less to find jobs for welfare recipients than to have them fulfill their obligation to society by doing some productive work. Also, when the experiments began, the basic AFDC grant varied from $140 per month in Arkansas to $526 in California.[8]

The San Diego Experiment

Of all the work and welfare experiments analyzed by MDRC, the one in San Diego received the most attention. Social scientists, congressional staffers, and welfare-reform buffs all know about San Diego's "6-percent differential." So do governors, senators, and representatives. It is the difference between the 61 percent job-placement rate for San Diego's treatment group and the 55 percent placement rate for the control group.

Actually, there is much more to the San Diego results than this 6 percent job-placement differential. The San Diego experiment was really several experiments. From October 1982 through August 1983, all 3,591 AFDC applicants (84.4 percent women) and all 3,406 AFDC-UP applicants (93.0 percent men) in San Diego county were randomly assigned to one of three groups (two treatment groups and a control group). Some of these applicants had worked in the previous year; some had not. Some had previously been on welfare; some had not. Data was collected quarterly, and over the two and a quarter years of the experiment the labor market changed significantly as San Diego came out of a severe recession.[9]

One treatment group participated in a three-week job-search workshop that began with a week of training. Then participants undertook two weeks of individual job search in a group environment designed to foster improvement in their job-seeking skills. A second treatment group participated in this same three-week job-search workshop, but those who did not obtain employment by the end of this search were assigned to a work-experience program involving thirteen weeks of unpaid work in a public agency or nonprofit organization. The control group was eligible to receive the normal services of the federal Work Incentive Program (WIN), but only a few engaged in any kind of job search.

In general, the treatments had the desired effect. More of those in the treatment groups than in the control group worked at least some time during the fifteen-month follow-up. Further, when the two treatment groups were compared with the control group, average number of quarters with some employment were up for the two treatment groups, average total earnings were up, and average AFDC payments were down. In general, these impacts were larger (and more statistically significant) for the treatment group that received both the job-search workshop and work experience than for the treatment group that received the job-search workshop only.

MDRC also sought to test "the findings from other studies that employment programs for welfare recipients have larger impacts on those who are more disadvantaged—that is, those with no recent employment experience or with some prior welfare dependency." In general, the impacts were larger (and more statistically significant) for those with no recent work experience. Similarly, MDRC found that net "impacts were larger for those who had received some welfare prior to application than those who had not."[10]

Analyzing these data further, Daniel Friedlander and David Long (both of MDRC) defined a "dependency score" that reflected an AFDC applicant's prior history of work and welfare. They found that the San Diego program "was somewhat less effective with applicants at the two ends of the dependency spectrum." Moreover, they also discovered a "threshold effect." For the most dependent AFDC applicants (those who had spent the most time on welfare and had the least work experience) the job-search and work-experience program had little effect on earnings. But above a certain threshold, the program began to make some difference. And as dependency decreased (as prior time on welfare went down and time working went up), the impact increased. But as dependency continued to decrease, the impact leveled off; for the least dependent, it began to decline. For the Baltimore program, Friedlander and Long found that these phenomena were even more pronounced.[11]

The 6 percent differential, then, is only one of many results of the San Diego experiment. Moreover, it is not a particularly large number. Nevertheless, a 6 percent impact, while numerically small, can be socially significant. Judith M. Gueron, MDRC's president, writes about these experiments:

In interpreting the results, one should remember that the impacts, or program effects, are expressed as averages for a large segment of the caseload: e.g., all Win-mandatory applicants, both program participants and nonparticipants. Thus, even relatively small changes—multiplied by a large number of people—may have considerable policy significance . . .

Programs do not necessarily have to effect dramatic changes to be worthwhile. In fact, small impacts can be significant if they are long-lasting or if they occur for a large number of people. Thus, the research points to an important finding about expectations. In the past, we have had to oversell social programs to convince policymakers that they are worthwhile investments. The data from these state programs suggest that this is not necessary.[12]

This is why the San Diego 6 percent can be important for public policy.

No Controlled Experiment for ET

The research of Mary Jo Bane and David R. Ellwood of Harvard University has revealed that half of all welfare recipients leave the rolls within two years.[13] And, notes Barbara Blum, formerly New York State's commissioner of social services and, later, president of MDRC: "In all probability many in this group do not require massive or intensive special assistance delivered through the welfare system. Temporary income support and modest help with finding child care or with conducting a job search may be all that is required."[14] This phenomenon, emphasizes Gueron, creates a problem for anyone who seeks to evaluate a welfare, training, and work program: "If a study estimates employment impacts or welfare savings based only on participants' behavior (e.g., their job placement or employment rates), it will overstate program accomplishments by taking credit for those who would have found jobs on their own. The challenge in measuring program impacts is to distinguish program-induced changes from the normal dynamics of welfare turnover. This requires data on what people would have done in the absence of the program: that is, data on a control group."[15] *The Washington Post* made a similar point in an editorial: "A governor can claim his work program moved some impressive percentage of mothers off welfare, and it turns out most of them would have moved off anyway."[16]

Writing about ET CHOICES, *Fortune* magazine observed that the data "seem impressive" but "are more than a trifle inflated. Massachusetts has not compared the ET graduates with a control group and is claiming savings from thousands of employed welfare recipients who probably would have found jobs anyway."[17] Spencer Rich, who reports frequently on welfare issues for *The Washington Post,* also has noted that "no controlled study has been done [for ET], and some observers think that favorable results may be attributable not to the program but to low unemployment in the state."[18] Using total placements to measure the program's success automatically exaggerates its accomplishments. It is as if a business firm used gross receipts rather than net profits to determine how well it was doing.

Robert Rector of the Heritage Foundation used a different metaphor: "It's roughly equivalent to claiming you have a miracle cure for cancer—without any proof. The poor deserve a lot better than some flimflam artist who's out there making all these grandiose claims." Rector was particularly critical of claims that ET could be a prototype for federal welfare reform. "They're saying this is a national model, a program that could serve four million people," said Rector. "But they're not willing to withhold it from several hundred people in order to find out if in fact it works."[19]

Why did ET receive more attention for its managers' unwillingness to conduct a controlled experiment with random assignment than do most government programs? After all, no one demands a controlled experiment to evaluate the net deterrence of the Stealth bomber. No one demands an experimental evaluation of the net impact of college-student loans on education attainment, on upward economic mobility, or on the gross national product. Nor does anyone demand an experimental evaluation of the social consequences of disability insurance. So why was ET the one public policy of the 1980s to become the focus of complaints about the lack of experimental validation?

The answer is threefold. First, the publicity generated by ET—particularly the news about the number of women placed in jobs—generated not only visibility but also skepticism and jealousy. Second, because Massachusetts's governor was running for president and touting ET as one of his major accomplishments, opponents and journalists instinctively looked for the program's flaws. Third, MDRC was already conducting experiments—lots of experiments—of other similar welfare, training, and work programs. If Dukakis had not run for president, and if ET placements had not repeatedly made national headlines, some in Massachusetts would still have complained that the program might not be doing everything that the welfare department claimed. But given that the governor was running for president, given the political publicity received by ET, and given that MDRC was evaluating similar programs, it was inevitable that some people would criticize Massachusetts for failing to conduct a controlled experiment.

"Creaming"

The voluntary nature of ET CHOICES exacerbates the problem of drawing inferences from the number of placements. Welfare recipients who are very job-ready and who might easily find a job on their own—that is, women who have the skills and motivation to get off welfare—will automatically be attracted to a program like ET. They will be the recipients that the department's social workers have the easiest time recruiting to participate in the program and the easiest time placing in a job. The voluntary character of ET combined with the focus on placements as the measure of success might have caused the department to devote significant job-placement or training resources to those women who, in Blum's words, need only "modest help with finding child care or with conducting a job search."

Using job placements as the measure of ET's success provided an incentive for "creaming." ET contractors had an interest in identifying recipients who were most job-ready and recruiting them to be their placements. Writes Gueron: "a program operator, using traditional measures of success—program placements or employment—naturally tends to serve the more 'advantaged' segments of the welfare population."[20] MDRC's analyses have indicated, however, that the largest net impact comes from concentrating not on the easiest-to-serve (or, for that matter, on the hardest-to-serve) but on the harder-to-serve.

Placement rates will, obviously, be largest for the most job-ready. But net impact upon earnings will be larger for those who are less job-ready. In Baltimore, for example, MDRC found that those with prior employment experience were much more likely to find jobs than those with no such prior experience. Further, Baltimore's Options program improved the chances that a welfare recipient would get a job—regardless of whether the woman did or did not have prior employment experience. The net impact of the treatment was greater, however, for those with no prior employment experience. (See Table 8.1.) Concludes Gueron, "A program that achieves high placement rates by working with people who would have found jobs on their own or cycled off welfare anyway may look successful but not have accomplished much."[21]

Making the definition of what job counts as a "placement" more stringent may create a further incentive for creaming. A welfare recipient might have enough education, training, and skills to get a full-time job at $4.50 per hour, or even a part-time job at $5.50 an hour. But if a placement will count toward a contractor's goal only if it is *full-time* and pays *more than $5.00 per hour*—and if this woman needs too many ser-

Table 8.1   Results from the OPTIONS Program in Baltimore

	Percent who found employment	
	Prior employment experience	No prior employment experience
Treatment group	52.9	23.1
Control group	50.0	16.8
Net impact	+2.9	+6.3

Source: Daniel Friedlander et al., *Maryland: Final Report of the Employment Initiatives Evaluation* (New York: Manpower Demonstration Research Corporation, December 1985), p. 138.

vices to get her to that level—then the contractor may choose to ignore her in favor of other, more job-ready recipients. Indeed, at the quarterly meetings that Commissioner Charles M. Atkins held with ET contractors, some of these organizations complained that other contractors were getting the better recipients to train or place.

The Task of Negating the Null Hypothesis

Despite the criticism leveled at the Massachusetts Department of Public Welfare for failing to undertake a controlled experiment of ET, and despite the obvious flaw in using gross rather than net data to describe the program's effects, the department's management was unwilling to conduct a controlled experiment to evaluate ET. Indeed, the vast majority of the policy experiments conducted in the last two decades were created to test theories about the effects of specific policies on human behavior. Few resulted from the request of a public manager for a scientific analysis of what an ongoing program was accomplishing.[22]

There should be little surprise that few public managers invite evaluations of their key programs or new ideas. The methodology of such evaluations is automatically biased against discovering that the program has any net impact. Any controlled experiment begins with the assumption that the policy being tested has no effect. This "null hypothesis" is assumed to be true unless it can be disproved. To negate the null hypothesis, the difference between the treatment and control groups must be sufficiently large that a statistical analysis will suggest that there is a very small chance that this difference could have come from randomness in the data.

For example, suppose that (in a particular local economy) 35 welfare recipients in a control group of 100 recipients found jobs at the end of one year, while 45 recipients out of 100 in a treatment group assigned to a training and work program also found jobs by the end of the same period. Clearly, this difference could result from pure chance. It is possible that, over the long run, welfare recipients in that region would have found jobs at an average rate of about 40 percent per year *and* that even those participants in this training and work program would still have found jobs at an average rate of only 40 percent per year. If this is the case, however, how likely is it that only 35 recipients in a control group of 100 would find jobs while 45 recipients in the treatment group of 100 would do the same? The answer, statistics tells us, is 7.5 percent.[23]

If a statistical analysis says there is only a 1 percent possibility that the difference observed could have come from pure chance, this result is said to be "statistically significant at the 0.01 (or 1 percent) level." If there is a 5 percent possibility that the result came from chance, it is said to be statistically significant at the 0.05 (or 5 percent) level. A statistical significance at the 10 percent level may also be given, but if there is greater than a 5 percent probability that the difference observed was a random outcome, the result is not usually considered statistically significant and the null hypothesis is not rejected. For example, the results of the hypothetical program described in the previous paragraph are not statistically significant at the 0.05 level, and thus the null hypothesis could not be rejected. That is (until more data are collected) the treatment would be assumed to have no net impact.

Failing to reject the null hypothesis does *not* prove that it is true. The treatment may indeed have an effect. All the data reveal is that you *cannot prove* that it had any effect.

As the San Diego Job Search and Work Experience Demonstration illustrates, in a real policy experiment, the data are not so pure or unambiguous as in this hypothetical example. For those AFDC applicants assigned to the treatment group, the program was "mandatory"—in theory. Reality, however, was somewhat different. First, approximately 10 percent of the recipients in the treatment groups did not participate in the initial one-day placement assistance. Second, after nine months, less than 50 percent in the treatment groups had participated in one or more days of the three-week job-search workshop. Slightly more than a quarter of those participating in the workshop found employment during these three weeks. Half of those participating completed the workshop but did not find employment. The remainder (about a fifth of those participating at all) did not complete the workshop.[24] Finally, of those assigned to the job-search *and* work-experience treatment group, less than a third started the job search but did not find a job. Of those, roughly 35 percent actually participated in the work-experience part of the program. Thus, of the original members of this treatment group, only 13 percent worked at least one hour in work experience.[25]

The San Diego program was hardly as "mandatory" as the word implies. Less than half of the treatment group received any services beyond the initial one-day assistance in job placement. Yet 61 percent of the original group found some employment at some point during the following *fifteen months* (compared with 55 percent in the control group). But look at the outcome of the job-search workshop: one-quarter of those who actually started the program found employment during these *three weeks* (and another 20 percent did not even finish this treatment).

Unfortunately, MDRC provides detailed data for only the entire treatment and control groups. But many of the people in the treatment group received very little treatment. What about just those AFDC recipients who actually began the three-week job search? These are the only people in whom society invested any real job-search resources. What about the AFDC recipients who began and either completed the job search or found a job? These are the only people for whom this three-week job-search treatment was really mandatory. What percentage of these subgroups were ever employed? Did they experience even higher earnings? Or did these recipients simply find jobs quicker but then lose them at the same rate as the controls? Did the large number of people in the treatment group who received little or no treatment mask a large net impact of the treatments that were really applied? Would a truly mandatory program generate a 10 percent differential? Would a three-week voluntary workshop produce a similar 6 percent differential?

Such questions cannot be answered from the summary data. While revealing only small net impacts, these data may hide even larger differentials—differentials between, for example, the controls and those who actually received some significant treatments. But the rules of social science are unambiguous: if you cannot find a differential between those assigned randomly to the treatment and control groups, you have to assume that the null hypothesis holds—that there is *no* net impact.

Given the multitudinous difficulties in collecting social data and given the bias of social science toward the null hypothesis, should anyone really be surprised that the standard conclusion about social policy is that "nothing works"? Should anyone be surprised that program managers or agency heads are reluctant to call up their local social scientists and invite them to conduct social experiments of their key programs?

Evaluation as a Conservative Force

"Research and evaluation tend to be a conservative force" in social policy, write David H. Greenberg and Philip K. Robins, economists at the universities of Maryland and Miami, respectively, and "experimental research is a more conservative force than nonexperimental research."[26] Henry J. Aaron of the Brookings Institution has offered several reasons why the very processes of social science make research and experimentation "an intellectually conservative force in debates about public policy."[27]

First, the search in social science for "simplicity and 'elegance'"—a credendum borrowed from the natural sciences—requires abstraction, which, writes Aaron, "makes it almost impossible to identify policies that may be necessary, but not sufficient, to achieve some objective."[28] For example, a welfare, training, and work program might prove unsuccessful if it provided training in specific job skills, but failed to offer tutoring in the proper on-the-job attitudes and behavior. Moreover, the same result might occur if it only offered tutoring in the proper on-the-job attitudes and behavior, but did not provide any skills training. Together, however, the two policies might make a significant difference. The search for simplicity and elegance would lead researchers to check out each policy individually—and discover their independent inadequacies. Neither alone is sufficient. Yet both policies might be quite important. Both might be necessary. But how many scholars will bother to check all the various policy combinations to determine the individual policies that might be necessary and the collections that are sufficient?

Further, even if a researcher does collect the necessary data and discover something that is sufficient—some combination of necessary policies that, together, do work—an army of scholars will be ready to do battle for an alternative explanation. "The incentives in the academic world will encourage people," writes Aaron, "to discover facts not consistent with previous theories and to devise new theories to explain them." Academic prestige, argues Aaron, goes to those who "point out anomalies between facts and existing theories and . . . develop new theories to resolve the anomalies."[29]

As a result, continues Aaron's argument, "at any given time there will coexist several theories consistent with any given set of facts." These inevitable differences among scholars—encouraged by the incentives of the profession—are enough to force the "prudent person" to defer any significant policy decision "until the controversial issues have been settled." Thus the "internal laws [of social science research] guarantee that it will corrode any simple faiths around which political coalitions ordinarily are built."[30]

Indeed, any public manager would have to worry that exposing a program to a major controlled experiment would attract swarms of scholars to the data, some of whom would inevitably massage that data in such a way as to confirm the null hypothesis—to "prove" that the program "doesn't work." The resulting controversy would certainly cause the prudent legislator to wonder about voting to allocate additional resources for the program.

But there could well be an additional, internal impact. Implementation of the program also depends upon simple faith. Legislators vote for money on faith. Public employees work hard on faith. The public manager has few rewards with which to motivate his agency's line workers. But if he can convince them that what they are doing is important—that the program they administer and the policies they carry out are having a significant social benefit—he may also be able to convince them that they want to work hard. Again, however, an honest controversy among social scientists over the efficacy of the program can easily undermine this faith and the individual energies that this faith generates.

Drawing "policy lessons" from the results of several experiments, Gary Burtless, of the Brookings Institution, and Robert H. Haveman, from the University of Wisconsin, have written that "if you advocate a particular policy, do not press to have it tested."[31]

Evaluators and Managers

Those who manage public programs and those who evaluate them are both concerned with results. They both collect data and seek to learn as much as possible from them. Indeed, both want these data to tell them what works. Nevertheless, there is an inherent tension between the task of management and the task of evaluation.[32]

Each task has very different rules. The manager thinks that the evaluator has rigged the rules. It is almost impossible for the manager to prove—playing by the rules of social science—that any program is working. Conversely, the evaluator thinks that the manager has no rules. The manager will use any evidence that suggests his program is producing results. Moreover, the manager conveniently ignores alternative explanations and avoids collecting data that are likely to question the program's efficacy. Thus, while the manager dislikes the bias in the evaluator's rules, the evaluator disdains the manager's unwillingness to play by any set of rules.

For the evaluator, one of the critical rules is constancy. To evaluate any public program, it is necessary to collect a lot of observations of people, behavior, and outcomes. This requires that the program remain unchanged for a moderately long period of time—usually several years. Only after collecting enough data under similar conditions can the evaluator do the necessary statistical tests.

The manager, however, cares little for the evaluator's needs. Making the program work is the manager's job, and this requires improvement—constant improvement. Consequently, any time the data suggest how to improve the program, the manager will quickly institute the implied change. The manager accepts that the first guess at the program's design may not be the best; indeed, the manager recognizes it as only a guess. So the manager collects all sorts of data—from carefully coded statistics to stories about how one field office has increased performance through clever marketing. The manager is constantly groping along and is unwilling to keep everything identical for several years so the evaluator can collect the data required by statistical theory.

Moreover, a public manager does not have much time.[33] The press, the legislature, and the voters are not content to wait several years while the manager gets the program working. The stakeholders want results, and they want them now. Thus the manager's ego and possibly his job security are caught up in the enterprise: if the program does not work, it will be his fault. He is naturally eager for any information that can be used to improve the program. In contrast, the evaluator may have little attachment to the program; indeed, the evaluator's ego is engaged in the task of debunking the conventional wisdom. If this means deflating the manager's claims about the program's efficacy, so be it.

For the manager, there are additional reasons why constant change is desirable. The world changes, and public programs must change with it. Further, change offers opportunities to provide new ways to make the program work. Change provides new challenges to the agency's middle managers and line workers and prevents them from becoming stale or bored through repetition. Change also provides sources of new stories for journalists, who are important to the manager's ongoing credibility. Finally, change gives the manager visibility with his superiors and the legislature. For the manager, constant change may be critical to doing a good job. For the evaluator, in contrast, change may prevent him from doing any job.

What sustains the public manager through all this change is faith. The manager believes in his program. The business entrepreneur does not say: "Prove to me—by the rules of social science—that there is a market for this new product, and then I will open the plant to produce it." The flaws in that reasoning are clear. The only way to *prove* that the market exists is to produce the product. No test would have proved the vast market for Apple's first personal computer or 3M's little Post-Its. The entrepreneurs behind those products could only produce and market them on faith. Similarly, the public manager needs confidence in his program. With so many people telling him that the program is all wrong, he will never be able to sustain the energy necessary to make the program work unless he believes that it will.

The manager assumes that the program has an impact unless others can prove to him that it does not. The only question for the manager is how to make it work. In contrast, the evaluator is a skeptic. The evaluator believes in the null hypothesis. The evaluator assumes that the program has no impact, unless the data can prove it does.

Clearly, the gestalts of evaluation and management are very different. The evaluator is patient. The manager is passionate. Little wonder that evaluators and managers are often in conflict.

Indeed, managers often see evaluators as the enemy.[34] From the perspective of the manager, there is only a down side to evaluation. The evaluator will never say that everything is working smoothly. The evaluator will never confirm all the claims that the manager has made. What better way to start a convention of public managers guffawing than to announce: "I'm an evaluator, and I'm here to help you."

Evaluators have a choice. They can remain true to the norms of their profession. Or they can try to be of real help to public managers. The latter course is not easy. Some individuals and some organizations have proved themselves most valuable to managers,[35] but that is not the profession's dominant reputation. Managers will be skeptical. Individual evaluators will have to build trust. They will have to learn how managers think and function. They will have to understand the behavior of large organizations and appreciate what it takes to manage and lead them. If evaluators want to have an impact on how social services are delivered, they will have to build alliances with public managers.

Faith Alone Is Not Enough

Leadership requires faith. Faith is essential to launch a new enterprise and keep it going through the inevitable setbacks. But faith alone is not enough. Neither the press, the legislature, nor the public will support a public enterprise on faith alone. Eventually, they will want results. Often, they will demand very quick and visible results. And, over the long run, they may even occasionally require a credible evaluation of what is actually being accomplished.

With a new program, the manager needs some quick, visible results. Without them, social scientists offering alternative explanations, opponents arguing for budget cuts, and even supporters who believe in different approaches can all speedily undermine the manager's vision. These initial results need not meet any test except that of public acceptance. They need not demonstrate that the program is really accomplishing something—only that it has the clear potential to do so. Assembling a group of former welfare recipients turned productive employees before the TV cameras does precisely that. No one believes that the stories of these few individuals are enough to justify expenditures of millions. But the stories do demonstrate that the concept of the program is justified. At least for a while.

But quick, visible results will not give the manager permanent credibility. Such results only buy time. They allow the manager opportunity to work on the more intractable long-term problems, and to initiate more fundamental changes. Quick, visible results may be a necessary condition to managerial success. But they certainly are not sufficient.

Eventually, the manager's program has to stand up to increasingly sophisticated scrutiny. And to answer the questions he is asked, the manager needs to provide increasingly sophisticated answers. This does not necessarily mean control groups and random assignments. Indeed, established programs are rarely subjected to such experimental evaluations that question their basic existence. Nevertheless, the manager may find it quite helpful to take a quasi-experimental approach—using multiple measures and lots of data to help sort out the alternative explanations.

The history of American public policy is replete with examples of obviously ineffective and even dysfunctional policies that have been kept alive by powerful interest groups. An entrenched constituency need not subject its favorite program to a controlled experiment or worry much about the results of one. But even those public managers who are absolutely convinced of their programs' effectiveness will need to convince others. And they will want to find ways to improve these programs. To do both, some kind of evaluation will help.

Information for Motivation, Improvement, Evaluation

Any public manager needs information—lots of information for lots of purposes. In particular, the manager needs information for evaluation, for improvement, and for motivation.

The manager needs information for evaluation. The manager's program needs resources. And to convince the voters and legislators who provide these resources, the manager must demonstrate that his agency's program is accomplishing something. Legislators and the public are growing more sophisticated, and they are demanding more analysis. They may not insist on a formal social experiment, but they may expect some kind of careful quasi-experimental evaluation that attempts to compare what is happening with the program to what would have happened without it.

In addition, the manager needs information for improvement. The diligent manager is constantly looking for ways to improve his program. To do this, the manager needs to know what is working, why, and how it can be replicated throughout the agency. Conversely, the manager needs to know what is going wrong so that it can be fixed.

Finally, the manager needs information to motivate. To get his agency to achieve its mission, the manager needs to set specific goals for the entire agency and for each unit, and then to collect the information necessary to determine which units are achieving their targets.

In theory, the manager can easily collect information for these three different purposes. In reality, however, collecting information for one purpose may conflict with the achievement of another purpose.

Perhaps the most obvious conflict is between the collection of information for evaluation and for improvement. The public manager wants to collect as much information as possible about the agency's problems and then use that information to fix these problems. But even the most ethical public manager does not want to expose, unnecessarily, all of his organization's weaknesses to the world. Any effort to discover what needs to be fixed can quickly produce new headlines. Further, if any outside evaluation is also under way, the manager will be necessarily worried that any negative information may prejudice interpretations of the final, published results. A fair, open, and unbiased evaluation can be useful. But if information about the agency's deficiencies only titillates journalists and prejudices the public, the manager will wonder whether the benefits of collecting such information to fix operational problems is worth the costs.

But this is not the only conflict. Collecting information to motivate people can inhibit efforts to improve the program. If managers are judged primarily by their achievement of very specific goals, they may well be afraid to tell their superiors about their mistakes. Despite his stress on "bottom-line goals," Atkins was as successful as perhaps any agency head can be in convincing his line managers to be forthcoming about their problems and mistakes. Nevertheless, whenever a manager collects information so that he can measure performance, he necessarily inhibits his ability to collect information about his agency's mistakes.

Finally, there is the conflict between collecting information for the purposes of motivation and evaluation. Motivation requires a single, explicit, clear goal. Moreover, the goal should also be simple. There is an advantage in measuring the performance of a local welfare office in terms of the number of jobs found for welfare recipients. The goal is unambiguous; it is easy to determine whether the office has reached its target. It might, of course, make sense to base a local office's placement goal not only on its caseload but also on the region's unemployment rate. Further, it might make sense, as Friedlander and Long of MDRC argue, to count the job placements for people with little or no past income more than placements for others.[36] Whatever performance measure is used, however, it has to be simple to be an effective motivator.

In contrast, any evaluation is complicated. Whether it is being done to check for distortions in the use of a single management goal or to determine the program's true impact, any serious evaluation requires multiple measures. Inevitably, some of these measures will suggest that the program is effective while others will lead to the opposite conclusion. Consequently, the evaluation will undermine faith in the program.

Moreover, collecting information may disturb the program itself. In physics, this phenomenon is called the "Heisenberg uncertainty principle": You cannot determine precisely both the location and the momentum of a subatomic particle because merely looking at the particle—which requires you to bounce some light off it—disturbs the particle's location and momentum. Similarly, collecting information about a public program affects it. When a public manager collects information, he affects the organization's behavior and, perhaps, disturbs it. Indeed, to collect the information necessary to conduct a social experiment—that is, to assign individuals randomly to treatment and control groups—not only may change the behavior of individuals within the organization, but may require a change in the nature of the program itself.

The Manager's Dilemma

These conflicts over the collection of information create a dilemma. The manager must balance motivation, improvement, and evaluation. Collecting information solely to motivate not only corrupts the information needed to uncover and fix problems but also destroys the credibility of any evaluation conducted using strictly that data. Collecting just the information needed to fix problems undermines motivation and also ensures that the only "evaluation" that the voters and legislators will receive is journalistic reports of the inevitable failures. And collecting information strictly for evaluation will undermine the manager's efforts both to motivate performance and to uncover problems that need to be fixed.

Dilemmas, by definition, cannot be solved. They can only be resolved within the context of the particular circumstances. Public managers need to worry about motivation, improvement, and evaluation. They need to collect information for all three purposes. Evaluators should not be surprised when agency heads, rather than being concerned solely with evaluation, choose to balance these three managerial responsibilities.

9

Evaluating
ET CHOICES

In January 1986, the Massachusetts Department of Public Welfare released *An Evaluation of the Massachusetts Employment and Training Choices Program*, prepared by the department's Office of Research, Planning and Evaluation (RP&E). The evaluation was designed to answer "questions concerning numbers and characteristics of program participants." For example, the report stated that although ET participants "were, for the most part, representative of the AFDC population," they "were somewhat more job-ready." More ET participants had "some past work experience" (87 percent) than did AFDC recipients in general (73 percent).[1]

RP&E also examined "the impact of the program on the employment experiences and welfare dependency of participants, as well as on welfare savings." For example, the report stated: "The average hourly wage for full-time jobs obtained through the Training and Placement Services of ET was $5.11, more than twice the income from the average AFDC grant, and 53% above the minimum wage." It also noted that the "average monthly grant savings for a job obtained through Training and Placement Services is $219."[2]

The department's evaluation suggested three ways in which ET could be improved: (1) by closing the wage gap between whites and minorities, (2) by finding higher-paying jobs, and (3) by putting a greater emphasis on training as opposed to direct placement:

Among individual components, the Training components—Skills Training and Supported Work—had the highest proportions of job finders with closed cases. This last finding demonstrates the value of upgrading clients' vocational skills through intensive training services as a central strategy for reducing welfare dependence. It is especially significant in ET because the participants in these components were less job ready than participants in the Placement components when they began.

Devoting greater resources to more intensive training services might, in the short run, decrease marginally the number of ET job placements, since people stay in the program longer when receiving skills training or education. In the long run, however, it would result in better jobs for ET participants and greater savings for the Commonwealth. While skills training services are more costly, they are also more effective than less intensive job development and placement services in helping people prepare for and find jobs that will enable them to move and stay off welfare.[3]

This evaluation did not contain all the department's data and analyses on ET. RP&E was constantly collecting information and examining it. Sometimes RP&E simply summarized these data in charts for publications or briefings. Sometimes it used such data in internal memoranda. Sometimes speechwriters for Governor Michael S. Dukakis quoted the data. Sometimes the department used the data to explain to the press and public how ET was working. And annually, the department used these data and analyses to explain its budget submission to the legislature.

At the same time, none of the data collected could show what would have happened in Massachusetts without ET CHOICES. The department wanted to know how the program was working and how it could be improved. Thus it made a significant effort to collect information that would help answer these questions.

Estimating Caseload Reductions and Budget Savings

The department was looking, however, to show that ET CHOICES was reducing the caseload and thus saving the state money. For example, in its FY 1987 "Program Plan and Budget Request" for ET, the department noted that from January 1983 to July 1985, the state's AFDC caseload declined by 9.4 percent—the biggest drop in the twelve states with the largest caseloads (six of which actually had increases). During this period, the unemployment rate declined in all twelve states, with five experiencing larger decreases than Massachusetts. "A strong economy in and of itself is not sufficient to result in a large decrease in AFDC rolls," concluded the budget document.[4] An additional explanation, it argued, was needed.

"In Massachusetts," stated the budget, "ET Choices has become one of the primary factors leading to the caseload decline." The budget also contained a graph contrasting the caseload with a "projected caseload without ET." Stated the accompanying text: "The AFDC caseload in November 1985 would have been 95,945 compared to 85,411 were it not for ET."[5] The budget did not, however, contain any of the calculations that converted the 23,000 ET placements into a drop of 10,500 in the caseload. Nor did it describe the method employed to obtain these estimates.

The following year, the department's "Program Plan and Budget Request" for FY 1988 contained more caseload data: "The AFDC caseload has declined by 4.2%—from 88,414 in October 1983 when ET began to 84,693 in December 1986—despite significant upward pressure on the caseload from a 32% increase in benefits, a 35% increase in the AFDC eligibility standard, and an 87% increase in the number of single parent families in the past decade. In contrast, the AFDC caseloads in the twelve largest welfare states increased, on average, by 6% during the same period . . . The Department projects that without ET, the AFDC caseload would have been as high as 100,000."[6] Again, however, the department did not explain how it estimated what the caseload would have been without ET.

But the FY 1987 budget did explain how the department had concluded that ET had already saved the state's budget $69 million. The total cost to place 23,000 ET participants had been $71 million (for an average cost per placement of about $3,100). The average annual cost for an AFDC case was $6,100. Thus, the total annual unincurred expenditures for 23,000 cases was $140 million. The difference between ET expenditures of $71 million and unincurred AFDC expenditures of $140 million was the estimated net savings of $69 million.[7]

In August 1987, the Massachusetts Taxpayers Foundation ("whose purpose is to encourage state government to work more efficiently") published its own evaluation of ET including an estimate of budget savings. Assuming that 60 percent of placements resulted in case closings, and "that those who leave welfare through ET would have been on AFDC for an additional year if not for the program," the Taxpayers Foundation projected five-year savings of $150 million through June 1988.[8] Annual savings peaked in FY 1986 and then declined because of increases in the average cost per ET placement.

In estimating budget savings, both the department and the Taxpayers Foundation assumed that none of the recipients placed in jobs would have left AFDC without ET. Thus, both calculations overestimated ET's savings. The department's calculation further overestimated savings by assuming that every ET job placement automatically resulted in a closing of the AFDC case (reducing this AFDC grant to zero). Yet, the department's own evaluation revealed that, during the first two fiscal years of the program, only 45 percent of ET placements resulted in case closings. Thus, at least for this period, the Taxpayers Foundation calculation (which assumed 60 percent of ET placements resulted in a case closing) also overestimated the savings.

Both the Taxpayers Foundation and the department further assumed that former AFDC recipients who found jobs through ET were off the caseload for only one year. This assumption might have underestimated ET's savings. If, on average, former ET participants stayed off welfare for two years, actual savings would have been more than double the estimate. Clearly, efforts to estimate the budget savings of any welfare, training, and work program are sensitive to many assumptions.

There is, however, a simpler way to test whether such a program is cost effective. Ignore the issue of whether a recipient would have gotten a job (or gone off welfare) without ET. Instead, focus on the question: How many months *before* she would otherwise have left AFDC on her own does the average ET participant have her case closed? Suppose (as stated in the FY 1987 budget) the average cost per ET placement was $3,000 and the average annual cost for an AFDC case was $6,000; then if, on average, ET participants left AFDC six months early, the program saved money in the short run. If the cost of a placement was $5,100 and the annual cost per AFDC case was $8,700 (the Taxpayers Foundation's numbers for FY 1987), the department needed to get the average ET participant off welfare seven months early to ensure immediate savings.

If a welfare, training, and work program passes this short-term test of net savings due to early case closings, it is clearly cost effective. This test would, however, underestimate in two ways the total budget savings from the program. First, this test ignores the savings that result from a part-time job that causes a reduction in an AFDC grant. In addition, this test ignores some potential long-term savings. If, because of their ET training, some women did not return to AFDC—or merely stayed off welfare for a longer period of time before they returned—additional savings would accrue in the future. Obviously, any such savings are even more difficult to estimate.

Indeed, any effort to estimate the budget savings caused by ET CHOICES dramatizes the difficulty of evaluating any public program without a control group.

Designing a Policy Experiment for ET CHOICES

Suppose that Massachusetts's political leaders wanted to evaluate ET CHOICES with a policy experiment. The design of such an experiment would have to reflect the nine key characteristics of the program:

1. ET should be voluntary. Women should not be coerced into participating, nor should their benefits be cut if they decide not to.

2. To ensure that every welfare recipient knows about ET and can take advantage of the program, the welfare department should devote significant resources to outreach—to informing recipients about the program, to convincing them that they have the intelligence necessary to complete a training program, to assuring them that they have the personal character required to become economically independent, and to recruiting them to participate.

3. This marketing effort should be complemented by one directed at the department's own employees to convince them that recipients can become productive citizens and by another targeted at the state's employers to persuade them that welfare recipients want to work and that it makes good business sense to hire them.

4. ET should be conducted statewide. Every woman on welfare in the state should have an opportunity to participate.

5. A branch office of the state's employment-service agency should be located adjacent to each welfare office, thus providing services to recipients more directly and effectively.

6. A wide variety of educational, job-training, and placement services should be provided to ensure that every ET participant can find a program that fits her needs. These services should not be provided by the welfare department but by organizations already in this business. This is to ensure that (a) the program uses the state's best job-training people and (b) these organizations do not cut back on the services they are already providing to welfare recipients. (A maintenance-of-effort clause is to be included in all contracts with these organizations.)

7. Unfortunately, those designing ET are not sure how precisely the program will function (for this depends upon the uncertain interaction of local economic conditions, the political culture, the characteristics of the caseload, and the individual and collective behavior of social workers). Thus, the effectiveness of various program components should be continuously appraised and the lessons learned and ideas generated from these assessments immediately adopted to improve the program.

8. Despite this uncertainty about program implementation, ET's mission is very ambitious. The purpose is not just to raise the earnings (and incomes) of welfare recipients or to reduce welfare expenditures. The purpose is to convert welfare recipients into economically independent and socially productive citizens.

9. Finally, the state's political leadership has concluded that its welfare benefits are too low. Consequently, it has decided to raise benefit levels and to broaden eligibility.

A researcher would have to be careful, when attempting to design an experiment to evaluate ET, not to introduce anything that might undermine any of these characteristics.

Any welfare, training, and employment program with these nine characteristics could produce results that would be open to many alternative explanations. How could such a program be evaluated? In particular, how would an evaluator design a controlled experiment to eliminate as many of these alternative explanations as possible and determine the net impact of the ET program?

Creating a Control Group

The first task would be to develop a mechanism for randomly assigning recipients to treatment and control groups. After all, comparing the job-finding rates of ET participants who volunteer for the program with nonparticipants who do not volunteer does not eliminate one obvious explanation for any differential: those recipients participating in the program might be more successful simply because they were more motivated. To judge the net impact of this program alone—to eliminate as many alternative explanations as possible—it would be useful to assign randomly some of the volunteers to the treatment group and the rest to the control group.

But these volunteers are recruited through an aggressive marketing campaign. Some of this marketing is done wholesale (with fliers and videos). Most is done "retail"—person to person—with a caseworker explaining to a recipient all the benefits of the program and convincing her that ET can improve her life. But if the recipient will be participating in a controlled experiment, the caseworker's marketing pitch will be necessarily constrained: "This program is really super. You should sign up. It will help you live a better life. Your income will go up. You'll be proud of yourself. Your kids will respect you more. So sign up. Then those running the experiment will flip a coin, and if it comes up Heads you get in."

One of the things that the Massachusetts Department of Public Welfare learned about marketing was that once a social worker got a welfare recipient excited about ET, the social worker should sign her up without delay. The social worker should not send the recipient home to call up an ET worker to arrange an appointment but should instead immediately walk the recipient over and introduce her to the ET worker. This suggests that the mere existence of a controlled experiment might undermine one of ET's key components; even the volunteer who gets Heads and is admitted to the program may have her motivation reduced by this uncertainty in the department's promise of help. Operationally, random assignment is incompatible with a voluntary program that depends heavily on person-to-person, worker-to-recipient marketing that is quickly followed by entry into some component of the program.

In addition, there is the ethical problem of denying services to people. If a state does not have enough resources to provide training and employment services to every recipient, random assignment may be one way to determine who gets them. But if the state does have enough resources, how can it deny these services to someone who wants to get a job? Taking a position "on ethical grounds," Richard P. Nathan, provost of the Rockefeller College at the State University of New York and chairman of the board of directors of the Manpower Demonstration Research Corporation (MDRC), writes that if a policy is "universal . . . one is hard put to argue that the policy should be suspended for some otherwise eligible participants in the interest of science."[9]

This ethical dilemma influenced the design of MDRC's evaluation of Arkansas's WORK program. MDRC employed random assignment "in two of the eight original counties, Jefferson and Pulaski South [Little Rock], the only areas in which eligible people outnumbered program slots by a level high enough to allow for this technique."[10] For Project Redirection, a program to assist teenage mothers, MDRC used a quasi-experimental approach because random assignment was, observed Nathan, "infeasible for political reasons."[11]

Still, the political leaders who conceived ET might be willing to market it aggressively *and* to deny participation to half of the volunteers. And caseworkers might make a personal and enthusiastic pitch to every woman knowing she would have only a fifty-fifty chance of getting into the program. Even then, however, those assigned to the control group might still receive ET services.

In fact, a woman assigned to the control group still has access to nearly identical services. She needs only to persist in her quest. Having become enthusiastic about getting a job, she can walk out of the welfare office, down the corridor, and into the employment-service office. Or, if she wants training, she can search out an organization that provides it under the Job Training Partnership Act. Any JTPA agency that has a contract under the ET program needs (in addition to recipients in the department's treatment group) to enroll additional welfare recipients to satisfy its maintenance-of-effort clause. Thus the JTPA agency will also be recruiting recipients and may have an easier time signing up a woman who has already volunteered once for the welfare department's program.

Further, consider the social worker who has just delivered an animated sales pitch to convince a welfare recipient of the many benefits and joys of training and employment, only to discover that the fickle flip of the coin has randomly assigned this woman to the control group. Not only is the welfare recipient deflated; so is the social worker. Now the social worker (or the director of the program) faces what Nathan calls the "program director's dilemma." Should the social worker tell the recipient how to find the nearest JTPA office?[12] Indeed, how many social workers can resist the temptation to do so?

Defining and Standardizing the Treatment

Beyond the difficulty of creating a control group, there is also the problem of defining the "treatment" and ensuring its uniformity. Is the treatment just the specific job-counseling, education, job-training, and job-placement services provided by the department to those in the treatment group? Or does it include the changes made in the attitudes of welfare recipients, social workers, and business executives? If the only treatment that counts is the direct provision of a specific social service, the task of evaluation is somewhat simplified.

Still, how can the evaluators be sure that the quality of the treatment is uniform? For example, if the treatment group receives job-training services, is the caliber of this training consistent enough and high enough to ensure that everyone in the treatment group has received treatment—a real treatment, and the same treatment?

For the polio vaccine or the negative income tax, the treatment is narrow and relatively easy to define and control. It is a simple action: injecting a vaccine into an individual's arm; injecting money into a family's bank account. The quality of an antipolio vaccine can be controlled and kept constant. And whether a welfare family receives new crisp dollar bills, old faded ones, or a check will not affect its economic behavior. Thus, conducting a controlled experiment for vaccines and straightforward social policies (such as giving people money) is a *relatively* easy task. But this ease is only relative. Maintaining uniform standards for AFDC payments is a major problem, and quality-control efforts to keep down the error rate absorb significant resources in every welfare department. Further, the multiple volumes written about the negative-income-tax experiments reveal that the evaluation of this comparatively simple social policy was not all that simple.[13]

A welfare-to-work program might also be a relatively simple social policy. It might consist of a single, simple action—e.g., a group job search. Even for such a modest undertaking, however, defining and standardizing the treatment can get complex. For example, the quality of the job-search activities provided could vary quite markedly; some job counselors might prove quite effective while others have little impact.

Yet how would anyone know? Researchers might compare different social workers and different job-search activities. But that would create an experiment within an experiment. If some activities or social workers produced results while some did not, evaluators could test whether this difference was statistically significant. But what then? Should policymakers ignore the results of the ineffective treatment?

Such an approach might make sense for different job-search activities. The experiment would have revealed that some activities worked and some did not. But should policymakers also disregard results from the ineffective social workers? That seems much less legitimate. It might be acceptable if the characteristics of the ineffective social workers can be (a) clearly identified, and (b) positively eliminated in the future through either the selection of social workers or their training. Otherwise, however, the reported results would apply only to the best social workers rather than to the average. The results would be no more legitimate than those of the "researchers" on parapsychology who discard the results of their experiments when the subject exhibits no talent for ESP or when a subject who has previously exhibited such "talent" has an "off day."

Moreover, none of this ensures that job-search activities that prove effective in one locale will work in another. It is quite possible that some aspects of a job-search program could prove appropriate for the San Diego economy of 1982–1984, while others had no effect—though these might work well in New Jersey in 1984–1986. Do the 1982–1984 results from San Diego apply to Arkansas in 1990 or to San Diego in 2005?

All these problems in standardizing the treatment dramatize why the San Diego 6 percent differential is significant. As easy as it is to describe, even the San Diego program did not provide one single, simple treatment. During the two and a quarter years of the experiment, there must have been clear differences in the quality of the job-search and work-experience services provided—and perhaps even in the nature of these services. After all, the program and the evaluation started at the same time; there was no opportunity to work out the inevitable kinks or to learn how to ensure uniformity. Given that discovering the 6 percent differential required a positive disproof of the null hypothesis, given that some of the services undoubtedly had little effect on the ability of welfare recipients to find jobs, and given that many of those in the treatment group received few services, that MDRC could detect any net impact at all was indeed significant.

The Rosenthal Effect

Compared with the San Diego job-search program, ET CHOICES was quite complex, for it provided a number of different counseling, education, training, and job-placement services. Moreover, these services were provided by a large number of welfare offices, employment-service offices, and small contractors across the state. Some were effective. Others were not. Uniformity is difficult to establish—unless it is through tight bureaucratic controls that push uniformity toward the lowest common denominator on any effectiveness scale.

In addition, ET also attempted to influence the attitudes and behavior of the welfare recipients *and* everyone else who came into contact with them—social workers, educators, and employers. For example, when the vice president of a manufacturing firm told the press, ''These people really want to work . . . We've got four winners here, and we'd like to have more like them,''[14] it helped to break down the normal skepticism of other employers about hiring welfare recipients.

If all the journalists clearly reported that ''these people,'' ''winners,'' and ''more like them'' were only those welfare recipients who were ET graduates, this publicity and any accompanying change in attitudes might not have complicated any controlled experiment. But if other employers interpreted ''winners'' to mean welfare recipients in general, there would be a problem. Now this aspect of the ''treatment''—affecting the attitudes of potential employers—might help not only those in the treatment group. It might also help the controls find jobs. An AFDC recipient might be motivated by ET's aggressive marketing efforts, placed in the control group, find her way just around the corner to the employment-security office, directed to a training contractor (which needs to meet its maintenance-of-effort requirements), and then get a job—because the employer no longer thought that hiring a welfare recipient was a big risk.

How often would this happen? Not very often. It might be a minor roadblock to conducting a controlled experiment of ET CHOICES. Still, if the differential between the treatment and control groups for which we are looking is only 6 percentage points, then several small problems such as this one can, collectively, be troubling.[15]

Moreover, the component of the program that seeks to affect attitudes can have a potentially bigger impact. The demeanor with which the services are delivered can be as consequential as the services themselves. Are the social workers friendly, helpful, and encouraging? Or surly, uninformative, and disdainful? The attitude of the social worker can easily send strong signals to the welfare recipient: ''You can do it. You can get a job." Or: "You are worthless. No one will hire you." One component of ET that might be most important is the major effort to affect the attitudes of all the employees in the welfare department.

Specifically, the management of the state's welfare department attempted to convince its social workers of several key ideas:

- All of us are and should be in the business of helping welfare recipients find employment and become economically independent.
- Most welfare recipients are capable—if given the right education and training—of finding and keeping a job.
- To do this, it is necessary for us to treat every recipient as an individual and design an individualized program that reflects her needs.

If there is to be a controlled experiment, however, and if attitude is part of the treatment, there needs to be one more component to that message.

- Oh, and by the way, only affect these new attitudes when you talk with recipients assigned to the treatment group. When dealing with those in the control group, please be your old, indifferent selves.

Obviously, it is impossible to withhold the attitudinal component of the treatment from the control group. If the attitude with which the service is delivered is important, and if the managers of ET want to influence this attitude, they need to inject this new attitude into every communication they have with their department's social workers.

The attitude with which any service is delivered can prove critical. Over a quarter of a century ago, Robert Rosenthal, of Harvard University, discovered that the expectations of the teacher can affect the learning of the student. Rosenthal tested children, randomly assigned 20 percent of each class to the treatment group, and then told their teachers that the treatment group's "scores on the 'test for intellectual blooming' indicated that they would show unusual intellectual gains during the [coming] academic year." Eight months later, Rosenthal readministered the test; those children who the teachers were told would make unusual intellectual gains, indeed, had higher gains. The direct treatment was what Rosenthal told the teachers. But there was also an indirect treatment: how the teachers treated students in the treatment group compared with how the same teachers treated the controls.[16]

Similarly, for ET, the department's leadership attempted to apply both a direct treatment (what the leaders told the social workers) and an indirect treatment (how the social workers treated the recipients). The direct treatment was the various messages designed to convince social workers that they could help welfare recipients find jobs and that the welfare recipients could function productively in these jobs. Then these social workers would apply the indirect treatment by working with the welfare recipients.

The Placebo Effect

Parallels to this "Rosenthal effect" can be observed in other fields. A physician's "bedside manner," long an important tool of the family doctor of the past, dropped out of favor with the advent of high-tech medicine. Now it is receiving increased attention as an essential part of any doctor's skills. The best doctors, it appears, possess both technical competence and personal compassion.[17]

Indeed, the field of medicine has provided us with the famous "placebo effect." Give a patient a sugar pill and say it is the latest drug; the patient improves. (For some inexplicable reason, pills that are very large and brown or purple, or very small and yellow or red, produce better results. And the worse it tastes, the more effective a placebo is.[18]) The placebo effect applies not only to drugs but even to surgery. Thirty years ago, patients with coronary heart disease reported fewer chest pains after a surgical procedure that consisted of opening the chest cavity and tying off an artery. But some physicians wondered whether the effect was physiological or psychological. So they ran an experiment. Those in the treatment group had their artery tied off; the controls merely had an incision made in their chest and were then sewn back up. Oops. No difference.[19]

The Hawthorne Effect

The Rosenthal effect in teaching and the placebo effect in medicine have a parallel in management: the Hawthorne Effect. In 1924, in an effort to determine how illumination affected industrial production, the National Academy of Sciences and Western Electric conducted a series of experiments at the Hawthorne Works, a Western Electric plant outside Chicago. Management turned the lights up in one part of the plant. The treatment group increased its productivity. So did the control group. Again management turned up the lights for the treatment group. Again productivity went up. Again for both groups. Then management turned the lights down. Still productivity went up—and for both groups. Obviously, changes in the lighting were not influencing productivity. Rather, what appeared to make the difference was the attention management was giving to both groups—treatment and control. To conduct the experiment and collect the data, management had to devote a lot of attention to the people working in both sections of the plant. This attention was the factor that distinguished the time prior to the experiment with what happened after it began.[20]

Medical research attempts to distinguish between treatments that have a physiological effect and those for which the effect is purely psychological. Why pay for an expensive drug when a sugar pill will do? But the desire to eliminate the placebo effect when testing pharmaceuticals does not mean it should be eliminated when practicing medicine. Indeed, the placebo effect is an important part of the doctor's array of treatments: "Here. Take this medicine. It *will* make you better." Similarly, the "Rosenthal effect" is an important tool for the teacher: "You can learn this. I know you can." Doctors and teachers not only need to apply the latest technology of their professions; they also need to influence the attitude of the individual being treated or taught.

The same applies to public policy. Not all the tools of public policy are technological. Some of the most important may be psychological. For social workers trying to help welfare recipients become financially independent, part of the task is technical: training the welfare recipient to run a lathe. But another part of the task is psychological: convincing the welfare recipient that she can run a lathe, get along with the boss, manage to get the children in day care, and handle the inevitable personal crises while still arriving at work on time.

Welfare commissioners trying to convince their states' employers to hire these women also have both a technical and a psychological task. They have to demonstrate concretely to potential employers that the recipients have the required skills. They also have to convince these same employers that they and the welfare recipient can work well together. Indeed, part of the commissioner's job is to make hard-headed business executives feel good about hiring welfare recipients. The psychological part of the treatment may be more significant than the technological. The manager of any training and employment program wants to take full advantage of the Rosenthal effect.

Similarly, any welfare commissioner (indeed, any public manager) wants to take full advantage of the Hawthorne effect. If paying attention to social workers has an impact on their effectiveness, a welfare commissioner wants to do it. If getting media coverage for the program makes those who work on the program, those who are welfare recipients, and those who would hire them feel that people are paying attention to them, then the commissioner wants to do all that too. Maybe mandatory job search, or voluntary training, or any other feature of a training and employment program is no more important than the lighting in the Hawthorne plant. Maybe what counts is the attention the managers give to those individuals whose actions are necessary to make the program work.

If the "treatment" can be administered individually and impersonally to each member of the treatment group—and can also be positively denied to the members of the control group—then it does make sense to call any difference between the outcomes for treatment and control groups the "net impact." But if the treatment cannot be denied to the control group, it is hard to argue that the failure to discover any difference between the treatment and control groups—the failure to disprove the null hypothesis—also establishes that the program has no net impact. Moreover, if, to achieve the purpose of the program, its managers have designed it to ensure multiple access to treatment, it is absurd to modify significantly some components of the program just to make other components more amenable to evaluation.

Do the most effective social policies consist of only one critical component? Hardly. To attack problems like welfare dependency requires policies with multiple components (and with the flexibility to treat different individuals with different components). Moreover, several of these components may themselves be necessary for the overall policy to prove successful. For such policies, it is most difficult to determine a net impact. And again, it would be foolish to limit our choice of social policies to those that social science can easily evaluate.

Getting to the Front of the Line

Durgin-Park is one of Boston's most famous restaurants. Located behind Faneuil Hall, it was for years in a dismal section of the city; when Quincy Market was renovated, however, the locale improved significantly. But the Durgin-Park formula remained the same: thick slices of roast beef, modest prices, long tables with red-checked tablecloths, surly waitresses, and long lines. But there was a "secret"—so everyone knew. If you bought a drink at the bar, you would get placed near the front of the dining-room line.

This system does not serve more dinners to more people more quickly. It simply rearranges the queue. The people who stand in the regular line have to wait longer for their dinner. The dining room has a fixed number of seats.

Perhaps that is all any welfare, training, and work program ever does. Maybe in San Diego some of the welfare recipients in the control group who did not get jobs would have gotten jobs without the program. Maybe what the program really did was move those in the treatment group to the front of the employment queue, while denying the jobs to some from the control group.

Suppose a controlled experiment of ET CHOICES did reveal a net impact. There are still two alternative explanations: (1) those recipients in the treatment group came out of this program with better skills and better attitudes toward work, or (2) the marketing and placement components of the program convinced prospective employers to hire ET participants rather than other applicants. Those in the treatment group might have displaced other welfare recipients from these jobs. Or they might have displaced married women who, because of ET, could not find a job to supplement their families' income.

If the supply of people willing and able to take entry-level jobs exceeds the demand for these jobs so that (after a short transition period) every one of these jobs is filled, then any training and employment program accomplishes little. It affects *who* gets these jobs, but it contributes nothing to the economy (unless it improves *how* these employees perform at these jobs). The program might, however, reduce welfare expenditures and affect the distribution of income. The unmarried women who get jobs through the program would leave welfare, increasing their income and eliminating their cases from the welfare budget; they might take jobs that would otherwise have been filled by married women who now remain housewives in families with a lower (one wage-earner) income that is nevertheless above the welfare level.

If, however, the supply of people willing and able to take entry-level jobs exceeds the demand, but the jobs are not filled (primarily because the employers cannot find these potential employees or vice versa), then a training and employment program could be quite important. The job-placement activities of such a program might provide employers with workers they could not otherwise find and provide employment for those who would otherwise be on welfare. Or if many of these entry-level jobs go unfilled because of a lack of applicants with the minimum skills, the training of welfare recipients will have some positive impact on employment, the welfare budget, and total family income in the state. Indeed, it will have a positive economic impact by helping to expand the state's entire economy. (In any case, Massachusetts's "Economic Miracle"—about which Governor Dukakis spoke frequently as a presidential candidate—was less dependent on the graduates of ET training programs than it was on the graduates of M.I.T.)

An educational program—be it a JTPA contractor training welfare recipients or a university training MBAs—may place its graduates into jobs, but that does not mean it is accomplishing a social purpose. The education may give the graduates knowledge and skills to perform more effectively in their jobs. Or this education may do little more than give these graduates a credential that puts them at the front of the employment queue. On the job, these "well-educated" job candidates may not perform any better than people with similar backgrounds but without this education and credential.

Nevertheless, to simplify their task of finding employees, employers can decide (arbitrarily but not unintelligently) to consider only those who have the credential. Because these people perform adequately on the job (due to their backgrounds, not their training), employers may limit their recruiting efforts to those with the credential. This will drive up the demand for this training credential (and thus its price). After all, it has become the ticket to employment (just as buying a drink at the Durgin-Park bar is the ticket to its dining room). But it will do little for society's economic productivity.

Even if a controlled experiment for ET was to reveal a net impact, there is still an alternative explanation. Is the program little more than an educational Durgin-Park, inviting those with the necessary background, skills, and attitudes to have an expensive drink at the bar, before putting them at the front of the employment queue? No controlled experiment can answer this question.[21]

The social experiment is a valuable but sometimes beguiling concept: Randomly divide people into two groups. Give one group the treatment and withhold it from the other. Then use statistical tests to see if there is any real difference in the success rate.

If the treatment is a medical drug, the experiment can be powerful indeed. After all, the treatment is a single, simple act that can be given or denied with certainty, and the formula does not change. Moreover, the number of successes or failures is not fixed. If one individual fails to get a disease, the probability that another person will get it does not increase (although if there is an epidemic, the chances of people in both groups getting the disease will rise).

But if the treatment is a social program with multiple components, a social experiment may not be so effective at sorting out cause and effect. For example, it may simply be impossible to withhold some critical components from those in the control group. In such a situation, the results of the experiment may underestimate the impact of the program. Or, if the success sought is a full-time job with a decent wage and health benefits, the number of successes may be fixed, so that all the program does is influence who gets those successes. In such a situation, the results of the experiment may overestimate the impact of the program. Furthermore, whenever the political leaders who created the program learn something that can improve it, they will quickly make the necessary modification.

Policymakers who love to boogie to the music of The Control Group should save the first dance for some careful thinking about what a social experiment for any specific program with specific characteristics really can or cannot prove.

How and When to Measure Success?

Getting to the front of the employment queue would not, however, be good enough for ET. ET's mission was not to increase the earnings of welfare recipients or to reduce welfare expenditures. The designers of this program set a higher standard. Their mission was to help welfare recipients escape poverty permanently. Consequently, it would be inappropriate to evaluate this program by comparing the average earnings of the treatment and control groups. A treatment group might have statistically higher earnings and still be making few strides toward economic independence.

To evaluate ET CHOICES in terms of the mission established by its creators, an evaluator must compare the treatment and control groups in terms of their welfare status. How many are still receiving welfare? How many have become financially independent? The evaluator needs to check these differences not only after thirty days or one year but also after, say, five years.

This raises what Lester Salamon, now of Johns Hopkins University, has called "the time dimension in policy evaluation." When should this program be evaluated? Can an evaluator test a program for results immediately? Or must an evaluator check for important "letdown effects"—such as a return to welfare of those who worked for, say, two years. After all, the Rosenthal effect on attitudes may have a very short half-life. Conversely, there may be some "latent effects"—recipients who first took part-time jobs but eventually found full-time employment—as well as "sleeper effects"—recipients who finally got jobs two years after their training ended. Should an evaluator wait? And if so, for how long?[22]

MDRC's evaluation of Project Redirection, which was designed to help teenage mothers, illustrates the importance of timing in evaluation. After one year, those teenagers who received the services of Project Redirection did better than the comparison group, but "this advantage largely disappeared at two years." After a five-year retrospective evaluation, however,

MDRC reported some "important new findings." The mothers who participated in Project Redirection "were working more hours per week and had higher weekly earnings; were less likely to be receiving welfare; and scored higher on a widely used test of parenting ability." Moreover, the children in the treatment group "showed better cognitive skills, as measured by a test of vocabulary knowledge; and exhibited fewer behavioral problems."[23] The services provided by Project Redirection, concluded MDRC's President Judith M. Gueron, "can make an enduring difference."[24]

How long should the evaluator wait? In particular, how long should the evaluator wait if the managers are trying to improve the program? Should the evaluator wait two years? Will that give the program's managers enough time to get the program right? Or at least substantially right? Or, because the program is very complicated, does the evaluator need to wait five years? This program—any program—will never be perfect. The managers will always be using new information and new capabilities to improve the program. When is the best time to evaluate it?

San Diego's initial job-search/work-experience program was also its final one. The formal features of the program did not change. Consequently, the evaluation and the program could (and did) begin at the same time. What was being evaluated was what the policy's designers really wanted.

In contrast, ET CHOICES was a constantly evolving program. No one pretended that the ET of the first year was the ultimate program. The objective—as ET's management team frequently emphasized—was to get the program up and running and *then* to "fix it." From the beginning "case management" was to be an important part of ET. Yet it was not until the fifth year of ET's operation that case management began to become reality.

A program manager can always say, "Not yet. We have just initiated some important improvements in the program. You can't really evaluate it until these changes are working properly." But the program will never be perfect. It will always be changing. A. Ernest Fitzgerald, who blew the whistle on the cost overruns on the Air Force's C5A cargo plane, has summed up this problem in Fitzgerald's First Law: "There are only two phases of a program. The first is 'It's too early to tell.' The second: 'It's too late to stop.'"[25]

Evaluating Ongoing Programs

Nathan distinguishes between "*demonstration research* to test possible new programs and policy approaches" and "*evaluation research* to assess the effects of existing programs." These differences, he continues, "have not been sufficiently appreciated or taken into account."[26]

By demonstration research, Nathan means the kind of work that MDRC did in San Diego, Arkansas, and Baltimore. Policymakers have an idea: they believe that some kind of action might produce some kind of result. But they want to be sure that the action will, indeed, produce the desired result. To test the idea, they sponsor several demonstrations, such as the series of negative-income-tax experiments, or MDRC's Demonstration of Work/Welfare Initiatives. In demonstration research, only a limited number of people are involved; usually some of these people are randomly assigned to the treatment group while the others are used as the control, though Nathan includes quasi-experimental approaches for creating a comparison group as legitimate forms of demonstration research. If the idea makes sense on a small scale—that is, if the experiment produces desirable results—then the idea can be converted into a full-blown policy.

In contrast, evaluation research focuses on policies that have been fully implemented across a large political jurisdiction. Evaluation research, Nathan argues, differs from demonstration research in three important ways. First, evaluation "researchers have less control over the conditions under which an evaluation study is carried out." Second, it is "more difficult to establish the counterfactual state"—to determine what would have happened without the policy. Third, "evaluation research is more likely to focus on institutional impacts as opposed to individual impacts."[27]

To "establish the counterfactual state," control groups are ideal. Unfortunately, it is difficult to create one for an ongoing program. "Random assignment," writes Nathan, "is extremely difficult to bring to bear in evaluating an ongoing program once it has been adopted."[28] With a demonstration program, random assignment means selecting a few people to receive the treatment that theory, at least, suggests is beneficial. With an ongoing program, however, random assignment really means random denial: the flip of the coin will determine the people who will be denied the (presumed) benefits that everyone else will be receiving. Both ethically and politically, that is very hard to do. Thus, for evaluation research, quasi-experimental approaches often make the most sense.

Further, Nathan argues that evaluation research will often address different questions, particularly "institutional impacts": how "different types of governments, organizations, and political actors respond to policy changes."[29] The policy idea has moved from the demonstration stage to becoming a complete program. But will an idea that worked well in a small, experimental setting produce similar results when implemented by a large, established bureaucracy? How will an experimental program that produced results when applied to 3,500 AFDC applicants in San Diego work when it is adopted for all AFDC recipients in California? Institutional research examines both organizational behavior and human attitudes.

For ET, any institutional research would address questions such as: What do the social workers think about ET? How do their attitudes affect how they implement the program and deal with individual recipients? What are the characteristics of the recipients with whom the contractors choose to work? Whom do the contractors seek for their training programs? What type of people do they place? How do the contractors respond to the incentives in the performance-based contracts? How well does the employment security agency work with the welfare department? Has ET been able to change the way those who work in the large state agencies and local nonprofit organizations think about the task of providing training and employment services to welfare recipients and how they go about performing that task?

Institutional research is important because "politicians often act by indirection," writes Nathan. "They seek to change the behavior of institutions in the hope or belief that such changes in institutional behavior will influence the services and activities of these institutions in ways that will eventually affect individual citizens."[30] Public services—be they training and employment services for welfare recipients, road repair services for drivers, or defense services for everyone—are provided by large organizations. Thus evaluators need to determine how public managers can affect the behavior of these organizations so that they do a better job delivering these services.

He Who Lives by the Caseload, Dies by the Caseload

On October 29, 1985, Governor Dukakis announced that, since he had taken office two and a half years earlier, the AFDC caseload had dropped 9.5 percent. And, of the twelve states with the largest number of AFDC cases, Massachusetts's decrease was the greatest. "The difference is unquestionably ET," the governor told the press. "There is no other way to explain the numbers."[31] Naturally, any social scientist could easily come up with a dozen alternative explanations. Still, the governor attributed the drop in the AFDC caseload directly to ET. A year and a half later, Dukakis again linked the declining caseload to ET: "I can't explain the difference or the dramatic reduction in longterm [AFDC clients] any way other than ET."[32]

Perhaps the governor's statements merely reinforced that relationship in most people's minds. Maybe the public was already using the size of the caseload as a measure of ET's success. After all, people would have little difficulty linking the two. Each year, the department was placing over 10,000 welfare recipients in jobs. With a caseload of 85,000, people would naturally expect 10,000 placements to have a noticeable impact. Yet decreases in the caseload did not approach the number of placements. Over five years, the department made over 50,000 placements but the caseload dropped by only 5,500.

To many, the purpose of any training and employment program for welfare recipients is to reduce the welfare rolls. That was not the objective that motivated Commissioner Charles M. Atkins or the other managers of the department. "We never set out to say 'Let's lower the welfare caseload,'" said Deputy Commissioner Thomas P. Glynn. "We wanted a program to get people out of poverty."[33] But because others cared about the caseload, the department's leaders had to pay attention to it. By 1988, the famous sheets that Atkins circulated to local office directors to dramatize how well they were doing against their ET placement goals were accompanied by sheets showing how each office was doing in reducing the caseload.

Unfortunately, neither the local-office directors nor the department's top managers could control the caseload. While ET placements were reducing it, other pressures were working in the opposite direction. In October 1987, Atkins sent a memo to Philip W. Johnston, the state's secretary of human services, describing three factors that were driving up the AFDC caseload: (1) AFDC benefits, (2) the characteristics of children and families, and (3) migration into Massachusetts.[34]

During the first four years of ET, Massachusetts had increased AFDC benefits by 47 percent. Further, the federal government had broadened the eligibility standards. Thus not only were more women eligible for AFDC, but the increased benefits made signing up more attractive.

Massachusetts had also experienced some significant demographic changes. Since 1980, children born to unwed mothers had increased by 33 percent. In three years, the number of single-parent families had grown by 23 percent, and the proportion of AFDC cases headed by unwed women was up from 37 percent in 1983 to 53 percent in 1987. Increasingly, the AFDC caseload seemed to be composed of families with very few resources.

Finally, in-migration was pushing the caseload up. Between January

1985 and October 1987, cases headed by an individual whose Social Security number had been issued in Massachusetts were off by a thousand, while the number of cases headed by an individual whose Social Security number had been issued in another state grew by a thousand. And the number of cases headed by an individual whose Social Security number had been issued in Puerto Rico was up by nearly 2,000. Over the first four years of ET, the number of white and black families on AFDC dropped by 11 percent, while the Hispanic caseload was up 32 percent. At a time when pressure to keep the caseload down was increasing, the local-office directors were frustrated by the growth in the Hispanic caseload; for a number of reasons, it was even harder to find jobs for these recipients.

Despite all this, in October 1987, Massachusetts's AFDC caseload stood at 85,300—down 4 percent from 88,600 four years earlier. Moreover, there were some other gains during ET's first four years. The number of two-parent families on AFDC-UP had been cut in half—down from 2,836 cases to 1,163. The time families headed by women were staying on AFDC had also dropped significantly. The total number of families on AFDC for five years or more was off 29 percent—down from 20,800 to 14,700. Another measure—the average time spent on AFDC—had dropped by nearly a year, from 37 to 28 months. These statistics provided further evidence, Atkins wrote Johnston, of his department's "success . . . in reducing welfare dependency."

Yet such measures of "success" rarely came to the attention of any but the cognoscenti. Nor did the upward pressures on the caseload receive much attention. To the journalist, such a story was too complicated and too abstract. So the public never learned to even think about other ways of evaluating ET. And thus many legislators did not care either. To many people, there were only two measures of success: total ET placements, and the total caseload. And of those two, the one that really mattered was the caseload. As one of the department's top managers recognized, the caseload was the "soft underbelly" of ET CHOICES.

Playing the Numbers Game

Any public manager—particularly a new manager—needs to produce results. The new manager needs to show legislators, stakeholders, journalists, and the public that he or she can get things done. The new manager also needs to show the people working within his organization that he is serious about his goals and that together they can achieve some significant accomplishments. Often, the new manager needs a small but visible win.

The easiest way to do this is to establish a clear target and go after it right away. The target must be significant; it helps if it also appears difficult to achieve, though if the new manager is clever he will select a target that appears to be more difficult than it is. In October 1983, for example, Atkins set out to find 6,000 jobs for AFDC recipients in the next nine months. Although, for many people, this might have appeared impossible, Atkins understood that the target was quite achievable. Atkins "knew" he could get the Division of Employment Security to produce job placements "because (1) Kristin [Demong, Atkins's wife] was there [as its director] and (2) it was easier to and quicker to place people into a job than to train them." Then, in June 1984, the announcement that the goal had been achieved sent some very strong messages about the intentions and capacities of the department's management to those on the inside and the outside.

Obviously, this is not the only style the new manager can choose. Some will carefully avoid playing this "visible-claims game." They will still try to find jobs for welfare recipients. But they will be reluctant to set specific targets for either external or internal consumption. They will also be reluctant to announce that they have achieved even their own private goals. For once the public manager starts playing the numbers game, he can never stop. Once he has demonstrated his ability to find jobs for 6,000 welfare recipients in nine months, he has to repeat the trick. The manager will always have to answer the question: What have you done for me lately? (In the private sector, of course, the manager has little choice. He has to worry about the critical number—profits— every year.) Some public managers would prefer never to get on this treadmill.

But there is another danger in playing the numbers game. Suppose the target you select for your first, small win is not the one you want to pursue in the second or third years? The use of any single goal can distort organizational behavior. It can also distort citizens' expectations. Focusing attention on direct job placements can mean that the public will ignore the complications of training, which, after the first year's small win, may be a central part of the program. Yet the press will continue to report only stories that are simple, personal, and symbolic.

Focusing public attention on the caseload is fraught with long-run dangers. Maybe the public would have fixed on the size of the AFDC caseload even if Governor Dukakis had not given it such prominent exposure. Maybe the legislature would have been concerned about the caseload even if the department had not linked ET to the caseload in its annual budget request. Maybe everyone would have expected ET placements to reduce the caseload. But the governor's very public remarks, just two years into the program, ensured that many people would use the size of the caseload to evaluate ET. Given that ET was only one of many factors that influenced the caseload, and given that most of the other factors were beyond the control of the department, the legislature, and the governor, to claim that ET was the sole cause of the decline in the caseload was bound—eventually—to boomerang.

In 1988, June O'Neill of Baruch College set out "to measure the extent to which the ET program has reduced the welfare caseload and saved taxpayers money." In her analysis, published in March 1990, she concluded that ET did neither. "Little if any of the decline" in the caseload, wrote O'Neill, "can reasonably be attributed to ET."[35] On the back of the report were the traditional endorsements. "O'Neill's analysis certainly indicates that ET has not cut the caseload or welfare expenditures enough to offset its immediate expense to the Massachusetts taxpayer," said Alice Rivlin of the Brookings Institution. "However," continued Rivlin, "it is important to keep in mind that there are larger issues such as possible long-term benefits to ET participants, not addressed in this study." Indeed, nowhere in her report did O'Neill examine these "larger issues." ET was created to help welfare mothers become economically independent. But O'Neill's focus on the size of the caseload easily attracted attention. On May 1, 1990, the headline in *The Boston Globe* read: "Bay State's solution to welfare load said lacking." He who lives by the caseload, dies by the caseload.

The Urban Institute's Evaluation

In 1987, the Massachusetts Department of Public Welfare contracted with The Urban Institute to conduct an evaluation of ET. In its request for proposals (RFP), the department made it clear that a controlled experiment with random assignment was not an acceptable research design: "ET Choices . . . is based on the notion of client choice, which facilitates clients taking a more active role in the delivery of service. Making individual choices the cornerstone of this program fosters a sense of control in clients' lives. Therefore, methodologies involving random assignment of clients to a control group and various treatment groups would deny the client choice on which this program is based. The Department of Public Welfare considers random assignment a methodology diametrically opposed to the basic philosophy of the ET Choices program."[36]

The decision to use a quasi-experimental design[37] rather than random assignment meant, wrote Demetra Nightingale, Lee Bawden, and Lynn Burbridge of The Urban Institute team that did the research, that "the evaluation has already been criticized before it has even begun."[38]

In the RFP, the department indicated that it was motivated less by a desire to determine if the program was working than to learn how to make it work better. "Of particular interest to program administrators," wrote Nightingale and her colleagues, "is an analysis of differences between components and among different groups of participants."[39] Indeed, the department's RFP raised numerous management issues:

- "Are some ET components more successful than others in helping clients to move off and stay off welfare?"
- "Which job finders in each component are most successful in finding jobs and moving off welfare?"
- "To what extent do clients keep their jobs: How many are still employed one year after finding their ET jobs? How many clients are still off welfare a year later?"
- "Are some types of clients more likely to keep their jobs and stay off welfare than others?"
- "To what extent is the extended provision of day care services by the ET program a factor in helping clients to keep their jobs and stay off welfare?"[40]

"The primary purpose of the evaluation," wrote the Urban Institute team, "is to determine which components of the ET program work best for which types of AFDC clients."[41]

In September 1990, The Urban Institute released its report describing ET as "fairly successful." In particular, the study found:

- "Participation in ET, on average, reduced the median length of the current spell on AFDC by a little over four months, or about 29 percent."
- "Participation in ET, on average, reduced the average monthly grant by over $25 per month, a decrease of about 8 percent."
- "Participation in ET, on average, is estimated to have increased employment . . . by 8.2 percentage points (from 36.3 percent to 44.5 percent . . .)."
- "The average estimated effect of participating in ET was to increase earnings over the six months by $390, or approximately 34 percent."

All of these findings were statistically significant at the 1 percent level, and the estimated impacts were "slightly larger than those found in welfare-reform demonstrations in other states." For example, ET's effect on earnings (up $390 over six months) was "a somewhat greater dollar impact than found for other programs, which range from about $100 a year to about $470 a year in the first year after participation." ET did not, however, have any "effect on the rate at which former recipients returned to welfare."[42]

The Urban Institute did not attempt to determine the impact of ET on the caseload or to conduct a benefit-cost analysis. But it did further analyze the effects of the various components of ET, and their differential impacts were quite predictable:

- Basic education actually increased both the time spent on AFDC and the monthly grant, while reducing employment and earnings. Those AFDC recipients who need basic education (such as English as a second language) are the least employable; their decision to seek such education is also a decision to delay seeking employment until they have completed that education. But The Urban Institute found that "those who do become employed after participating in remedial education tend to remain employed longer than others who become employed."[43]
- Direct job search had "positive impacts" that "were higher than found in other studies" but "short-term only." ET participants who opted for job search "had shorter periods of employment than other ET job finders."[44]
- "The most intensive components offered by ET—supported work experience and occupational training—had" a "greater observed impact." For example, supported work increased six-month earnings by $885 and employment by 42 percent.[45]

"These results are consistent with other studies," concluded The Urban Institute team, "confirming that investment in more intensive (and costly) activities is worthwhile given the greater observed impact. That is, intensive services such as supported work are fairly expensive, but the impacts are also high."[46]

Of the jobs found by ET participants, 48 percent included health coverage. Moreover, those with health insurance had "an employment exit rate approximately 50 percent less than" those without any health insurance—suggesting "a difference in the median duration of employment of over 106 percent." But, The Urban Institute cautions, correlation is not causation: The health insurance may not be the reason that former ET participants leave these jobs less quickly. Rather, health insurance "may simply be correlated with 'good' jobs." It may just be that jobs with health insurance are better jobs; they may pay more and have better working conditions, stability, and other benefits.[47]

To the evaluator, who is concerned about alternative explanations, the causation in this correlation is suspect. Yet to the manager, who is concerned about producing results, this correlation may itself be quite valuable. The manager does not care that the health insurance may not be the cause of longer employment. All that matters to the manager is that health insurance looks like a reliable indicator of a good job. What is a "good job"? What are the characteristics of a good job and how can they be combined into a single, simple index of job quality? That might be worth another study. But the manager need not wait. For he already has a most useful indicator of job quality: whether the job includes health coverage. And how is a "good job" defined in this case? To the manager, the answer is quite simple: A good job is one that lasts approximately 106 percent longer than others.

Managers and evaluators view even the smallest piece of data quite differently. That is because managers and evaluators have different jobs and thus different perspectives and different priorities. They view the tasks of designing, evaluating, and managing public programs quite differently. Evaluators would like to design ET to ensure that it can be evaluated. But ET cannot be evaluated—at least not with the evaluator's definitive tool, the social experiment—without modifying some of the program's characteristics that the political leadership consider central to its purpose and effectiveness. We can no more determine definitively how much ET helps welfare recipients find a route out of poverty than we can determine definitively how much the Stealth bomber deters Soviet aggression.

10

The Necessity
of Leadership

Those who seek to achieve public purposes through government tend to emphasize either policy, or administration, or leadership. Some adopt the Policy Metastrategy and worry about establishing policies and regulations. Others pursue the Administrative Metastrategy and concentrate on creating administrative structures and systems. Still others employ the Leadership Metastrategy and focus on the mission and goals of their agency.

These three metastrategies are not, however, mutually exclusive. For example, a manager who emphasizes policy does not have to neglect administration or leadership. In fact, anyone who seeks to accomplish public purposes will have to employ some combination of all three approaches. After all, none of the three is, alone, sufficient. Nevertheless, those in government tend to rely most heavily on just one of these three metastrategies while ignoring the other two.

The Policy Metastrategy

For over two decades, welfare policy has been on the national agenda. In 1969, President Richard M. Nixon proposed the Family Assistance Plan. In 1977, President Carter offered his Program for Better Jobs and Income. In 1967, Congress passed the Work Incentive (WIN) program, which it made mandatory for all states in 1971. Then in 1981, as part of the Omnibus Budget Reconciliation Act (OBRA), Congress modified WIN to permit states to experiment with various welfare, training, and work programs. And the 100th Congress adopted the Family Support Act of 1988 to provide education, training, and employment to move people from welfare to work.

Each of these initiatives was based on the assumption that policy is important. Improving the welfare system (if not solving the poverty problem), for example, requires Congress to pass the right legislation—to enact the right policy. Certainly Massachusetts needed the right policy; without OBRA, ET CHOICES could not have been created. Legislation is important because it provides funding, offers guidelines, establishes rules, and creates incentives. So do the subsequent regulations issued by the executive branch.

For a policy to work, however, the legislators and the regulators have to get it right. If these policymakers do not provide enough financial support, no one can accomplish anything; if their funding level is too high, money—and political support—will be squandered, creating a public backlash. If policymakers do not have the right guidelines, people may not understand what is to be accomplished. If they do not have the right rules, people can distort the spirit of the policy while still abiding by the formal constraints. If the policymakers do not build the right incentives into the policy, people will respond to the incentives that are implicitly there and, in doing so, thwart the true purposes of the policy.

For years, the national debate over welfare reform has focused on several critical components of policy: Who should pay for what parts of the program? What rules should the federal government establish, and how much flexibility should it give to states and municipalities that administer the program? Who should be required to seek work, to actually work, or to participate in training? How do you get the financial incentives correct without driving expenditures unacceptably high? If you reduce a welfare recipient's benefits sharply when she takes a part-time job, you also reduce her incentive to seek employment. But if you don't cut back the benefits somewhat, you encourage people who are not currently eligible for welfare to sign up.[1] Policy is important because if government does not get the incentives, funding, rules, and guidelines right, it will not accomplish much.

The policy metastrategy—particularly the emphasis on the incentives inherent in legislation and regulations—flows from welfare economics. Economists from Adam Smith to Charles L. Schultze have argued that people respond to incentives. This is true of people as consumers, people as workers, people as investors, and people as politicians and bureaucrats. People respond to the incentives created by the guidelines, rules, and funding of any public policy. Thus, argues Schultze, the key to good policy is to get the incentives right:

> Societies seeking to achieve a high standard of living have three major options in organizing individual citizens toward that end: coercion (by democratic majority or authoritarian dictate), self-interest

incentives, and what we might loosely call the "emotional" forces [of compassion, patriotism, brotherly love, and cultural solidarity] . . . Harnessing the "base" motive of material self-interest to promote the common good is perhaps *the* most important social invention mankind has yet achieved . . . In most cases the prerequisite for social gains is the identification, not of villains and heroes but of the defects in the incentive system that drive ordinary decent citizens into doing things contrary to the common good.[2]

Whether the policy area is poverty, agriculture, or international trade, those who employ the policy metastrategy focus on the incentives that influence the behavior of people and organizations.

Getting the policy right is necessary, but not sufficient. It is the Legislator's Conceit, as noted in Chapter 7, to assume that once the policy is determined everything else is mere detail—that people will behave exactly as the creators of the incentives, rules, and guidelines intended. Legislators may believe that if their brilliantly conceived policy does not have the intended consequences it is because of executive-branch incompetence. (The same thinking applies to executive-branch regulators, who also are in the business of making "policy" by providing the details about funding, guidelines, rules and incentives that convert vague legislation into specific programs.) They may believe policy is all important because policymaking is what they do. Still, enough has been written about the difficulties of implementation to disprove this legislative presumption.[3]

At a seminar sponsored by the Council for Excellence in Government, two former federal officials analyzed government's emphasis on policy. In government, people spend 80 percent of their time on policy and 20 percent on implementation, observed Philip Odeen, formerly a deputy assistant secretary of defense and now with Coopers and Lybrand. In business, however, people spend 20 percent of their time on policy and 80 percent on implementation. "There is the assumption in government that the important thing is policy," commented Alan K. Campbell, former director of the Office of Personnel Management and former vice chairman of ARA Services, Inc.; in government, people assume that once you get the policy right you have solved the problem.

Get the policy wrong, and everything is a disaster. This statement is true enough. But that does not mean there is any truth in the converse: Get the policy right, and everything is okay. Yet this policy myth lives on.

The Administration Metastrategy

Once Congress has passed legislation, the relevant federal department has promulgated the necessary regulations, and the state legislature has added its own guidelines, rules, and funding, state and municipal agencies still have to convert these policies into a specific program for local offices to operate.

To do this, public agencies create administrative systems. These systems are designed to facilitate—though too often to control—the behavior of the line staff. Usually the administrative objective is to create an idiot-proof system—to delineate a series of tasks so simple that no one can botch them. The result is a thick procedures manual specifying what to do in every conceivable circumstance. Of course, the authors of the procedures manual cannot conceive of every possible circumstance. Reliance on a supposedly all-encompassing manual is but one fallacy of the administrative strategy.

Administrative systems include everything from the structure of the organization to the content of the forms that people will use. These systems designate how and to whom this paperwork flows. In the case of welfare, administrative systems specify who is eligible for what services. They indicate who determines eligibility and how. They provide all the necessary specifics for the appeals process. The administrative strategy concentrates on getting all the bureaucratic routines working properly.[4]

In traditional public administration, "administration" is distinct from "policy." In 1900, Frank J. Goodnow argued that policy should be determined by the politicians.[5] Then, by creating various administrative systems, the value-free and politically neutral public administrator implements this policy as efficiently as possible. Luther Gulick captured the concern for such systems with his acronym POSDCORB, which stands for Planning, Organizing, Staffing, Directing, COordinating, Reporting, and Budgeting.[6]

As an intellectual ideal, the dichotomy between policy and administration has gone out of fashion. Few talk about it any more. Too much has been written about how a wide variety of nonelected officials—from federal cabinet secretaries to street-level bureaucrats—all make policy.[7] Neutral administration does not exist; every administrative action contains policy implications. Even the word "administration" has become antiquated, replaced by the more modern term "management."

Still, professional myths do not die easily. Indeed, the constant cry for government to adopt the techniques of business management reflects this search for efficient administrative systems. The language may be more modern—"management" not "administration"—but the core of the administration myth still lives.

In the 1980s, the General Accounting Office began conducting "management reviews" of federal agencies,[8] but in reality GAO's work concentrates on the efficiency of administrative systems. The generic title for a

GAO report reads: "Department X would have saved millions of dollars if it had better administrative systems."[9] During the Reagan administration, the Office of Management and Budget (OMB) issued a management report, *Management of the United States Government, FY 1988.* Yet this document focused almost exclusively on the financial savings generated by credit, financial, and procurement systems.[10] "Perhaps," wrote Mark A. Abramson, of the Council for Excellence in Government, this report "should be titled *Administrative Processes of the United States Government.*"[11] Both GAO and OMB have substituted the modern word "management" for the discredited one of "administration" and, if asked, would declare that the policy-administration dichotomy is dead. But their own reports belie any such obituary. The legacy of traditional public administration is repeatedly reincarnated.

The emphasis on administrative systems flows less, however, from the writing of Goodnow and Gulick than from Max Weber's beliefs in the efficiency of bureaucracy[12] and Frederick Winslow Taylor's advocacy of "scientific management." Under Taylor's scientific management (which he argued was "far better" than the "old school" of "management of initiative and incentive"), managers gather "the great mass of traditional knowledge, which in the past has been in the heads of the workmen . . . and, in many cases, finally reducing it to laws, rules, and even to mathematical formulae."[13] The purpose of these rules is to "replace the judgment of the individual workman," to provide for "absolute uniformity": "The work of every workman is fully planned out by the management at least one day in advance and each man receives in most cases complete written instructions, describing in detail the task which he is to accomplish, as well as the means to be used in doing the work . . . This task specifies not only what is to be done but how it is to be done and the exact time allowed for doing it."[14] Whether the policy area is welfare, or agriculture, or international trade, those who employ the administrative metastrategy focus on the detailed description of exactly what every individual in the organization should do.

Again, however, getting the administrative systems right is necessary, but not sufficient. In fact, it is the Administrator's Conceit to assume that once all of the administrative systems have been specified everything else is trivial—that everything will flow smoothly and as intended.[15] If somehow things do not go as planned, it is because the line workers are not following their clearly stated assignments or the line supervisors are subverting the central office's procedures. (In reality, to get the administrative systems to function properly, individuals may have to ignore the manual and work around the official but counterproductive procedures.)

Much evidence suggests that even a carefully designed administrative system can run in perverse or unintended directions, disproving this administrative presumption.[16]

Design the administrative systems badly, and nothing will work right. Again, that is obvious. But, again, one should not leap from there to the converse: Design the administrative systems correctly, and everything will work all right. Yet this administrative myth also lives.

The Leadership Metastrategy

There exists a third approach for producing results in government: the Leadership Metastrategy. This approach begins not with a "policy" or an "administrative system." Rather, the cornerstone is an inspiring mission combined with a specific goal. For example, the mission might be to move families from welfare to work; the accompanying goal would be to place 50,000 welfare recipients in jobs over the next five years. "Whenever anything is being accomplished," writes Peter Drucker, "it is being done, I have learned, by a monomaniac with a mission."[17]

The next step is not, however, to develop the correct "policy" for accomplishing the mission. Nor is the next step to design an administrative structure for achieving the objective. Rather, the first step is simply to concentrate on the mission and its coordinate goal. Following this metastrategy, the manager talks constantly about the mission. Boldly and repeatedly, the manager proclaims both mission and goal. The manager leaves no doubt about what the goal is. Nor, when the time comes, will there be much doubt about whether the goal has been achieved.

Next the manager takes an unorthodox step, telling every individual in the organization what he or she must accomplish to achieve the agency's overall goal. No longer are people solely responsible for carrying out policy. No longer are people solely accountable for following administrative procedures. Now they too have both a mission and a specific goal to go with it. Now each subunit—and each manager of each subunit—has its own, visible, unambiguous goal, and there can be little doubt about whether this goal has been achieved. And attached to these individual goals are rewards: praise, thanks, public recognition.

But, complain the troops, "This cannot be done. No one has ever done this before. We don't know how to do it. And besides, we don't have the resources." To which the manager replies:

Whether it has been done before is irrelevant. It *can* be done. And we will do it. Your job (or the job of your successor) is to do your part.

> Moreover, your job is to figure out *how* to do it. I don't know how to do it. I'm sitting here in my ivory tower at headquarters. You out there in the field have a much better idea about how to do it. My job is to help you figure out how to do it. Furthermore—and this may be more useful—my job is to keep you informed about what other people, in other parts of the organization, have figured out.
>
> Also, my job is to get you the resources necessary to achieve your objective. So don't tell me that you can't achieve the objective. Tell me what you need to do it, and I'll get it for you.

The manager has reversed the traditional responsibilities. Headquarters will not promulgate detailed routines that tell everyone exactly how to do everything. The field will figure out how to do it. And when the field explains what resources it needs to do it, the overhead units have the job of getting the resources for the line workers. The leadership metastrategy is, in fact, precisely what Taylor called the "old school"—the "management of initiative and incentive."[18]

This approach requires chutzpah. The manager must define success and then attempt to achieve it. He places himself squarely on his own line—in front of his organization, the legislature, his elected political boss, the press, and the voters. The manager must produce against a very specific benchmark that he has created.

The leadership metastrategy flows from the ideas of Thomas J. Peters and Gordon Chase. Both emphasize purpose—the mission of a government agency or business firm—what Peters calls "the dominating value" or the "singleness of focus."[19] As head of New York City's Health Services Administration (HSA), Chase met with his top managers: "I would . . . ask them what they'd been doing—what their agencies or units or programs had been up to in the last few weeks or months or years. Some of these senior officials would start by telling me how many meetings they had attended, how many memos they'd written, how many staff they'd hired, and similar benchmarks of bureaucratic activity. I'd look at them and say: 'But whom did you make healthy today (or last week, or last year)? Did you make anybody in New York healthier—and how do you know?'"[20] A leader must communicate a purpose throughout the organization. Moreover, cautions Peters, a manager's "overt verbal communications are only part of the story. Consciously or unconsciously, the senior executive is constantly acting out the vision and goals he is trying to realize."[21]

Next, the manager assigns responsibilities for producing results. At the same time, he provides resources and flexibility to ensure that these results can be achieved. "Performance—the ability to deliver against multiple odds, and to deliver quickly and consistently—is what matters," writes Chase. "As manager, your mission must be, first and foremost, to make government work—to decide what values you have, how they relate to government's role, how that translates into government programs, and how you can make those programs work."[22]

The Leader's Conceit is to assume that setting goals, measuring results, and rewarding performance is all the manager need do. Indeed, Peters has been accused of ignoring the importance of the more traditional factors of production that are necessary to achieve a business firm's goals.[23] Similarly, following the leadership metastrategy in government, a manager might ignore the need for adequate authorizing legislation, sufficient budgetary or personnel resources, or the appropriate administrative support (such as systems for computers, personnel, procurement, or contracting).

Mark H. Moore of Harvard University has critiqued Chase's approach to public management. Chase made "extravagant promises that could not be reliably fulfilled," writes Moore. "And his commitment to evaluating them and finding out whether they were really successful was quite weak compared to his zeal for launching them." Further, Moore argues, Chase's penchant for undertaking special innovative projects—in areas such as lead poisoning and methadone maintenance—meant that, as HSA's administrator, he ignored most units within the organization and "did not . . . reposition its main line operations to increase their productivity and value."[24]

Moore also emphasizes Chase's failure, at HSA, to make any long-run improvements in administrative systems. "He found ways to circumvent and avoid the overhead agencies that managed money, people, and contracts," writes Moore. "Thus, the financial systems, the civil service system, and the contracting system remained much as he found them—obstacles to effective innovation, and for that reason, obstacles to re-positioning organizations for improved performance."[25] The leadership presumption—that the mission is all that really counts—can lead one to ignore the need for adequate support from formal policy and administrative systems.

Chase was a project manager. At HSA, he took on a series of projects: testing children for lead poisoning; providing methadone to heroin addicts; delivering health care to prison inmates. Such project management is "more visible and glamorous" than operations management, observes Stephen R. Rosenthal of Boston University. In government, continues

Rosenthal, "project management gets more than its share of the lime-light. Ongoing management of day-to-day public services deserves greater attention from everyone who wants to help government produce more and better results."[26]

In contrast, Charles M. Atkins, commissioner of the Massachusetts Department of Public Welfare, converted project management into operations management. Taking the concepts of project management that he had learned from Chase, he applied them to the task of organization management: he made everyone part of his agency's one big project, ET. But rather than work around his dysfunctional overhead units, Atkins changed them significantly. When he left the department after nearly six years, these units were major contributors to the mission of the agency.

Fail to establish a mission and set goals, and little or nothing happens. With only policy and administrative systems, no one is responsible for producing results. Process reigns. The overhead units run the organization. People will follow the regulations and the procedures, but they will pay little attention to making sure that their work achieves any purpose.

Get the goals wrong, and the wrong things happen. People will pursue these goals in ways that contravene the true mission of the agency. Thus, defining the mission and selecting the goals is a major task of leadership. Not only does the manager want to avoid the creation of perverse incentives; he also wants to define a single, specific goal such that the efforts to achieve it also result in the realization of secondary, ancillary goals, all of which contribute to the necessarily less well defined, less easily measurable mission of the agency.

Again, however, the converse does not hold. Even if the manager gets the mission and goals right, there is no guarantee of success. To assert otherwise would be to create a leadership myth. To accomplish the mission, the manager needs policies and administrative systems to support those charged with achieving the accompanying objective. For success—for results—the manager must put together policy, administration, and leadership.

These three metastrategies are not mutually exclusive. As described here, they are extreme or ideal types—caricatures that are rarely found in the real world. They might be more appropriately called not "strategies" but "emphases," or "approaches," or "styles." Someone who is concerned primarily with the design of a policy has taken a "policy emphasis." Someone who focuses on the creation of an administrative system has assumed an "administrative style." Someone who concentrates on articulating a vision and achieving some very specific goals has adopted a "leadership approach."

The Relation between Policy, Administration, and Leadership

A public manager cannot pursue such a leadership approach independent of existing policy. Fortunately, such policies are usually (and necessarily) vague, giving a manager some flexibility in establishing a mission, in setting goals, and in achieving them.

ET CHOICES was obviously dependent upon the policies of the federal government. The original mandate from Secretary of Human Services Manuel Carballo to his Work and Welfare Advisory Task Force was to design a program compatible with federal policies. ET had to mesh with both WIN and AFDC. Indeed, the 99 percent reimbursement provided by WIN and the 50 percent reimbursement available under AFDC were important to ET. Similarly, ET was dependent upon numerous state policies. At the beginning, the funding for WTP in Governor Edward J. King's last budget was crucial, as was the policy that permitted the new commissioner to reorganize his executive staff.

ET CHOICES could not have been created as it was without numerous policies of the federal and state governments. But those policies were not the driving force behind ET. Rather, ET was designed with existing policies in mind and shaped in several important ways to mesh with them. Further, those policies were not constraints to be feared but opportunities to be exploited. ET, a *de facto* voluntary state program, operated under WIN, a *de jure* mandatory federal program, because the program's managers saw how to fulfill the letter—and, in many ways, the spirit—of the federal regulations while still pursuing their own mission.

Having established mission and goals, the manager may still need some new policies. For example, when the state of Washington developed its new welfare, training, and employment program, it designed one that actually required new federal legislation. If given a choice, however, most public managers prefer to function with existing (albeit inadequate) legislation, rather than open their agency to additional legislative scrutiny and perhaps to legislation that creates as many new constraints as opportunities. And even if the legislature enacts precisely the bill that the manager wants, it can take months—often years—to pass the new policy.

Similarly, adopting a leadership strategy does not mean that the agency head can ignore administrative systems. They are critical for any organization. But they do not come first. Rather, as the line units answer their headquarters' question, "What resources does your unit need to achieve your objectives?" headquarters can begin to provide those resources, including the supporting administrative systems.

Indeed, the Massachusetts Department of Public Welfare spent over five years developing and searching for effective administrative systems —everything from the proper mix of contractors that local ET workers could use to achieve their goals, to improved eligibility forms, to information about how the best local offices actually go about using these contractors and other resources to move recipients from welfare to work. And this search for better administrative systems goes on.

As welfare commissioner, Atkins could undertake to move people from welfare to work because this mission was consistent with the purposes of his agency. It fit the broad mandate that his department had from both the state legislature and the federal government. If he had chosen to build housing for AFDC families, he could easily have found himself in conflict with local housing authorities and the state's Executive Office of Communities and Development. In fact, in attempting to educate, train, and find jobs for Massachusetts's poor, Atkins could have placed himself in direct conflict with the Department of Social Services (DSS). After all, what social service could be more important than helping a chronically unemployed person become financially self-sufficient? But DSS chose to define its mission narrowly—to focus on providing protective services for children. That focus gave Atkins the policy opportunity to pursue his mission (with his leadership strategy).

Similarly, Atkins could undertake to help welfare recipients find a route out of poverty because the administrative systems were in place to do so. Semiannually, at the time of eligibility redetermination, his agency had personal contact with every welfare recipient in the state. Moreover, there existed the Division of Employment Security, which knew how to find jobs for people (if not specifically for welfare recipients). And there existed the Office of Employment and Training and its regional contractors, which provided job training under the federal Job Training and Partnership Act. The basics of the administrative apparatus necessary to run ET already existed when Atkins became welfare commissioner, again providing him with the opportunity to pursue his mission (with his leadership strategy).

Atkins was free to focus his department's energies on moving people from welfare to work because there already existed a policy and administrative foundation on which to build. That the policy was not all that explicit and the administrative system rudimentary did not deter him. A public manager can rarely expect otherwise. But to make the existing administrative structure achieve the policy, Atkins needed a leadership strategy.

Dumb Luck

In American government, the leadership strategy has been under utilized. Yet it was clearly the approach taken by Atkins. Moreover, he recruited people such as Deputy Commissioner Thomas P. Glynn and Associate Commissioners Jolie Bain Pillsbury and Barbara Burke-Tatum who shared his perspective. Was their success a consequence of their leadership approach? Certainly, there can be alternative explanations. After all, the basic policies and administrative systems already existed. Maybe ET's leadership team was simply lucky.

Maybe inspiring leadership had nothing to do with ET's success. Maybe they did not grope along intelligently. Maybe they just stumbled along unwittingly. Maybe they were not especially smart or even particularly good managers. Maybe they were merely in the right place at the right time. In science, write Nathan Spielberg and Bryon D. Anderson, professors of physics at Kent State, "Often dumb luck, sometimes called serendipity, plays a role either in revealing a key piece of information or in revealing a particularly simple solution."[27] Maybe what happened in Massachusetts was just "dumb luck"—the fortuitous coincidence of several factors.

The Massachusetts economy. During most of the 1980s, the state's economy was booming. In 1983, the unemployment rate in the United States was 9.6 percent, but only 6.9 percent in Massachusetts. A year later, the U.S. figure was 7.5 percent, while in Massachusetts it was 4.8 percent.[28] Obviously, welfare recipients will find jobs much more easily when there are fewer other job seekers with whom to compete. Said Atkins at the first Framingham press conference in June 1984: "I think it would be very difficult to do if it weren't for the economy."[29]

Personnel flexibility. Atkins inherited from the King administration the ability to reorganize the managerial structure of his department. He could create new positions and set higher salaries for these positions; he could recruit into his agency new, talented managers who would be loyal to him and his mission. A new manager who lacks the ability to make staff changes will find the task of moving the organization in a new direction difficult and time consuming.

A state-run welfare system. In two-thirds of the states, AFDC is administered by county welfare departments. In the other one-third (including Massachusetts), AFDC is run directly by the state welfare department. Given Atkins's management style, the state's administrative arrangement was essential. Indeed, in 1983, Atkins was so concerned about his ability to influence the local directors that only some very determined aides were able to dissuade him from advertising and refilling every one of these management jobs. How does a state welfare commissioner influence the behavior of local-office directors who are hired by the county commissioners? Only indirectly. Atkins's system of setting goals, monitoring results, and rewarding success could not have worked as it did if every local-office director reported to the local political establishment.

An existing program. When ET was designed in 1983, Atkins did not have to create an entirely new program, policy, or administrative apparatus. He could simply modify WTP. He needed to have the federal policy regulators sign off on his changes. But that was the only approval he needed. He did not need to go to the state legislature for new authorizing legislation or for more funds. The fewer people who must approve an initiative, the easier it is to get it up and running.

"The best thing that happened to us," said Burke-Tatum, "was to never have [to submit new] legislation, which could get amended [to] where it didn't even look like it made sense." For an agency head who is pursuing a leadership metastrategy, the need to obtain additional legislation can create numerous problems. The proposed legislation can, as Burke-Tatum observed, be amended—or even replaced with new language that does not provide the necessary authorizations. New, conflicting, or absurd guidelines, rules, and incentives can be locked into law. Moreover, to win new legislation, the manager must go public and sell his program; to put together a legislative majority, the manager may have to overpromise on future results—an easy ticket to failure. Or some enthusiastic legislative aide may write unrealistic deadlines into the bill.[30]

The legislature did not create ET CHOICES. The executive branch developed it almost exclusively. Thus Atkins and company could grope along, adjusting the program as they learned (rather than having to explain inadequacies to the legislature and seek legal modifications to make the necessary alterations). ET did not develop along the lines of a traditional multi-phase model of the policy process: from the "recognition" of a problem, through the "selection" of a policy by the legislature, and on to "implementation" of this policy by the legislatively designated agency.[31]

Rather, because no legislation was required, the department could do everything from problem recognition to program revision. The department's leaders had their own idea; they wanted to make it work; and they provided their own internal motivation to make it happen. And because they did not really need much additional authorization, they did not seek it.

Little (early) criticism. During the first year of ET CHOICES, there was no criticism from academics, state legislators, federal regulators, or the press. The program was an internal undertaking; it was invisible. Because so few people knew about it, no one criticized it. And the longer one can avoid outside scrutiny, the easier it is to work out the problems inherent in any new endeavor. As Atkins wrote to Burke-Tatum, "It is not often in government that one has an opportunity to both implement a program *and* fix problems which may be clear only after the program has been in operation for a year or more."[32]

In contrast, the process that produced California's welfare, training, and work program (called Greater Avenues for Independence, or GAIN) was very public. The authorizing legislation, enacted in 1985, was a compromise between the Republican governor, George Deukmejian, and the Democratic legislature. The program began on July 1, 1986, and a year later was operating in ten of the state's fifty-eight counties (which administer AFDC in California). Soon state legislators, academics, and journalists were offering analyses, criticisms, and recommendations for major modifications of the program. GAIN's visibility prevented its managers from quietly fixing the program as they went along.[33]

Conjugal coordination. When Atkins agreed to manage the welfare department, Kristin Demong, his wife, was already the director of the Division of Employment Security. What luck! A manager with any talent ought to be able to gain some cooperation from another agency headed by his or her spouse.

Gubernatorial support. At the first press conference in Framingham, Governor Dukakis became an enthusiastic champion of ET CHOICES. Observed a panel from the National Academy of Public Administration: "A strong commitment from the governor is necessary to make a cross-cutting [welfare-to-work] program like this work."[34] At the same time, what public manager could not produce results if he reports to a popular elected official who is a passionate and persistent partisan of his key program? "Big and bold initiatives like ET require the support of the Governor," said Atkins. "If you don't have the Governor's support, you have to be prepared to adjust your goals downward. If you do have his support, you have to be prepared to raise your goals if he wishes."[35] Dukakis liked ET so much that, in January 1985, he decided—without consulting his commissioner—to raise the five-year goal from 40,000 to 50,000 placements.

Managerial continuity. "Here is an irony," writes Rosabeth Moss Kanter of Harvard University: *"change requires stability."* In particular, change requires stability in leadership: "Continuity of people is a related requirement, or else one is constantly beginning again, without progress."[36] Atkins, Glynn, Burke-Tatum, and Pillsbury—all four of ET's top managers—spent at least four and a half years in the welfare department. They provided consistent direction and created an ongoing commitment to ET. If the leadership had been constantly changing—as is common in public agencies—they would have been unable to focus energies and attention on making ET work.[37]

Wisdom and Luck in Management

Atkins, Dukakis, and Massachusetts were indeed lucky in many different ways. When arguing that any success of ET was due to dumb luck, not managerial skill, detractors most frequently mention the Massachusetts economy. But other circumstances that Atkins and Dukakis inherited were at least as important: personnel flexibility, a state-run welfare system, and an existing program. In fact, of these four factors, the state-administered AFDC program was the most crucial to how ET CHOICES was managed; Atkins's approach to managing for performance would not have been as productive if the local-office directors had not reported to the state department.

But none of these four inherited circumstances—not even the booming Massachusetts economy[38]—guaranteed success. Each stroke of luck provided an opportunity. Yet Atkins's management team had to exploit each lucky strike. The low unemployment rate told the department's managers that there were jobs available; but it did not tell them where these jobs were located or how to prepare welfare clients to fill them. (During Dukakis's first term, the unemployment rate dropped from 12 to 6 percent, while the AFDC caseload grew 15 percent. "A booming economy has nothing to do with welfare," argued Atkins. Those on welfare "don't get a shot at those jobs without a high-school diploma and someone to look after their kids."[39]) WTP, a state-run welfare system, and personnel flexibility provided something with which to work. But when Atkins, Glynn, Burke-Tatum, and Pillsbury took over in 1983 there were no memos on their desks explaining how to do it. Luck requires wisdom— the ability to recognize when circumstances are propitious and to know how to take advantage of them.

The other four fortunate factors—little early criticism, conjugal coordination, gubernatorial support, managerial continuity—were not merely inherited circumstances. They may appear to be the product of dumb luck but in fact they were at least partially created.

The existence of WTP helped insulate ET from early criticism. But in

August 1983 when the WIN Waiver was submitted, or 45 days later when the waiver was approved and the program began, Governor Dukakis could have announced ET with much fanfare. This is traditional when employing the policy metastrategy: create a program—or merely the idea for a program—and proclaim it to the world. But Dukakis and Atkins kept quiet until they had something specific to announce. And when they did go public, it was not with a proposal, which is easy to attack, but with their first year's results, which were difficult (without some sophisticated analysis) to criticize.

Similarly, the marriage of the welfare commissioner and the DES director was no guarantee that these agencies would cooperate. Obviously it facilitated communication between the two agency heads; it even ensured that their key deputies would not want to be caught failing to return each other's phone calls. But it was no guarantee that the directors of a pair of local welfare and employment-security offices would work in harmony; nor did it ensure the cooperation between individual employment-security and ET workers that was necessary to move specific recipients from welfare to work.

Dukakis's support for ET was obviously important. When a manager's governor regularly participates in his various awards ceremonies and brags about the manager's program on national television, it helps in many ways: it convinces people inside the agency that their work is important, and it helps gain cooperation from those outside. Yet Dukakis's passion for ET did not just happen. Rather, Atkins, Glynn, and Lee Chelminiak (the director of communications) helped to create that enthusiasm with the original Framingham press conference, from which both ET and the governor received significant press coverage. Once that press event worked so well, the department had no trouble convincing the governor to do the next one. Moreover, whenever there was good news about ET—or about the AFDC error rate—Atkins did not announce it. He asked the governor to do that. Dukakis became a vocal advocate for ET because its management team provided a mechanism for him to be one and (in the process) to gain positive attention from journalists and the public. Then Atkins made that gubernatorial support work for him inside and outside his organization.

The continuity in ET's leadership did not just happen, either. Traditionally, the political managers who head agencies in government are in-and-outers, staying two or three years before moving on to bigger jobs and better opportunities. For managers who generate attention, these job opportunities can come frequently. Write Sapolsky, Alsenberg, and Morone: "A governor or commissioner, anxious to create an innovative administration, may bring into state government a team of able assistants to design new programs. However, the presentation of new ideas often brings the designers widespread attention and career opportunities such as the chance to serve in a larger jurisdiction—the Call to Rome perhaps. The reward for creativity draws talent away from state government at the point when the ideas are being implemented and refined. The understandable urge to seize opportunities for advancement removes the very people best able to complete the process of innovation."[40] Further, a governor is tempted to "make better use" of his best managers: "If this guy has done such a good job in the welfare department, why don't I move him over to mental health where I really have problems?" Dukakis, however, resisted this temptation. In fact, he even called a local "emperor" to ensure that one of his best managers did not get such a "Call to Rome." Atkins worked to ensure that Dukakis was continuously supporting ET; Dukakis worked to ensure that Atkins was continuously managing it.

Certainly, Dukakis, Atkins, Glynn, Pillsbury, and Burke-Tatum were lucky—just as a scientist making a new discovery is lucky. But the luck of the scientist stumbling upon some new experimental evidence comes only after hours of thought and toil. This work creates the circumstances from which the evidence emerges—apparently serendipitously. And even the scientist who is exposed to such new evidence still must be wise enough to recognize its implications. ET's managers worked to create the circumstances out of which could flow some serendipity and, then, were able both to recognize this dumb luck and exploit it.

You Can't Do Only One Thing

Being lucky is not easy. Even if you create the necessary circumstances, even if you recognize your luck, and even if you understand how to exploit these opportunities, you may despair at the magnitude of the task confronting you. To be lucky, you can't do only one thing.[41]

A welfare, training, and work program has many components: career-assessment, day care, child support, education, training, job placement, and transition services. In addition to these formal pieces, there is the more amorphous, psychological component of convincing welfare recipients not only to enroll in the program but to really try—to try to make the day-care arrangements successful, to try to learn the material in the training program, to try to find a decent job, to try to be successful in that job, and to try to cope with the inevitable crises that (without some serious effort) can easily drive a family back to welfare. To make a welfare, training, and work program work, you can't do only one thing. To move families from welfare to work, the manager has no programmatic silver bullet.

Similarly, to make all those programmatic components work, the manager has no managerial silver bullet. Articulating a mission that reflects the mood of the times is not, itself, enough. Measuring results alone will not accomplish much. Neither will marketing. Creating an organization with simultaneous loose-tight properties is not, singly, of much value. Nor are persistence and enthusiasm, by themselves, adequate. To attack any specific task effectively, the manager must discriminatingly deploy an entire corps of managerial concepts. (Or, to switch metaphors: To create any culinary delicacy, the manager uses not just a single ingredient but artfully adapts a standard recipe, carefully blending in those ingredients listed on the recipe and those suggested by experience.)

Although the public manager may focus on one mission—with one goal to motivate performance—he cannot concentrate on only one action to achieve that goal or accomplish that mission. The manager can't do only one thing right and be successful. He needs a multifarious strategy that reflects the mission to be achieved and the goals to be met, the existing (and potential) capabilities of the organization, the opportunities for funding, the need to motivate people, the personalities who hold power in the legislature, and the behavior of journalists. To be effective, the public manager must exploit the available opportunities while, somehow, overcoming the most critical barriers.

Context Is Everything

The specifics of the leadership metastrategy used to manage ET CHOICES in Massachusetts cannot be replicated anyplace else. They won't work. Atkins, Glynn, Pillsbury, and Burke-Tatum cannot be cloned. Nor can ET. The political, organizational, and economic environment will be different. So must the strategy.

But the general principles of public management employed by Atkins, Glynn, Burke-Tatum, and Pillsbury to make ET work can be adapted in other states to run other welfare, training, and work programs. In fact, the principles are very adaptable. These general concepts of leadership and management can be applied to manage public enterprises from the federal Department of the Interior to a municipal fire department.

Moreover, none of the management concepts employed by the Massachusetts Department of Public Welfare is new. Every management idea that they used has been discussed extensively in books and articles. Atkins did not undertake to invent an entirely new management system. Rather, he put into practice the ideas taught to him by his mentor Gordon Chase.

But do not belittle the accomplishment. After all, there may be very little left about management to invent. In *The Classic Touch: Lessons in Leadership from Homer to Hemingway,* John K. Clemens and Douglas F. Mayer, of Hartwick College, argue: "the problems that are central to effective leadership—motivation, inspiration, sensitivity, and communication—have changed little in the past 3,000 years. These problems were faced by the Egyptians when they built the pyramids, by Alexander when he created his empire, and by the Greeks when they battled the Trojans."[42] Modern managers, conclude Clemens and Mayer, have much to learn from the classics. Argues Rosabeth Moss Kanter, "The problem before us [managers] is not to invent more tools, but to use the ones we have."[43]

Fledgling managers should not expect to find—either at the central office of the Massachusetts Department of Public Welfare or the corporate headquarters of Hewlett-Packard—people inventing brilliant new managerial concepts. Rather, they should look for people applying standard managerial ideas to new management problems. The challenge to the manager is not to develop new ideas. The manager's challenge is to select from the vast array of existing ideas those that are most appropriate for the current task, and then to adapt these ideas to the unique features, complications, and circumstances of this undertaking.

In management, context is everything. What Edmund Burke said about the principles of politics applies equally to the principles of management: "Circumstances . . . give in reality to every political principle its distinguishing colour and discriminating effect. The circumstances are what render every civil and political scheme beneficial or noxious."[44] The value of any managerial concept lies not in its abstract beauty but in its ability to help managers cope with a diversity of managerial challenges. Conversely, the manager's skill lies in understanding the current circumstances, selecting the most appropriate concepts from his own repertoire of approaches, and fitting these approaches to the circumstances.

The Tasks of Leadership

To achieve public purposes, leadership counts. What influences the quality of the education in an elementary school? Leadership by the principal.[45] What determines the quality of life in a prison? Leadership by the warden.[46] What affects the performance of a welfare, training, and employment program? Leadership by the department's top managers.

The 100th Congress debated whether welfare, training, and work programs should be voluntary or mandatory. And yet this policy choice—despite its obvious ideological symbolism—may not have been the important issue. The determining question may still remain: How best to manage the policy that the Congress did adopt? Whether the JOBS program (Job Opportunities and Basic Skills) contained in the Family Support Act of 1988 is managed well or badly will have more impact on welfare expenditures, welfare caseloads, and welfare dependency than whether it is voluntary or mandatory.[47] A well-managed mandatory program will be significantly better than a poorly managed voluntary program. Conversely, a well-managed voluntary program will be much better than a poorly managed mandatory one.

Making a welfare, training, and employment program work is a complex task. To achieve the program's objectives, the heads of state and local welfare agencies will have to solve several specific management problems:

- The coordination problem—getting the various governmental and nonprofit organizations that are responsible for different parts of the program to work together in providing useful assistance to people with an array of individual and special needs.
- The motivation problem—getting (for example) social workers whose primary responsibility has been determining who is eligible to receive public assistance to concentrate their intelligence and their energies on an entirely different mission.
- The technical problem—determining precisely what mix of specific services will prove most effective in moving people from welfare to work.
- The budgetary problem—finding the resources and flexibility to undertake such a major new initiative at a time when federal funding for innovative social programs has almost disappeared.
- The overhead-agency problem—making sure that the people who run the support units (from procurement to personnel) are not so enamored with the details of their rules and regulations that they lose sight of the mission that they are supposed to support.
- The political problem—generating the understanding and support from constituent groups, legislators, journalists, public-employee unions, and the electorate that is necessary for any public program to succeed.

Moving people from welfare to work is not like innoculating people with the polio vaccine or writing checks to welfare recipients. A welfare, training, and employment program is really an interrelated collection of many programs that have to function in concert. Occasionally, the effectiveness of a single one of these activities may be enough to move a family from welfare through training to work. In most circumstances, however, the failure of any one of the components—an inability to locate a job that matches the individual's training, a breakdown in day-care services—can convert a would-be success story into another long-term welfare case. To produce meaningful results—not simply for one welfare family, but for many such families—the program must be well managed.

The leadership team at the Massachusetts Department of Public Welfare solved the coordination, motivation, technical, budgetary, overhead-agency, and political problems required to make ET CHOICES work. Not completely, not permanently, not universally, and not even to their own satisfaction. Compared, however, with many other public agencies (not just compared with other state welfare departments, but also with federal agencies, municipal offices, and even many businesses), the department's leadership had some significant managerial successes:

- Different state agencies that once barely knew of each other's existence actively cooperated.
- People who never thought of trying to help a welfare recipient find a job did so aggressively; welfare recipients who had never tried to look for work did so successfully.
- Across the state, local welfare offices offered a combination of different services—basic education, job training, employment search, day care, transportation, medical care, and counseling and follow-up.
- The department designed a program to take advantage of the available federal funding and then convinced the budget bureau, the governor, and the legislature to provide the rest.
- The overhead units within the department actually operated under the principle that the staff should serve the line.
- Many welfare recipients, corporate executives, legislators, journalists, union leaders, and citizens understood the program, what it did, how it worked, and what it accomplished—and they supported it.

Even those who think ET did not place enough welfare recipients in jobs or that the only measure of the program's success is the reduction in the caseload will recognize these managerial achievements. Anyone familiar with the efforts of public agencies to undertake programs of similar complexity will appreciate the management accomplishment of ET CHOICES.[48] The program is worthy of analysis. It provides important lessons that will prove helpful to managers of welfare, training, and work programs, to managers of state welfare departments, to managers of other public agencies, and—perhaps—to managers of a few businesses.

Over the first five years of ET CHOICES, the leadership team at the Massachusetts Department of Public Welfare demonstrated that leadership counts.

Notes

Preface

1. John J. Mitchell, Mark Lincoln Chadwin, and Demetra Smith Nightingale, *Implementing Welfare-Employment Programs: An Institutional Analysis of the Work Incentive (WIN) Program* (Washington, D.C.: The Urban Institute, October 1979), p. xiii. See also Mark Lincoln Chadwin, John J. Mitchell, and Demetra Smith Nightingale, "Reforming Welfare: Lessons from the WIN Experience," *Public Administration Review*, 41 (May/June 1981), pp. 372–380.
2. In a study of WIN programs in New York State, Lawrence M. Mead also found a set of characteristics of local offices that distinguished the high performers including "innovative, entrepreneurial leadership," "an informal management style," "clear accountability for performance," "personnel with energy, commitment, and a sense of responsibility for results." See Mead, *Beyond Entitlement: The Social Obligations of Citizenship* (New York: The Free Press, 1986), p. 151.

Prologue

1. Richard Gaines and Michael Segal, *Dukakis and the Reform Impulse* (Boston: Quinlan Press, 1987), p. 120; Charles Kenney and Robert L. Turner, *Dukakis: An American Odyssey* (Boston: Houghton Mifflin, 1988), p. 90.
2. Barry Friedman et al., *An Evaluation of the Massachusetts Work Experience Program* (Waltham, Mass.: Center for Employment and Income Studies, Heller Graduate School, Brandeis University, October 1980). See also Gaines and Segal, *Dukakis and the Reform Impulse*, p. 146; Kenney and Turner, *Dukakis*, pp. 102–104.
3. Michael S. Dukakis, "Inaugural Address," January 6, 1983, mimeo, p. 2.
4. "Governor Dukakis Appoints Charles M. Atkins Commissioner of Public Welfare; Dr. Bailus Walker to Be Commissioner of Public Health," press release issued by the office of Governor Michael S. Dukakis, May 9, 1983.

5. Eileen McNamara, "Welfare snag leaves mother, girl homeless," *The Boston Globe*, May 13, 1983.

6. Ibid.

7. Eileen McNamara, "Welfare counsel fired by Atkins," *The Boston Globe*, May 14, 1983.

8. Letter from Charles M. Atkins to JoAnne Ross (acting associate commissioner for family assistance, Department of Health and Human Services), August 16, 1983.

9. "Jobs plan pays off" (editorial), *The Boston Herald*, June 28, 1984.

10. William Raspberry, "Choosing Work Over Welfare," *The Washington Post*, July 6, 1984.

11. Michael S. Dukakis, "Opportunity for All," State of the State Address, Delivered before Both Houses of the General Court of Massachusetts, January 16, 1985, pp. 12–13.

12. "13,000th recipient off welfare, into job," *The Patriot Ledger* (of Quincy, Mass.), February 11, 1985.

13. Don Ebbeling, "Welfare agency lauded," *The Morning Union* (in Springfield, Mass.), June 5, 1985.

14. Kenneth J. Cooper, "Dukakis says job program has cut state's welfare rolls," *The Boston Globe*, October 30, 1985.

15. Michael K. Frisby, "Job-training program may end, officials say," *The Boston Globe*, April 20, 1986.

16. Massachusetts Taxpayers Foundation, "MTF's Outstanding Public Servant for 1986," December 1986.

17. Joan Fallon, "Taxpayers' group honors welfare chief for quiet efficiency," *The Middlesex News*, December 20, 1986.

18. "Credit where due" (editorial), *The Boston Herald*, December 18, 1986.

19. Lou Storrow, "Atkins edit" (letter to the editor), *The Boston Herald*, January 1, 1987.

20. "Exclusive Interview with Dukakis," *Boston Business Journal*, January 1987.

21. Photocopy of "Opening Remarks" of various individuals at the announcement of Dukakis's presidential candidacy.

22. Michael S. Dukakis, "Statement on the Occasion of the Announcement of His Candidacy for President of the United States of America," Boston Common, April 29, 1987, p. 4.

23. David S. Broder, "Dukakis Joins '88 Race with 'Growth' Theme," *The Washington Post*, April 30, 1987.

24. Tom Morganthau, "Welfare: A New Drive to Clean Up the Mess," *Newsweek*, February 2, 1987, p. 25.

25. Ronald Brownstein, "Running on His Record," *National Journal*, July 18, 1987, p. 1832.

26. Nicholas Lemann, "Welfare Goes 'Constitutional,'" *The Washington Post*, March 13, 1987.

27. Robert R. Bliss, "Dukakis uses some hoopla to tout ET program," *The Evening Gazette* (in Worcester, Mass.), June 23, 1988.

28. Massachusetts Department of Public Welfare, "ET Fact Sheet Update," June 20, 1988.

29. Eric Fehrnstrom, "Duke calls for reform of welfare," *The Boston Herald,* June 23, 1988.

30. Judy Katz, "Dukakis hails 50,000th success scored by welfare job program," *The Berkshire Eagle,* June 23, 1988.

31. Madeline Patton, "Dukakis drops a local name during his speech to the nation," *The Evening Gazette* (in Worcester, Mass.), July 22, 1988.

32. Neal R. Peirce, "His Name Is Mud, But Dukakis Still Innovates," *National Journal,* October 28, 1989, p. 2648.

33. Mark Starr, "The Fall of Michael Dukakis," *Newsweek,* January 8, 1990, p. 39.

34. M. E. Malone, "The budget: grim history, future doubts," *The Boston Globe,* August 1, 1990.

35. David Nyhan, "Keverian says House would pass tax hike if Dukakis resigned, Sees lawmakers swayed by anger at governor," *The Boston Globe,* April 12, 1990.

1. The Idea behind ET CHOICES

1. Office of Research, Planning and Evaluation, *An Evaluation of the Massachusetts Employment and Training Choices Program: Interim Findings on Participation and Outcomes, FY84–FY85* (Boston: Massachusetts Department of Public Welfare, January 1986), p. 1.

2. One such source, based on a study of Massachusetts welfare recipients, is Leonard Goodwin, *Causes and Cures of Welfare: New Evidence on the Social Psychology of the Poor* (Lexington, Mass.: Lexington Books, 1983). Judith M. Gueron, president of Manpower Demonstration Research Corporation (MDRC), draws the same conclusion from the numerous evaluations her organization has conducted of welfare, training, and work programs: "These results are consistent with the findings of prior studies that show that the poor want to work and are eager to take advantage of opportunities to do so. As one of MDRC's field researchers observed: These workfare programs did not create the work ethic, they found it." Gueron, *Work Initiatives for Welfare Recipients* (New York: Manpower Demonstration Research Corporation, March 1986), p. 14.

3. Robert R. Bliss, "Dukakis outlines ET accomplishments," *The Evening Gazette* (in Worcester, Mass.), September 30, 1986.

4. Charles M. Atkins, "Evaluation of Employment and Training Contractors: Corrective Action Plan," February 20, 1986, p. 4.

5. David T. Ellwood, *Divide and Conquer: Responsible Security for America's Poor* (New York: The Ford Foundation, 1987), p. 13.

6. Office of Research, Planning and Evaluation, *An Evaluation of the Massachusetts Employment and Training Choices Program,* pp. 8–9.

7. Lucy A. Williams et al., "Recommendations of the Work and Welfare Advisory Task Force," May 13, 1982, Executive Summary, pp. 1–2.

8. National Academy of Public Administration, "Welfare Reform Dialogue: Implementation and Operational Feasibility Issues," proceedings of a panel dis-

cussion (July 21, 1987) conducted for the General Accounting Office at the request of the Committee on Governmental Affairs of the United States Senate, January 1988, pp. v–vi.

9. Lawrence M. Mead, *Beyond Entitlement: The Social Obligations of Citizenship* (New York: The Free Press, 1986), p. 160. Mead was not, however, the first one to reach this conclusion. See, for example, John J. Mitchell, Mark Lincoln Chadwin, and Demetra Smith Nightingale, *Implementing Welfare-Employment Programs: An Institutional Analysis of the Work Incentive (WIN) Program* (Washington, D.C.: The Urban Institute, October 1979), p. 161.

10. Kevin Landrigan, "Dukakis balks at welfare mother job plan," *The Sun* (of Lowell, Mass.), February 20, 1987.

11. Scott Lehigh, "Welfare Warfare: Dukakis and the alms race," *The Boston Phoenix,* January 13, 1987.

12. Charles M. Atkins, "20,000 Choose Paycheck over Welfare Check: Massachusetts' ET Is Different because of Choice," *Public Welfare,* Winter 1986, p. 21.

13. There are also some practical disagreements. Are voluntary programs harder to implement because they require social workers to recruit volunteers? Or are mandatory programs harder to implement because social workers have to devote time to sanctioning nonparticipants?

14. Mead, *Beyond Entitlement.*

15. Charles Murray, *Losing Ground: American Social Policy, 1950–1980* (New York: Basic Books, 1984).

16. Joseph F. Sullivan, "Kean Aims for Welfare Reform That Works," *The New York Times,* January 18, 1987.

17. Bob Kuttner, "Place to squeeze the poor," *The Boston Globe,* October 26, 1986.

18. Mary Jo Bane, "Welfare Reform and Mandatory versus Voluntary Work: Policy Issue or Management Problem?" *Journal of Policy Analysis and Management,* 8 (Spring 1989), p. 285.

19. Ibid., pp. 285–286.

20. Harvey Sherman, *It All Depends: A Pragmatic Approach to Organization* (University, Ala.: University of Alabama Press, 1966), pp. 18 and 20.

21. Bane, "Welfare Reform," p. 288. Bane also notes that "bad management can subvert either," although she believes that "the dangers of slipping into those bad management practices characteristic of mandatory programs are probably greater than of falling into the pitfalls of voluntary programs." For further discussion of the management differences between mandatory and voluntary programs, see (in the same issue of the *Journal of Policy Analysis and Management,* 8) the other articles in a symposium organized by Laurence E. Lynn, Jr., pp. 284–306.

22. Judith M. Gueron, *Reforming Welfare with Work* (New York: The Ford Foundation, 1987), p. 30.

23. Warren Bennis and Burt Nanus, *Leaders: The Strategies for Taking Charge* (New York: Harper & Row, 1985), pp. 89 and 90.

24. Ibid., p. 91.

25. Bane, "Welfare Reform," p. 12.

2. The Birth of ET CHOICES

1. Supported work is tightly supervised, federally subsidized, entry-level employment; the recipient begins with minimal responsibilities that increase as her job aptitudes and skills also increase. The hope is that at the end of the four- to nine-month supported-work program, the private employer will hire the participant as a regular employee. See also Chapter 3, note 2.
2. Meredith and Associates, Inc., "Massachusetts Department of Public Welfare Employment and Training Program," August 1983.
3. Dee Oliver and Kathy Dunham, letter of March 4, 1983, to Manuel Carballo and Phil Johnston.
4. Lucy A. Williams et al., "Recommendations of the Work and Welfare Advisory Task Force," May 13, 1983, Executive Summary, p. 1.
5. Ibid., Executive Summary, pp. 1–2.
6. Ibid., pp. 2, Executive Summary 3, 6, 3.
7. "In Memoriam," *John F. Kennedy School of Government Bulletin,* Spring/Summer 1980, p. 36.
8. Alan Werner, "From Welfare to Work: Push or Pull?—The Case of Massachusetts," paper presented at the Annual Research Conference of the Association for Public Policy Analysis and Management, October 20, 1984.
9. Charles M. Atkins and Barbara Burke-Tatum, "Massachusetts Department of Public Welfare Employment and Training Program, Amendment to WIN Demonstration Project," August 1983, p. 1.
10. Ibid., p. 4.
11. Ibid., p. 1.
12. Ibid.
13. Ibid., pp. 7, 8, 12, and 24.
14. Eileen McNamara, "Welfare snag leaves mother, girl homeless," *The Boston Globe,* May 13, 1983.
15. Eileen McNamara, "Welfare counsel fired by Atkins," *The Boston Globe,* May 14, 1983.

3. The Structure of ET CHOICES

1. Stephen R. Rosenthal, "Employment and Training Choices (B)," Boston University, p. 10.
2. Suppose a firm had a specific job with a $7.00-an-hour wage. The firm might agree to hire a welfare recipient for this job at $1.20 per hour less than normal (i.e., at $5.80 per hour) with $1.30 of this wage being paid by a "grant diversion" from a reduction in the recipient's welfare check. Thus, the firm had a total subsidy of $2.50 an hour (the $1.30 grant diversion plus the $1.20 lower wage). But the firm got an employee who needed some significant help. Supported workers were usually placed in groups to provide peer support, had the responsibilities and stresses of their jobs gradually

increased, and were closely counseled by their supervisors. Supported work lasted only nine months. After that, the department hoped the participant would be hired by the firm; otherwise the contractor would seek to place her in another job.

3. Stephen R. Rosenthal, "Quality Control in AFDC (A)," School of Management, Boston University, 1983, p. 1.

4. "The 'Caseworker' Returns," *Public Welfare News,* May 1985, p. 3.

5. On January 1, 1988, DES and OTEP were merged into a new Department of Employment and Training (DET).

6. Rosenthal, "Employment and Training Choices (B)," p. 3.

7. OTEP could use different combinations, other than 913 placements and zero "positive outcomes," to earn the $4,215,000. For example, by giving the minimum 1,054 recipients (75% of 1,405) vocational training and then placing the minimum 685 in jobs, OTEP could earn $4,615 each, or $3.16 million. Then another 395 positive outcomes would earn it $2,665 each, or $1.05 million. Thus its total income would be $4.215 million. Or OTEP could make job placements that totaled somewhere between the 685 minimum and the 913 maximum (earning $4,615 for each) and make up the rest with "positive outcomes" (at $2,665 each). And for every job placement over the 685 minimum, OTEP earned a bonus of $876. If the wage was 10 percent over the regional "adult average wage standard" (which ranged from $4.65 to $5.47), OTEP earned another $200—$500 if it was 20 percent over this standard.

8. Charles M. Atkins and Barbara Burke-Tatum, "Massachusetts Department of Public Welfare Employment and Training Program, Amendment to WIN Demonstration Project," August 1983, pp. 2 and 5.

9. Massachusetts Department of Public Welfare, *Case Management Guide* (Boston: Massachusetts Department of Public Welfare, April 1987), pp. i and ii.

10. Massachusetts Department of Public Welfare, "The Challenge: Putting It All Together," a booklet on case management distributed at the Partners in Professionalism Conferences in April and May of 1987.

11. Ibid.

4. Managing for Performance

1. Each local office's placement goal was determined strictly by the size of its caseload; other factors, such as the local unemployment rate, were not taken into account. Two of the fifty-eight local offices, the ones on the islands of Nantucket and Martha's Vineyard, had no ET goals for FY 1984. The monthly goals for the fifty-six local offices totaled 658 placements and so the sum of the goals for the nine different months totaled slightly less than 6,000.

2. Table 4.4 dramatically illustrates Behn's First Law of Policy Analysis: "The data never add up right." Each row of data is from that month's "Internal Management Report." But it is impossible to add any month's data to the previous month's year-to-date figures to calculate the new year-to-date information. For example, the 1983 reports for October and November show 214

and 346 placements, respectively; these two numbers sum to 560, yet the November report lists year-to-date placements of 680. In part such discrepancies are explained by the constantly changing character of the information system. Even the forms themselves changed from month to month. The department's "get the program up and running and then fix it" approach also applied to its system of collecting data, which was modified many times. In addition, these discrepancies resulted from reporting lags. A welfare recipient who went to work in November may not have notified her social worker until December; thus this would be recorded later but still as a November placement. In December, the year-to-date figure would be adjusted accordingly, but the November report would never be modified.

3. "Governor Dukakis Praises Welfare Employees at Hyannis Conference," *Public Welfare News*, July 1984, p. 1.

4. "Dukakis Tells Welfare Case-workers—'You Are The Best,'" *Public Welfare News*, September 1985, p. 5.

5. Office of Research, Planning and Evaluation, *An Evaluation of the Massachusetts Employment and Training Program: Interim Findings on Participation and Outcomes, FY84–FY85* (Boston: Massachusetts Department of Public Welfare, January 1986), p. 60.

6. An untitled and undated collection of departmental charts.

7. Michael Lipsky, *Street-Level Bureaucracy: Dilemmas of the Individual in Public Services* (New York: Russell Sage Foundation, 1980).

8. Charles M. Atkins and Barbara Burke-Tatum, "Massachusetts Department of Public Welfare Employment and Training Program, Amendment to WIN Demonstration Project," August 1983, p. 1.

9. "An Open Letter to All Departmental Staff," *Public Welfare News*, January 1986, p. 2.

10. "Letter from the Commissioner," *Public Welfare News*, Winter 1987, p. 2.

11. "Commissioner's Corner," December 1986.

12. Massachusetts Department of Public Welfare, *Case Management Guide* (Boston: Massachusetts Department of Public Welfare, April 1987), p. i.

13. Morton H. Halperin, *Bureaucratic Politics and Foreign Policy* (Washington, D.C.: The Brookings Institution, 1974), p. 28.

14. Robert D. Behn, "Gordon Chase's Management Reporting System," unpublished manuscript.

15. Frederick Herzberg, "One more time: How do you motivate employees?" *Harvard Business Review* (January-February 1968), pp. 53–62.

16. Thomas J. Peters and Robert H. Waterman, Jr., *In Search of Excellence* (New York: Harper & Row, 1982), pp. 58 and 269.

17. "Governor Thanks E.T. Partners for an Unparalleled Success," *Public Welfare News*, October 1986, p. 1.

18. Peter G. Peterson, "Can Gorbachev Make His Reforms Work?" *The Washington Post*, April 4, 1987.

19. For a discussion of the "dysfunctional consequences" of setting goals for an unemployment agency, see Peter M. Blau, *The Dynamics of Bureaucracy* (Chicago: University of Chicago Press, 1963, second edition), pp. 44–47. For

an analysis of how using goals to measure performance can distort the behavior of local agencies doing training and job placement, see Katherine P. Dickinson, et al., *Evaluation of the Effects of JTPA Performance Standards on Clients, Services, and Costs* (Washington, D.C.: National Commission for Employment Policy, September 1988).

20. Congressional Budget Office, *Work-Related Programs for Welfare Recipients* (Washington, D.C.: Congress of the United States, 1987), pp. xiii and 21.

21. Actually, Daniel Friedlander and David Long concluded that employment and training programs have their greatest impact (in terms, for example, of gains of income) not on the easiest or the hardest to serve, but on those in between. Friedlander and Long, *A Study of Performance Measures and Subgroup Impacts in Three Welfare Employment Programs* (New York: Manpower Demonstration Research Corporation, March 1987).

22. Ibid.

23. To compare state WIN programs, the Urban Institute created a four-part performance measure: job entries per staff; welfare savings per participant divided by the state's average welfare grant; average WIN job-entry wage divided by the state's prevailing wage; and the ratio of placements expected to last thirty days to those that actually did. John J. Mitchell, Mark Lincoln Chadwin, and Demetra Smith Nightingale, *Implementing Welfare-Employment Programs: An Institutional Analysis of the Work Incentive (WIN) Program* (Washington, D.C.: The Urban Institute, October 1979), p. 21. As an evaluation tool, the various components of this performance measure help compensate for some important differences between states. Indeed, a department's managers might adapt this measure to monitor distortions. But such a complicated measure will not work to motivate performance.

24. Dickinson et al. found that for JTPA agencies there were fewer distortions when the agency had a strong sense of mission. Dickinson et al., *Evaluation of the Effects of JTPA*, p. 5 (Executive Summary).

25. How does this six-part process of managing for performance differ from management by objectives (MBO) as developed and popularized by Peter F. Drucker in *The Practice of Management* (New York: Harper & Row, 1954) and *Managing for Results* (New York: Harper & Row, 1964)? MBO was created for business, and has been predominantly used there. Rodney H. Brady has offered, however, one example of its use in government. "MBO goes to work in the public sector," *Harvard Business Review*, 51 (March-April 1973), pp. 65–74. Of the six components of managing for performance, only two and a half are part of the MBO system that Brady implemented as an assistant secretary at the Department of Health, Education, and Welfare. Brady's MBO system set specific goals. And Brady and the HEW secretary personally monitored the results. These goals were not, however, linked to any overall mission of the department; they were set independently by the manager of each program. Further, the goals were re-created annually, rather than linked to some long-term purpose. In a business, Brady emphasized, there is the "overall objective" of "maximizing return on investment" (p. 66). Thus, in a business it can make sense to have the goals set by the managers of different

divisions. Everyone understands that these goals must somehow relate to the accepted, long-term purpose of the firm. In a public agency, however, there is often a great deal of dispute about the institution's purpose. Thus, until the agency's leadership articulates an overall mission, any process of setting goals makes sense only at a micro-level.

Brady's MBO system placed little emphasis on rewards. Nor, predictably, did Brady appear to worry much about goal distortion; without an overall mission, it is difficult to think about how any specific goal distorts people's behavior from that mission. Brady did note that "changes inside or outside the agency" might require a change in the objectives (p. 71). And although these changes might reflect a concern over distortions from some unexplained long-term purpose (p. 73), a bigger concern seemed to be the need to change objectives "to conform to new initiatives" (p. 71). Management by objectives is part but by no means all of the process of managing for performance.

26. Judy Katz, "Dukakis hails 50,000th success scored by welfare job program," *The Berkshire Eagle* (in Pittsfield, Mass.), June 23, 1988. Eric Fehrnstrom, "Duke calls for reform of welfare," *The Boston Herald*, June 23, 1988. Peter B. Sleeper, "Dukakis says ET program has trained 50,000 for jobs," *The Boston Globe*, June 23, 1988.

5. An Emphasis on Marketing

1. Transcript from New England Newswatch, June 27, 1984, 6:00 to 7:00 P.M., Channel 4, WBZ-TV, Eyewitness News.
2. Transcript from New England Newswatch, June 27, 1984, 6:00 to 7:00 P.M., Channel 7, WNEV-TV, NEWSE7EN.
3. Transcript from New England Newswatch, June 27, 1984, 10:00 to 10:30 P.M., Channel 2, WGBH-TV, Ten O'Clock News.
4. The Associated Press, "Dukakis Declares Success in Welfare Jobs Program," *The Evening Gazette* (in Worcester, Mass.), June 27, 1984.
5. Kenneth J. Cooper, "6100 hired in optional 'workfare,' " *The Boston Globe*, June 28, 1984.
6. Ibid.
7. Jack Flynn, "Welfare-Job Plan Saves $16 Million," *The Daily News* (of Springfield, Mass.), June 27, 1984.
8. News Release from the Office of Governor Michael S. Dukakis, "Dukakis Calls New Employment and Training Program a Nationwide Model: Cites 6,000 Welfare Recipients Placed in Jobs," June 27, 1984.
9. Ibid.
10. Cooper, "6100 hired in optional 'workfare.' "
11. Robert Hoge, "State begins program for welfare jobs," *The Middlesex News*, June 28, 1984.
12. Transcript from New England Newswatch, June 27, 1984, 10:00–10:30 P.M., Channel 56, WLVI-TV, The News At Ten.
13. "From welfare to work," *The Boston Globe*, July 2, 1984.

14. "Jobs plan pays off," *The Boston Herald,* June 28, 1984.
15. "Jobs program leads the way," *The Sunday Republican* (in Springfield, Mass.), July 1, 1984.
16. Maureen Boyle, "New plan has jobs to escape welfare," *The Standard-Times* (in New Bedford, Mass.), July 27, 1984.
17. Jonathan Tilove, "Dukakis claims welfare success," *The Morning Union* (in Springfield, Mass.), August 9, 1984.
18. Office of State Services, "Management Brief: Capitol-for-a-Day Programs," National Governors' Association, March 21, 1988.
19. Joe Davidson, "More States Now Ask Recipients of Aid to Train and Take Jobs," *The Wall Street Journal,* July 23, 1986; "Massachusetts provides innovative welfare model," *The Atlanta Journal,* August 24, 1986.
20. Stuart Auerbach, "President Toughens U.S. Trade Policy," *The Washington Post,* September 24, 1985.
21. One of the "Six Principles of Communications" outlined by Steven Hull, communications director for Governor Bob Graham of Florida, at a seminar at Duke University on September 20, 1985.
22. Massachusetts Department of Public Welfare, *Case Management Guide,* (Boston: Massachusetts Department of Public Welfare, April 1987), p. 4.
23. John Herbers, "Job Training Efforts in Massachusetts and Michigan Move Poor off Welfare," *The New York Times,* March 30, 1987.
24. Michael Wiseman, "Workfare and welfare policy," *Focus* (Institute for Research on Poverty, University of Wisconsin), 9 (Fall and Winter 1986), p. 6.
25. Joe Klein, "Ready for the Duke?" *New York,* August 17, 1987, p. 30.
26. The Massachusetts Department of Public Welfare, "Employment and Training Choices: A Two Year Report," November 1985.
27. The San Diego Job Search and Work Experience Demonstration Program was "mandatory," yet less than half of the individuals for whom it was mandatory received any services beyond one day of placement assistance. Barbara Goldman et al., *Final Report on the San Diego Job Search and Work Experience Demonstration* (New York: Manpower Demonstration Research Corporation, February 1986).
28. The *threat* of sanctions may contribute to success, but their *actual use* apparently does not. In a study of the performance of local WIN programs in New York, Lawrence M. Mead found that "surprisingly, the procedures for adjudicating and sanctioning clients for noncooperation proved to be weakly or negatively linked to performance . . . Overall, the more registrants an office proceeded against in this formal way, the *worse* it performed." *Beyond Entitlement: The Social Obligations of Citizenship* (New York: The Free Press, 1986), p. 160.
29. Thomas J. Peters and Robert H. Waterman, Jr., *In Search of Excellence* (New York: Harper & Row, 1982), p. 193.
30. Publications and Outreach, Massachusetts Department of Public Welfare, "The ET Challenge: FY 1987 Marketing Plan," August 11, 1986.
31. Publications and Outreach, Massachusetts Department of Public Welfare, "Mailings and Response Rates," February 9, 1987.

32. Publications and Outreach, Massachusetts Department of Public Welfare, "Focus Group Report," July 21, 1986.
33. Publications and Outreach, "The ET Challenge."
34. Philip Kotler and Sidney J. Levy, "Broadening the Concept of Marketing," *Journal of Marketing,* 33 (January 1969), pp. 10–15.
35. Publications and Outreach, Massachusetts Department of Public Welfare, "Satisfaction Questionnaire Report," July 1986.
36. Joan Vennochi, "Dukakis: state welfare error rate dips to 2.1%," *The Boston Globe,* April 15, 1987.
37. Gordon Chase and Elizabeth C. Reveal, *How to Manage in the Public Sector* (Reading, Mass.: Addison-Wesley, 1983), pp. 48 and 59.

6. Making Government More Businesslike

1. The Massachusetts Civic Interest Council, " 'Once Is an Event; Twice Is a Tradition': An Analysis of Certain Expenditures by the Department of Public Welfare," plus the accompanying press release of January 14, 1987.
2. Robert M. Entman, *Democracy without Citizens: The Dilemma of American Journalism* (New York: Oxford University Press, 1989), pp. 49–50.
3. Press Release, Office of Senator William Proxmire, July 22, 1987.
4. Office of Senator William Proxmire, "Summary of Fleeces—1977."
5. "Watchdogs snap at Welfare Dept.," *Middlesex News,* January 15, 1987.
6. Randall Keith, "Welfare Department defends free meals," *The Patriot Ledger* (in Quincy, Mass.), January 15, 1987.
7. Frank Phillips, "It's party hearty time at Welfare: $143G spent on 'seminars,' " *The Boston Herald,* January 15, 1987.
8. Peter B. Sleeper, "Waste of $143,000 in Welfare Dept. is alleged," *The Boston Globe,* January 15, 1987.
9. Christopher Callahan, "Welfare Waste Is Charged," *The Gardner News,* January 15, 1987.
10. Transcript from New England Newswatch, January 15, 1987, 6:00 to 7:00 A.M., Channel 4, WBZ-TV, Eyewitness News First Edition.
11. Phillips, "It's party hearty time."
12. Callahan, "Welfare Waste."
13. Sleeper, "Waste of $143,000."
14. Keith, "Welfare Department."
15. "Who says no free lunch?" *Marlboro Enterprise,* January 20, 1987.
16. "Bring back the brown bag," *The Patriot Ledger* (in Quincy, Mass.), January 16, 1987.
17. Thomas J. Peters and Robert H. Waterman, Jr., *In Search of Excellence* (New York: Harper & Row, 1982), pp. 318–325, 201, 240, 322, and 322–323.
18. Gordon Chase and Elizabeth C. Reveal, *How to Manage in the Public Sector* (Reading, Mass.: Addison-Wesley, 1983), chap. 3, pp. 63–91.
19. Michael Lipsky, *Street-Level Bureaucracy: Dilemmas of the Individual in Public Services* (New York: Russell Sage Foundation, 1980).

20. Eileen McNamara, "Welfare snag leaves mother, girl homeless," *The Boston Globe*, May 13, 1983.
21. Eileen McNamara, "Welfare counsel fired by Atkins," *The Boston Globe*, May 14, 1983.
22. Peters and Waterman, *In Search*, pp. 241, 58, and 84.
23. Tom Peters and Nancy Austin, *A Passion for Excellence* (New York: Random House, 1985), pp. 252 and 260.
24. Peters and Waterman, *In Search*, pp. 157, 186, and 321.

7. Management by Groping Along

1. Office of Research, Planning and Evaluation, *An Evaluation of the Massachusetts Employment and Training Choices Program: Interim Findings on Participation and Outcomes, FY84–FY85* (Boston: Massachusetts Department of Public Welfare, January 1986), p. 26.
2. Meredith and Associates, Inc., "Massachusetts Department of Public Welfare Employment and Training Program," August 1983.
3. Martin A. Levin and Barbara Ferman, *The Political Hand* (New York: Pergamon Press, 1985), pp. 14–15.
4. Kenneth R. Andrews, *The Concept of Corporate Strategy* (Homewood, Ill.: Dow Jones-Irwin, 1971).
5. Robert D. Behn, "Leadership for Cut-Back Management: The Use of Corporate Strategy," *Public Administration Review*, 40 (November/December 1980), pp. 613–620.
6. For a discussion of getting people to "sign up" for a project rather than ordering them to participate, see Tracy Kidder, *The Soul of a New Machine* (Boston: The Atlantic Monthly Press, 1981), pp. 63–66.
7. Karl E. Weick, "Small Wins: Redefining the Scale of Social Problems," *American Psychologist*, 39 (January 1984), pp. 43 and 44.
8. Ibid., pp. 46 and 43.
9. From a seminar at Duke University on April 2, 1986.
10. Scott M. Matheson with James Edwin Kee, *Out of Balance* (Salt Lake City: Peregrine Smith, 1986), p. 225.
11. Thomas J. Peters and Robert H. Waterman, Jr., *In Search of Excellence* (New York: Harper & Row, 1982), pp. 119 and 155.
12. Ibid., p. 122.
13. Ibid., pp. 22–23. The most obvious deficiency of this research design is the lack of a comparison group. How do Peters and Waterman know that the management of nonexcellent companies is not also characterized by "a bias for action," etc.? For additional criticisms of Peters and Waterman's research design, see Robert T. Golembiewski, "Toward Excellence in Public Management: Constraints on Emulating America's Best-Run Companies," in Robert B. Denhardt and Edward T. Jennings, Jr. (eds.), *The Revitalization of the Public Service* (Columbia, Mo.: University of Missouri, 1987), pp. 177–198.
14. For example, Rosabeth Moss Kanter, *The Change Masters: Innovation and Entrepreneurship in the American Corporation* (New York: Simon and Schuster,

1983); Tom Peters and Nancy Austin, *A Passion for Excellence* (New York: Random House, 1985).

15. Henry Mintzberg, *The Nature of Managerial Work* (New York: Harper & Row, 1973), p. 31.

16. Ibid., p. 33.

17. Peters and Waterman, *In Search*, p. 124.

18. Mintzberg, *The Nature of Managerial Work*, p. 5.

19. Peters and Waterman, *In Search*, pp. 13–14 and chap. 5.

20. Mintzberg, *The Nature of Managerial Work*, pp. 39 and 52.

21. Ibid., p. 44.

22. For those whose scholarly sensibilities are offended by references to cartoons in *The New Yorker*, let me offer another source for this stereotype of the manager. John P. Kotter, *The General Managers* (New York: The Free Press, 1982), p. 131: "The professional manager in America exists above the industrial din, away from the dirt, noise, and irrationality of people and products. He dresses well. His secretary is alert and helpful. His office is as clean, quiet, and subdued as that of any other professional. He plans, organizes, and controls large enterprises in a calm, logical, dispassionate, and decisive manner. He surveys computer printouts, calculates profits and losses, sells and acquires subsidiaries, and imposes systems for monitoring and motivating employees, applying a general body of rules to each special circumstance." If you don't believe it, you can look it up—in *The New Yorker*.

23. Behn's Fifth Law of Policy Analysis: Analysis is much more helpful in exposing poor options than in identifying an optimal option.

24. Robert D. Behn, "Why Murphy Was Right," *Policy Analysis*, 6 (Summer 1980), pp. 361–363.

25. Kanter, *The Change Masters*, pp. 284–286.

26. Writes Weick in "Small Wins," p. 43: "A series of small wins can be gathered into a retrospective summary that imputes a consistent line of development, but this post hoc construction should not be mistaken for orderly implementation."

27. Friedrich Nietzsche, *The Gay Science* (New York: Vintage, 1974), p. 258.

28. Kanter, *The Change Masters*, p. 286.

29. Fortunately, our federal system gives us fifty state governments and thousands of municipal governments, each of whose certain prediction of how its perfect plan will work differs significantly from the equally certain prediction in the next jurisdiction. Individually each government can pretend that it knows exactly where it is going, while collectively we all continue to grope along.

30. Eric V. Denardo, *Dynamic Programming* (Englewood Cliffs, N.J.: Prentice-Hall, 1982).

31. Robert H. Hayes, "Why Strategic Planning Goes Awry," *The New York Times*, April 20, 1986.

32. In the terminology of control theory, management by groping along is a closed-loop control system; the feedback loop provides information that is used to correct deviations from the desired path. In contrast, comprehensive

planning is an open-loop control system. With no feedback loop, the system (once started) runs completely on dead reckoning.

33. From a meeting of governors, December 12–13, 1985, Stateline, Nevada.

34. Charles E. Lindblom, "The Science of Muddling Through," *Public Administration Review,* 19 (Spring 1959), pp. 79–88.

35. "Logical incrementalism," the approach of James Brian Quinn of Dartmouth College, has a number of similarities to Lindblom's "muddling through." *Strategies for Change: Logical Incrementalism* (Homewood, Ill.: Richard D. Irwin, 1980). Quinn is concerned primarily with the formulation of strategy for a corporation, though he pays some attention to the implementation of this strategy. Quinn argues that his business executives consider alternatives that are further from the status quo than do Lindblom's public-policy decision makers, and that they "take a much more proactive approach toward change" (p. 100). But compared with Atkins and his staff, Quinn's managers are extremely cautious. Rather than boldly proclaim that they are going to find jobs for welfare recipients, Quinn's business managers prefer to have others suggest what new goals might be, lest they become too publicly identified with new directions that the organization will not accept. See also James Brian Quinn, "Managing Strategies Incrementally," *The International Journal of Management Science,* 10 (1982), pp. 613–627.

36. Herbert A. Simon, Donald W. Smithburg, and Victor A. Thompson, *Public Administration* (New York: Knopf, 1950); Dan E. Schendel and Charles W. Hofer, *Strategic Management: A New View of Business Policy and Planning* (Boston: Little, Brown, 1979); and Balaji S. Chakravarthy, "Adaptation: A Promising Metaphor for Strategic Management," *Academy of Management Review,* 7 (January 1982), pp. 35–44.

37. Charles M. Atkins, "An Open Letter to All Department Staff," *Public Welfare News,* January 1986, p. 2.

38. Richard T. Pascale and Anthony G. Athos, *The Art of Japanese Management* (New York: Simon and Schuster, 1981).

39. Robert H. Hayes, "Strategic Planning—Forward in Reverse?" *Harvard Business Review,* 63 (November/December 1985), p. 118.

40. R. E. Miles and C. C. Snow, *Organizational Strategy, Structure and Process* (New York: McGraw-Hill, 1978).

41. Charles Atkins, "Comments," *Gordon Chase, 1932–1980* (Waltham, Mass.: Brandeis University, 1981).

42. Herbert A. Simon, "Information Processing Models of Cognition," *Annual Review of Psychology,* 30 (1979), p. 368; R. Bhaskar and Herbert A. Simon, "Problem Solving in Sematically Rich Domains: An Example from Engineering Thermodynamics," *Cognitive Science,* 1 (April 1977), pp. 193–215.

43. Robert D. Behn, "The Nature of Knowledge about Public Management," *Journal of Policy Analysis and Management,* 7 (Fall 1987), pp. 200–212.

44. Peters and Waterman, *In Search,* chap. 10.

45. Kanter, *The Change Masters,* p. 18.

46. Herbert Kaufman, *The Administrative Behavior of Federal Bureau Chiefs* (Washington, D.C.: The Brookings Institution, 1981), p. 82.

47. Richard E. Neustadt, *Presidential Power*, 1980 edition (New York: John Wiley & Sons, 1980), p. 89.

48. Herbert A. Simon, "The Proverbs of Administration," *Public Administration Review*, 6 (1946), pp. 53–67.

49. Peters and Waterman, *In Search*, chap. 11.

50. Kanter, *The Change Masters*, p. 44.

8. Managing and Evaluating Social Programs

1. Alicia H. Munnell, "Lessons from the Income Maintenance Experiments: An Overview," in Munnell (ed.), *Lessons from the Income Maintenance Experiments* (Boston: Federal Reserve Bank of Boston, 1987), pp. 20–21.

2. For a list of thirty-five such policy experiments, see David H. Greenberg and Philip K. Robins, "The Changing Role of Social Experiments in Policy Analysis," *Journal of Policy Analysis and Management*, 5 (Winter 1986), pp. 353–356.

3. For a general discussion of experimental design, see Donald T. Campbell and Julian C. Stanley, *Experimental and Quasi-Experimental Designs for Research* (Chicago: Rand McNally, 1966).

4. Thomas Francis, Jr., et al., "An Evaluation of the 1954 Poliomyelitis Vaccine Trials," *American Journal of Public Health*, 45 (1955), Table 2b, p. 25.

5. This is the result of two phenomena. The Income Effect suggests that if your income goes up you will work less. The Substitution Effect suggests that if your earnings per hour go down (as a result, in this case, of a tax on those earnings) you will also work less—substituting leisure for work. See any standard microeconomics textbook, for example, Jack Hirshleifer, *Price Theory and Applications* (Englewood Cliffs, N.J.: Prentice-Hall, 1976), pp. 100–101 and 386–390.

6. Suppose that without any welfare program, a family works 80 hours a month at a wage of $3.50 per hour so that its monthly income is $280. How much would it work under a negative-income-tax system? For example, suppose that without any income this same family is eligible for a welfare check of $400 per month that is reduced by 50 cents for every dollar earned. Thus if the family earns $100, it receives a welfare check of $350 for a total income of $450. With this negative-income-tax system, would this family still work 80 hours? If it did, it would earn $280 and receive a welfare check of $260 for a total monthly income of $540. Would the family reduce its work effort to 60 hours, for a total monthly income of $505? Or would it not work at all, and just take the $400 welfare check?

7. For a general discussion of the negative-income-tax experiments, see Munnell, *Lessons from the Income Maintenance Experiments;* Joseph A. Pechman and P. Michael Timpane, *Work Incentives and Income Guarantees* (Washington, D.C.: The Brookings Institution, 1975); Richard P. Nathan, *Social Science in Government* (New York: Basic Books, 1988), pp. 49–63.

8. Judith M. Gueron, *Work Initiatives for Welfare Recipients* (New York: Manpower Demonstration Research Corporation, March 1986), p. 1.

9. Barbara Goldman, Daniel Friedlander, and David Long, with Marjorie Erickson and Judith Gueron, *Final Report on the San Diego Job Search and Work Experience Demonstration* (New York: Manpower Demonstration Research Corporation, February 1986).

10. Ibid., pp. xx and 94.

11. Daniel Friedlander and David Long, *A Study of Performance Measures and Subgroup Impacts in Three Welfare Employment Programs* (New York: Manpower Demonstration Research Corporation, March 1987), pp. 51, xvii, and 51–55.

12. Gueron, *Work Initiatives*, pp. 14 and 24.

13. Mary Jo Bane and David T. Ellwood, *The Dynamics of Dependence: The Routes to Self-Sufficiency* (Cambridge, Mass.: Urban Systems Research and Engineering, 1983).

14. Barbara B. Blum, "Views of a Policymaker and Public Administrator," in Munnell (ed.), *Lessons from the Income Maintenance Experiments*, p. 239.

15. Gueron, *Work Initiatives*, p. 8.

16. "Warning on Welfare Reform," *The Washington Post*, January 19, 1988.

17. Monci Jo Williams, "Is Workfare the Answer," *Fortune*, October 27, 1986, p. 110.

18. Spencer Rich, "Workfare Experiments Hold Limited Promise," *The Washington Post*, December 11, 1986.

19. Quoted by Jon Sawyer, "Success Unbacked by Scientific Data," *St. Louis Post-Dispatch*, 1988.

20. Gueron, *Work Initiatives*, p. 22.

21. Ibid.

22. See Greenberg and Robins, "The Changing Role of Social Experiments."

23. Because the sample is large, this test can be conducted assuming that the distribution of the sample of each program and thus the distribution of the sample difference between the two programs is normal. Then, assuming the null hypothesis (the probability of finding a job is the same for people in both groups), the estimate of the probability of finding a job is 0.4 and the estimate of the variance of the difference is $(0.4)(0.6)(1/100 + 1/100)$ = 0.0048. Taking the square root of this number gives the estimate of the standard deviation: 0.06928. Thus, the t-statistic for the difference between the means is $(0.45 - 0.35)/0.06928 = 1.443$.

    We have estimated that the normal distribution for the difference between the job-finding rates of the two programs has a standard deviation of 0.06928. But the difference we observed is 0.1. Thus, this 0.1 observation is 1.443 standard deviations above the mean (of zero) for this distribution. For a normal distribution, the probability is 0.075 that a single observation will be 1.443 standard deviations or more away from the mean. Thus, *if* the null hypothesis were true—if the job-finding rates for the treatment and control groups were identical—there would still be a 7.5 percent chance that an experiment conducted with 100 people in the treatment group and 100 people in the control would result in a 10-percentage-point difference $(0.45 - 0.35)$ between the observed job-finding rates of the two groups.

For a normal distribution, there is a 68.3 percent chance that any single observation will fall within plus or minus one standard deviation of the mean. The chance that an observation will fall within plus or minus two standard deviations of the mean is 95.4 percent. The chance that a single observation will fall more than two standard deviations from the mean is just 2.3 percent. For a further explanation of this kind of analysis, see any standard statistical text, for example, Ralph E. Beals, *Statistics for Economists* (Chicago: Rand McNally, 1972), pp. 195–200.

24. Goldman et al., *Final Report on the San Diego Job Search and Work Experience Demonstration*, pp. 194 and 196.

25. Ibid.

26. Greenberg and Robins, "The Changing Role of Social Experiments," p. 345.

27. Henry J. Aaron, *Politics and the Professors* (Washington, D.C.: The Brookings Institution, 1978), p. 158.

28. Ibid., p. 156.

29. Ibid., pp. 158 and 156.

30. Ibid., pp. 158 and 159.

31. Gary Burtless and Robert H. Haveman, "Policy Lessons from Three Labor Market Experiments," in R. Thayne Robson (ed.), *Employment and Training R&D* (Kalamazoo, Mich.: W. E. Upjohn Institute for Employment Research, 1984), p. 128.

32. For a specific example of this tension, see Erwin C. Hargrove, "The Bureaucratic Politics of Evaluation: A Case Study of the Department of Labor," *Public Administration Review*, 40 (March/April 1980), pp. 150–159. Nathan, *Social Science*, p. 124, makes a similar point: "The differences in perspective between policy makers and researchers are likely to be substantial."

33. Joseph L. Bower, "Effective Public Management," *Harvard Business Review*, 55 (March/April 1977), pp. 31–40.

34. In the situation described by Hargrove ("The Bureaucratic Politics of Evaluation") the evaluators in the office of the assistant secretary for policy evaluation and research took an "adversarial stance" toward the programs they evaluated.

35. Hargrove (ibid., p. 152) provides an example of an evaluator with the "ability to answer the questions that managers ask."

36. Friedlander and Long, *A Study of Performance Measures*, p. 68.

9. Evaluating ET CHOICES

1. Office of Research, Planning and Evaluation, *An Evaluation of the Massachusetts Employment and Training Choices Program: Interim Findings on Participation and Outcomes, FY84–FY85* (Boston: Massachusetts Department of Public Welfare, January 1986), pp. i and 2.

2. Ibid., pp. i, ii, and 3.

3. Ibid., pp. 63–64.

4. Department of Public Welfare, *The Employment and Training Choices Program:*

Program Plan and Budget Request, FY87 (Boston: Commonwealth of Massachusetts, January 1986), pp. 6–7.

5. Ibid., pp. 7 and 17.
6. Department of Public Welfare, *The Employment and Training Choices Program: Program Plan and Budget Request, FY88* (Boston: Commonwealth of Massachusetts, February 1987), p. 8.
7. Department of Public Welfare, *Program Plan and Budget Request, FY87*, p. 16.
8. Massachusetts Taxpayers Foundation, *Training People to Live Without Welfare* (Boston: Massachusetts Taxpayers Foundation, August 1987), pp. ii–iii.
9. Richard P. Nathan, *Social Science in Government: Uses and Misuses* (New York: Basic Books, 1988), p. 125.
10. Daniel Friedlander, Gregory Hoerz, Janet Quint, and James Riccio, *Arkansas: Final Report on the WORK Program in Two Counties* (New York: Manpower Demonstration Research Corporation, September 1985), p. 9.
11. Nathan, *Social Science*, p. 80.
12. Ibid., p. 89.
13. See Chapter 8, note 7.
14. Kathleen Durand, "Dukakis praises employment program," *Fall River Herald*, September 11, 1985.
15. Nathan makes a similar point. He argues that demonstration research on income-maintenance programs, such as the negative-income-tax experiments, will not be as helpful as demonstration research on service-delivery programs such as welfare, training, and work programs. He reasons that a new, universal income-maintenance program would be enacted only after a "highly visible . . . national debate." As a result, it will be "widely known that the 'rules of the game' have been changed" by the new legislation, and thus "people exposed to this new policy would change their behavior in ways that could not be known in a research environment in which such a debate had not taken place." A small-scale demonstration of this income-maintenance program would not discover the changes in attitudes and accompanying changes in behavior because those in the treatment group would not be exposed to the publicity inherent in this national debate. In contrast, service-delivery programs can be instituted in "a much less intrusive way," so that they are "likely to be viewed as 'just another program.'" Concludes Nathan: "service-type delivery programs do not usually have the visibility and publicity that could in and of themselves change the expectations and behavior of large numbers of people." Nathan, *Social Science*, pp. 61–62 and 194–195.

   Of course, this does not describe ET at all. Atkins and company sought "visibility and publicity" for ET precisely because they wanted to "change the expectations and behavior of large numbers of people."
16. Robert Rosenthal and Lenore Jacobson, "Teachers' Expectancies: Determinants of Pupils' IQ Gains," *Psychological Reports*, 19 (1966), pp. 115–118. Rosenthal also did the same thing with rats rather than children. Robert Rosenthal and Kermit L. Fode, "The Effect of Experimenter Bias on the Performance of the Albino Rat," *Behavioral Science*, 8 (1963), pp. 183–189.

Robert Rosenthal and Reed Lawson, "A Longitudinal Study of the Effects of Experimenter Bias on the Operant Learning of Laboratory Rats," *Journal of Psychiatric Research*, 2 (1964), pp. 61–72. Psychology students were given rats randomly labeled "bright" or "dull" to teach to run mazes or perform other tasks. The rats the students believed were carefully bred to be bright performed better than those the students believed were bred to be dull, even though all the rats were randomly selected from the same litters. The student who believed his rat was bright "tended to be more enthusiastic, friendly, encouraging, pleasant, and more interested in S's [his rat's] performance. He liked S [his rat] more, watched him more intently." Rosenthal and Lawson, p. 71.

17. Phil R. Manning and Lois DeBakey, *Medicine: Preserving the Passion* (New York: Springer-Verlag, 1987).

18. Robert Ornstein and David Sobel, "Can the Brain Heal the Body?" *The Washington Post* (Outlook Section), May 3, 1987.

19. Robert G. Richardson, *The Surgeon's Heart: A History of Cardiac Surgery* (London: William Heinemann Medical Books, 1969), p. 146.

20. The results of the 1924–1927 illumination part of the Hawthorne Experiments were reported in C. E. Snow, "A Discussion of the Relation of Illumination Intensity to Productive Efficiency," *Technical Engineering News*, November 1927, pp. 257–282. In reality, however, the true "Hawthorne Effect" is the result of subsequent studies of five women who put together relays for telephones. See F. J. Roethlisberger and William J. Dickson, *Management and the Worker* (Cambridge, Mass.: Harvard University Press, 1939). As Chapter 8 suggests, these interpretations of the Hawthorne data have been challenged by other analysts. See H. McIlvanie Parsons, "What Happened at Hawthorne?" *Science*, 1983 (March 8, 1974), pp. 922–932; Richard Herbert Franke and James D. Kaul, "The Hawthorne Experiments: First Statistical Interpretation," *American Sociological Review*, 43 (October 1978), pp. 623–643.

21. Ralph E. Smith, *Work-Related Programs for Welfare Recipients* (Washington, D.C.: Congressional Budget Office, April 1987), pp. 11, 33–34, and 60–61.

22. Lester M. Salamon, "Follow-Ups, Letdowns, and Sleepers: The Time Dimension in Policy Evaluation," in Charles O. Jones and Robert D. Thomas (eds.) *Public Policy Making in a Federal System* (Beverly Hills, Calif.: Sage Publications, 1976), pp. 257 and 260–261.

23. Denise F. Polit, Janet C. Quint, and James A. Riccio, *The Challenge of Serving Teenage Mothers: Lessons from Project Redirection* (New York: Manpower Demonstration Research Corporation, October 1988), pp. 1 and 3.

24. Spencer Rich, "Welfare Mothers Show Benefits of Training," *The Washington Post*, October 7, 1988.

25. Molly Moore, "A. Ernest Fitzgerald: Analyst Who Knows the Price of Exposing Cost Overruns," *The Washington Post*, February 23, 1987.

26. Nathan, *Social Science in Government*, pp. 12 and 13.

27. Ibid., pp. 123–126.

28. Ibid., p. 126.

29. Ibid., p. 127.
30. Ibid., p. 128.
31. Kenneth J. Cooper, "Dukakis says job program has cut state's welfare rolls," *The Boston Globe*, October 30, 1985.
32. Irene Sage, "Merit of welfare-to-work program in dispute," *The Boston Globe*, February 2, 1987.
33. Maureen Dezel, "Is ET precious gem or just a zircon?" *Boston Business Journal*, November 10, 1986.
34. Charles M. Atkins, "AFDC Caseload Trends," memo to Philip W. Johnston, October 14, 1987. The data in the following four paragraphs come from this memorandum.
35. June O'Neill, *Work and Welfare in Massachusetts: An Evaluation of the ET Program* (Boston: Pioneer Institute for Public Policy Research, 1990), p. 4.
36. Office of Research, Planning and Evaluation, *Request for Proposal for An Evaluation of Employment and Training (ET) Choices* (Boston: Massachusetts Department of Public Welfare, August 1986), p. 3.
37. As a comparison group, Nightingale et al. used a stratified sample of non-ET participants with similar demographic characteristics. But what if those who volunteered for ET had higher motivation, more employable talents, or better interpersonal skills? If ET volunteers found more jobs, it might be because of these factors, not the program. But if this is true, these ET volunteers should have also had higher employment *before* they entered the ET program. Nightingale et al. found "no evidence" of such a "selection bias in the overall ET effect." Demetra Smith Nightingale et al., *Evaluation of the Massachusetts Employment and Training (ET) Program* (Washington, D.C.: The Urban Institute Press, 1991), pp. 151–157.
38. Demetra Nightingale, Lee Bawden, and Lynn Burbridge, "Summary of Massachusetts ET Choices Evaluation Design," paper presented at the meeting of the Association for Public Policy Analysis and Management, October 29, 1987, p. 5.
39. Ibid., p. 6.
40. Office of Research, Planning and Evaluation, *Request for Proposal*, pp. 2–3.
41. Nightingale et al., "ET Choices Evaluation Design," p. 9.
42. Nightingale et al., *Evaluation of the Massachusetts Employment and Training (ET) Program*, pp. 14, 82, 85, 89–90, 93, 97, and 9. The study analyzed AFDC recipients who had participated in "short-duration components" of ET (such as job search) between July 1986 and June 1987 and those who had participated in "long-duration" components (such as education or training) between January and December 1986. The duration on AFDC was measured from when the case was opened through December 1987. The monthly AFDC grant was measured between July and December 1987. Employment and earnings were measured between January and June 1988. Reentry to AFDC was measured through December 1987; this "finding . . . might have been different had the follow-up period been longer." Nightingale et al., *Evaluation*, p. 9.
43. Ibid., p. 11.

44. Ibid., pp. 10 and 14.
45. Ibid., pp. 9, 93, and 90.
46. Ibid., p. 9.
47. Ibid., p. 125.

10. The Necessity of Leadership

1. The issue of incentives has dominated much of the discussion and research about welfare policy. See for example, Henry Aaron, *Why Welfare Is So Hard To Reform?* (Washington, D.C.: The Brookings Institution, 1973); Congressional Budget Office, *Welfare Reform: Issues, Objectives, and Approaches* (Washington, D.C.: United States Congress, 1977).

2. Charles L. Schultze, *The Public Use of Private Interest* (Washington, D.C.: The Brookings Institution, 1977), p. 18.

3. For example, Jeffrey L. Pressman and Aaron B. Wildavsky, *Implementation* (Berkeley, Calif.: University of California Press, 1973); Eugene Bardach, *The Implementation Game* (Cambridge, Mass.: M.I.T. Press, 1977).

4. This view is expressed by James K. Conant, "Can Government Organizations Be Excellent Too?" *State and Local Government Review*, 19 (Spring 1987), pp. 47–53. A response is found in the same journal: Robert D. Behn, "A Curmudgeon's View of Public Administration: Routine Tasks, Performance, and Innovation," pp. 47 and 54–61.

5. Frank J. Goodnow, *Politics and Administration: A Study in Government* (New York: Russell & Russell, 1900).

6. Luther Gulick, "Notes on the Theory of Organization," in Gulick and Lyndall Urwick (eds.), *Papers on the Science of Administration* (New York: Institute of Public Administration, 1937).

7. For example, Michael Lipsky, *Street-Level Bureaucracy: Dilemmas of the Individual in Public Services* (New York: Russell Sage Foundation, 1980).

8. Leslie Christovich and Steve Martin, "Is Management Any Better, and How Can We Tell?" paper presented at the annual research conference of the Association for Public Policy Analysis and Management, October 27, 1988.

9. For example, *Tax Administration: IRS' Service Centers Need to Improve Handling of Taxpayer Correspondence* (Washington, D.C.: General Accounting Office, 1988), GGD-88-101; *Commodity Certificates: Backlog of 200,000 Unreconciled Certificates Affects Financial Reporting* (Washington, D.C.: General Accounting Office, 1988), RCED-89-14; *Air Traffic Control: Continued Improvements Needed in FAA's Management of the NAS Plan* (Washington, D.C.: General Accounting Office, 1988), RCED-89-7.

10. Office of Management and Budget, *Management of the United States Government, FY 1988* (Washington, D.C.: U.S. Government Printing Office, 1987).

11. Mark A. Abramson, "Review of *Management of the United States Government, FY 1988*," *Government Executive*, May 1987, p. 54.

12. H. Gerth and C. Wright Mills, *From Max Weber: Essays in Sociology* (New York: Oxford University Press, 1946).

13. Frederick W. Taylor, "Scientific Management," testimony before the U.S. House of Representatives, January 25, 1912, reprinted in Jay M. Shafritz and Albert C. Hyde, *Classics of Public Administration* (Chicago: The Dorsey Press, 1987), p. 30.

14. Frederick Winslow Taylor, *The Principles of Scientific Management* (1911; reprinted, New York: Norton, 1967), pp. 37, 36, and 39.

15. For one example of how establishing systems to achieve a purpose—in this case cooperation between school systems—does not automatically result in the realization of that purpose, see Janet A. Weiss, "Pathways to Cooperation among Public Agencies," *Journal of Policy Analysis and Management*, 7 (Fall 1987), pp. 94–117.

16. For example, Graham T. Allison, *Essence of Decision* (Boston: Little, Brown, 1971), chap. 4, pp. 101–143.

17. Peter F. Drucker, *Adventures of a Bystander* (New York: Harper & Row, 1979), p. 255.

18. Frederick W. Taylor (*Principles of Scientific Management*, pp. 25–26) wrote, "The underlying philosophy of all of the old systems of management in common use makes it imperative that each workman shall be left with the final responsibility for doing his job practically as he thinks best, with comparatively little help and advice from the management." This makes little sense, Taylor argues, because "there is always one method and one implement which is quicker and better than any of the rest." But, continues Taylor, "the workman who is best suited to actually doing the work is incapable of fully understanding this science without the guidance and help of those who are working with him or over him, either through lack of education or through insufficient mental capacity." The advocates of the leadership-management approach would offer three responses to Taylor's argument: (1) there is not necessarily one best way; (2) what works in one situation may not work in others; (3) those who have to do the work—produce the results—have some of the best ideas for improving this process.

19. Thomas J. Peters, "Symbols, Patterns, and Settings: An Optimistic Case for Getting Things Done," *Organizational Dynamics*, 7 (Autumn 1978), pp. 18 and 16.

20. Gordon Chase and Elizabeth C. Reveal, *How to Manage in the Public Sector* (Reading, Mass.: Addison-Wesley, 1983), p. 177.

21. Peters, "Symbols, Patterns, and Settings," p. 10.

22. Chase and Reveal, *How to Manage*, p. 178.

23. In a review of *In Search of Excellence* (coauthored with Robert H. Waterman, Jr.), Carroll argued that Peters and Waterman "apparently dismissed . . . such factors as proprietary technology, market dominance, control of critical raw materials, and national policy and culture." Daniel T. Carroll, "A disappointing search for excellence," *Harvard Business Review*, 61 (November/December 1983), p. 79.

24. Mark H. Moore, "Gordon Chase and Public Sector Innovation," paper presented at the ninth annual meeting of the Association for Public Policy Analysis and Management, October 30, 1987, pp. 13 and 16.

25. Ibid., pp. 16–17.

26. Stephen R. Rosenthal, "Producing Results in Government: Moving Beyond Project Management and Its Limited View of Success," *Journal of Policy Analysis and Management,* 8 (Winter 1989), pp. 114 and 110.

27. Nathan Spielberg and Bryon D. Anderson, *Seven Ideas That Shook the Universe* (New York: John Wiley & Sons, 1987), p. 12.

28. Division of Employment Security and the Center for Labor Market Studies, "Massachusetts Employment: Creating a Window of Opportunity in the Mid-1980's," Massachusetts Division of Employment Security, February 22, 1985, p. 11.

29. Kenneth J. Cooper, "6100 hired in optional 'workfare' " *The Boston Globe,* June 28, 1984.

30. For another illustration in a very different context, see William Ascher, *Scheming for the Poor: The Politics of Redistribution in Latin America* (Cambridge, Mass.: Harvard University Press, 1984).

31. Scholars offer different models of this policy process: Garry D. Brewer, "The Policy Sciences Emerge: To Nurture and Structure a Discipline," *Policy Sciences,* 5 (1974), pp. 239–244; Charles O. Jones, *An Introduction to the Study of Public Policy* (Belmont, Calif.: Duxbury Press, 1970); Harold D. Lasswell, *A Pre-View of the Policy Sciences* (New York: American Elsevier, 1971).

32. Charles M. Atkins, "Evaluation of the Employment and Training Contractors: Corrective Action Plan," memo to Barbara Burke-Tatum, February 20, 1986, p. 11.

33. Robert J. Waste, "Does Workfare Work? An Examination of Workfare Programs in California," paper presented at the Annual Meeting of the American Political Science Association, September 4, 1987.

34. National Academy of Public Administration, "Welfare Reform Dialogue: Implementation and Operational Feasibility Issues," proceedings of a panel discussion (July 21, 1987) conducted for the General Accounting Office at the request of the Committee on Governmental Affairs of the United States Senate, January 1988, p. 8.

35. Stephen R. Rosenthal, "Employment and Training Choices (C)," Boston University, p. 1.

36. Rosabeth Moss Kanter, *The Change Masters: Innovation and Entrepreneurship in the American Corporation* (New York: Simon and Schuster, 1983), pp. 122–123.

37. For another illustration in a different context, see William Ascher, "Risk, Politics, and Tax Reform: Some Latin American Experiences," in Malcolm Gillis (ed.), *Lessons from Fundamental Tax Reform in Developing Countries* (Durham, N.C.: Duke University Press, 1989).

38. Supporters of Dukakis might argue that his first-term economic policies (1975–1979) created the economic conditions that permitted ET to be a second-term success (1983–1987). One analysis of state economic policies under Dukakis and King concluded that these policies did little to start Massachusetts's economic boom but did help sustain it. See Ronald F. Ferguson and Helen F. Ladd, "State Economic Renaissance," in R. Scott Fosler (ed.),

The New Economic Role of the States (New York: Oxford University Press, 1988), pp. 21–62.

39. Carol Kreck, "Escaping Welfare," *The Denver Post,* December 8, 1987.

40. Harvey M. Sapolsky, James Aisenberg, and James A. Morone, "The Call to Rome and Other Obstacles to State-Level Innovation," *Public Administration Review,* 47 (March/April 1987), p. 135.

41. William Raspberry, "Healthier Babies, Fewer Babies," *The Washington Post,* June 18, 1984. Writes Raspberry: "You can't do [only] one thing."

42. John K. Clemens and Douglas F. Mayer, *The Classic Touch: Lessons in Leadership from Homer to Hemingway* (Homewood, Ill.: Dow Jones–Irwin, 1987), p. xiii.

43. Kanter, *The Change Masters,* p. 64.

44. Quoted by Irving Kristol in "Decentralization for What?" *The Public Interest,* no. 11 (Spring 1968), p. 19.

45. K. A. Leithwood and D. J. Montgomery, "The Role of the Elementary School Principle in Program Improvement," *Review of Educational Research,* 52 (Fall 1982), pp. 309–339.

46. John I. DiIulio, Jr., *Governing Prisons: A Comparative Study of Correction Management* (New York: The Free Press, 1987).

47. The Family Support Act of 1988 had many mandatory features. But these were all conditional on resources (including child care) being available to serve all welfare recipients. Thus, in reality, many state programs developed under the Family Support Act will look very voluntary.

48. How does a scholar conclude that an organization is well managed? The answer, concludes Richard P. Nathan, is "informed judgments," and "inductive research." Writes Nathan, "What researchers do in such a situation is *model the counterfactual* on the basis of available facts and experience and their knowledge of organizational behavior." Nathan, *Social Science in Government* (New York: Basic Books, 1988), p. 130.

Index

Aaron, Henry J., 163–164
Abramson, Mark A., 202
Accountability, 47–48, 60–63, 70–73, 121–122
Ackermann, Barbara, 1
Administration and Finance, Executive Office of, 32, 64
Administration Metastrategy, 198, 200–203
Administrator's Conceit, 202
Adult Basic Education (ABE), 37
Aid to Families with Dependent Children (AFDC): benefits, 6, 175, 191; caseload, 4, 6, 109, 172–174, 190–194, 212; error rate, 49, 51, 52, 55, 56, 63, 66, 104, 108–109, 213
Alcoholics-Anonymous assumption, 12–13
Alexander, Desi, 35
Alexander, Lamar, 135
Altman, Drew, 16
Anastas, Robert, 110
Anderson, Bryon D., 209
Atkins, Charles M., 2–5, 10, 13, 17–19, 23–35, 39, 41, 49–50, 58, 60–64, 66–68, 70–73, 76, 78–79, 81, 83–84, 89, 91–92, 95, 101–102, 105, 109–110, 116, 118–120, 121–122, 124–132, 136, 146–148, 150, 160–168, 191–193, 206, 208–215
Austin, Nancy, 124–125
Awards, 73–74, 78–79, 109–112, 114, 115–116, 124–126

Badger, Mary, 2, 31, 120
Baker, Russell, 8
Baltimore Options program, 154–156, 159–160, 189
Bane, Mary Jo, 16–17, 19–20, 157
Bawden, Lee, 195

Bay State Skills Corporation, 26, 72, 74
Behn's First Law of Policy Analysis, 226n2
Behn's Fifth Law of Policy Analysis, 233n23
Bellow, Jean, 34, 41, 133
Bennis, Warren, 19
Bergman, Terri, 95, 98
Blum, Barbara, 157, 159
Boston, welfare offices in, 41, 53, 60–63
Bouchard, Marie, 3, 86
Broder, David S., 5
Brownstein, Ronald, 6
Burbridge, Lynn, 195
Burke, Edmund, 216
Burke-Tatum, Barbara, 5, 10, 17–19, 25–26, 31, 33, 40–42, 47–48, 58, 64, 73, 76, 78, 84, 88, 96–97, 101, 107, 118–119, 124, 126, 129–131, 146–147, 150, 209–212, 214–215
Burtless, Gary, 164
Bush, George W., 7, 152

Campbell, Alan K., 200
Capitol for a Day, 86–88
Carballo, Manuel, 21–23, 25, 30, 35, 109, 128–129, 207
Carter, Jimmy, 198
Case management, 45–47, 60, 66, 68, 87–88, 106–108, 122
Chase, Gordon, 24–26, 32, 70, 101, 119, 128, 148, 204–206, 216
Chelminiak, Lee A., 34, 73, 84, 86–87, 213
Child support, 11, 37–38, 47, 52, 54, 79–80, 105–110, 112, 116, 214
Choices, 18
Clemens, John K., 216
Clusters of local offices, 39–40, 61–63
Cole, Roosevelt, 103
Commonwealth Service Corps, 26

Competition, 71–73, 80–81

Comprehensive Offender Employment Resources System (COERS), 74

Control group, 151–157, 161, 162, 176–178, 182, 184–185

Council for Excellence in Government, 200, 202

Creaming, 75–79, 129, 159–160

Cretella, Henry, 31

Cullen, Raymond C., Jr., 90

Danforth, John C., 87

Day care, 11, 23, 37–38, 42, 45, 85, 123–124, 214, 218

Deficit, Massachusetts budget, 1, 7–8

Demong, Kristin, 25, 84–85, 193, 211

Despres, Camella, 108

Diamond, Janet, 95–96, 99, 101, 121–122, 130–131

Dineen, William, 110

Drucker, Peter, 203

Dukakis, Michael S., 1–8, 10, 13, 21, 23, 30, 53, 56, 62, 67, 73, 82, 84–90, 101–102, 117, 145, 172, 185, 190–191, 193, 211–214

Economic Affairs, Executive Office of, 25

Eligibility Operations, Division of, 41–42, 46, 47, 121–122

Ellwood, David T., 11, 157

Employment and Training, Division of, 41–42, 47–48, 121–122, 208

Employment and Training program. See ET

Employment Security, Division of (DES), 14, 25, 36, 37, 42, 47–48, 72, 74, 84–85, 101–103, 127–130, 208, 211, 213

English as a second language (ESL), 37, 44, 130

Entman, Robert, 113–115

ET (Employment and Training): expenditures, 44, 173–174; placements, 2, 6, 27, 37, 49–82, 84, 128–129, 226n7; wage, 6, 55–59, 77, 84, 128

"ET Springs Forward," 58, 112, 114

Evans, Donna, 85

Family Independence Plan, 47, 132

Family Support Act of 1988, 15, 198, 217; JOBS program, 8, 15, 217

Farmer, Robert, 23

Ferman, Barbara, 131

Financial assistance social workers (FASW), 39, 46, 82, 91, 94, 101, 103, 111, 130

Financial assistance workers (FAW), 14, 39, 40, 46, 47

Fishman, Matthew E., 33

Fitzgerald, A. Ernest, 188

Focus groups, 95–96

Food stamps, 39, 51, 52, 54, 59–60, 65

Fouche, Gerald, 86

Frazier, Cassandra, 86

Friedlander, Daniel, 78, 156, 160, 169

General relief (GR), 33, 39, 51, 52, 54, 59–60

Glynn, Thomas P., 4, 14–19, 26–30, 33, 39, 41, 57–58, 63–64, 66, 73, 76, 84, 89, 91–92, 104–105, 118–119, 126–128, 146–147, 150, 191, 209, 212–215

Goals, 23–24, 27, 42–44, 49–82, 94, 112, 129–130, 169, 191–193, 203–207, 210–211, 215, 226n1

Goodnow, Frank J., 201–202

Graduate Equivalency Diploma (GED), 13, 100

Greater Avenues for Independence (GAIN), 211

Greenberg, David H., 163

Grove Hall, 35, 36, 37, 64, 103, 108

Gueron, Judith M., 17, 156–157, 159, 188, 223

Gulick, Luther, 201–202

Haley, David A., 102, 110

Halperin, Morton H., 68–69

Haveman, Robert H., 164

Hawthorne Effect, 182–184

Hayes, Robert H., 143–144

Health and Human Services, Department of (HHS), 2–3, 27, 146

Health care: Health Choices, 38, 47, 52, 54, 77, 101, 105–106; Medicaid, 33, 38, 39, 51, 52, 54, 108

Herbers, John, 88

Herzberg, Frederick, 73

Holmes, Walter E., Jr., 33, 63–64

Iacocca, Lee, 91, 97

Janusz, Lorraine, 85

JOBS program. See Family Support Act of 1988

Job Training Partnership Act (JTPA), 25, 37, 43–44, 72, 129, 177–178, 185, 208
Johnston, Philip W., 191–192

Kanter, Rosabeth Moss, 141, 150, 211, 216
Keverian, George, 7
King, Edward J., 1–2, 30–31, 33, 84–85, 128, 207; administration of, 12, 14, 39, 94, 95, 209
Kroc, Ray, 132

Lawson, Dawn, 6–7
Leader's Conceit, 205
Leadership, 18–20, 64, 66–80, 198–219; Leadership Metastrategy, 198, 203–208
Legislator's Conceit, 142, 200
Lemann, Nicholas, 6
Levin, Martin A., 131
Lewis, Gene E., 84
Liberatore, Cherly, 3
Lindblom, Charles E., 144–145
Lindsay, John V., 24
Lipsky, Michael, 67
Long, David, 78, 156, 169
Lukas, Carol VanDeusen, 34

Madison, Joseph, 34, 101, 106
Management by groping along (MBGA), 133–136, 140–150, 165, 210, 233n32
Management by objectives (MBO), 228n25
Management by wandering around (MBWA), 136–140
Mandatory employment and training programs, 1, 15–18, 30, 93–94, 154, 161–162, 183, 207, 224n21; sanctions, 12–13, 21–23, 25, 224n13, 230n28
Manpower Demonstration Research Corporation (MDRC), 17, 78, 154–168, 177, 179, 187–189, 223n2
Marketing, 25, 83–103, 176–178
Massachusetts Civic Interest Council (MCIC), 111–117, 125
Massachusetts Taxpayers Foundation (MTF), 4, 173–174
Matheson, Scott, 135
Mayer, Douglas F., 216
MBGA. See Management by groping along
MBO. See Management by objectives
MBWA. See Management by wandering around

McCue, Jeff, 124
Mead, Lawrence M., 13, 15–16, 19–20
Millett, Laurie, 106
Mintzberg, Henry, 137–138
Mission, 10, 67–70, 74–76, 82, 105–109, 118, 120, 123, 125–126, 187, 203–208, 215
Moore, Mark H., 205
Motivation, 51, 73–74, 116, 124–126, 130, 164, 167–170, 210, 215, 217, 228n25
Mudd, John, 25
Mulligan, Margaret, 34
Munnell, Alicia H., 151
My eyes glaze over (MEGO), 114
My Mom and ET, 99–100, 117

Nanus, Burt, 19
Nathan, Richard P., 177–178, 188–190
Negative income tax, 151, 153–154, 178, 235nn6,7
Nietzsche, Friedrich, 141
Nightingale, Demetra, 195
Nixon, Richard M., 198

O'Connor, Tom, 69
Odeen, Philip, 200
O'Meara, Marianne, 83, 85
O'Neal, Robert, 102
O'Neill, June, 194
O'Neill, Thomas P., 139
O'Sullivan, John, 133

Partners in Professionalism conferences (PIPs), 104–108, 111–112, 117–119, 122, 124
Pedroli, Richard P., 65
Perdue, Frank, 97
Perryman, Janice, 87
Personnel Administration, Department of (DPA), 32–33, 39, 102
Peters, Thomas J., 73, 95, 117–118, 124–125, 136–139, 150, 204, 232n13
Pillsbury, Jolie Bain, 4, 17–19, 33, 39–42, 47, 58, 61–64, 73, 76, 81, 87, 92, 104–108, 117–119, 121–124, 126, 130, 132–133, 146–147, 150, 209, 212, 214–215
Pilot projects, 26, 128
Placebo effect, 153, 182–183
Policy experiments, 151–158, 174–187
Policy and procedures unit, 92, 124

Policy Metastrategy, 198–200
Polio-vaccine experiment, 153, 178, 217
Project Redirection, 187–188
Proxmire, William, 114
Public Employees Roundtable, 4, 92
Publications and Outreach, Office of
  (P&O), 95–98, 130

Random assignment, 151–156, 158,
  176–178, 186, 189, 194–195
Raspberry, William, 3
Reagan, Ronald, 15, 146
Rector, Robert, 158
Reneghan, Dorothy, 34, 92–93
Research, Planning and Evaluation, Office
  of (RP&E), 55–57, 77, 131, 171–172
Revenue, Department of, 80
Rich, Spencer, 157
Risner, Sandra, 91
Rivlin, Alice, 194
Robins, Philip K., 163
Rosenthal, Robert, 181; Rosenthal Effect,
  182–183, 187
Rosenthal, Stephen R., 205–206
Route out of poverty, 10–11, 19, 46, 60,
  68, 71, 75, 105, 108, 132–133

Salamon, Lester, 187
Sampson, Ruby, 5, 96, 108
Sanctions. *See* Mandatory employment
  and training programs
Sanders, Ronnie, 25
San Diego Job Search and Work Experi-
  ence Demonstration, 154–157, 161–
  162, 179–180, 184, 188–190
Sasso, John, 88
Schultze, Charles L., 199–200
Sellers, Thomas P., 65–66
Sherman, Harvey, 17
Simon, Herbert, 150
Skarmos, Florence, 110
Smith, Adam, 199
Social experiments. *See* Policy experiments

Social Services, Department of (DSS), 38,
  39, 42, 47, 208
Speilberg, Nathan, 209
Strategic planning, 142–144
Stratton, Catherine N., 25
Sununu, John, 143–144
Supplemental Security Income (SSI), 33
Supported work, 37, 42, 45, 225n1,
  225–226n2

Taylor, Frederick Winslow, 202, 204
Tawa, Chela, 22, 34
Training and Employment Policy, Office of
  (OTEP), 25, 37, 42–44, 47, 74,
  226nn5,7
Transportation, 11, 23, 37–38, 85
Tuoey, Jane, 128

Urban Institute, evaluation of ET,
  194–197

Voluntary employment and training programs, 12–13, 15–18, 22, 30, 85,
  93–95, 154, 159, 162, 174, 176–178,
  207
Vorenberg, Elizabeth, 33

Waddell, Howard, 33, 92, 94–99, 101,
  130–131
Waddy, Benita, 86
Waterman, Robert H., Jr., 73, 95, 117–
  118, 124, 126, 136–139, 150, 232n13
Weber, Max, 202
Weick, Karl E., 134–135
Werner, Alan, 25
Whiteway, Diana, 4
Williams, Jack, 83
Work and Training Program (WTP), 12,
  21–23, 25, 27, 40, 85, 94, 128–129,
  207, 210, 212
Work Incentive (WIN) Program, 12,
  21–22, 27, 45, 67, 156, 198, 207, 213,
  221n2, 228n23